STRAIT OF GEORGIA

Sucia I.

Matia I.
Puffin I.

Lummi
Bay

Bell

Barnes I. Clark I.

t Sound
Crescent
Beach

Mt.
Constitution

Lummi
I.

Port Langdon

Rosario

ISLAND

Pt. Lawrence

Doe
Bay

Cascade Bay

Olga

Sinclair (Cottonwood I.)
I.

stone

Obstruction Pass

Obstruction I.

Peavine Pass

R O S A R I O   S T R A I T

Cypress
I.

Samish
I.

Upright Hd.

Blakely
I.

Strawberry Bay

Guemes
I.

Port
Stanley

Frost
I.

Guemes Channel

n's

Decatur
I.

Anacortes

Lopez
Sound

Fidalgo
Hd.

Sperry Pt.

Fidalgo
I.

chardson

Chadwick
Hill

Watmough
Hd.

Deception Pass

Skagit
I.

Swinomish Slough

LaConner

Whidbey
I.

Smith I.   Minor I.

PIG
WAR
ISLANDS

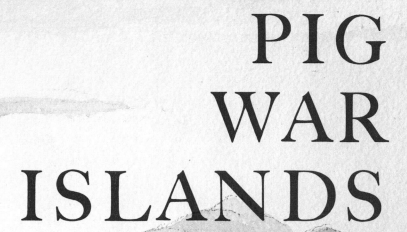

PIG
WAR
ISLANDS

DAVID RICHARDSON

ORCAS PUBLISHING COMPANY
EASTSOUND, WASHINGTON, U.S.A.

1971

GRUEYER/71

published by
ORCAS PUBLISHING COMPANY
POST OFFICE BOX 104
EASTSOUND, WASHINGTON, U.S.A. 98245

LIBRARY OF CONGRESS CATALOG CARD NUMBER 70-149337

designed and printed in Canada by
MORRISS PRINTING COMPANY LTD.
VICTORIA, BRITISH COLUMBIA

to the memory
of
my grandparents

Ivan & Lulu Blair

CONTENTS

CHINOOK WORD-LIST

As recently as a generation ago, many long-time residents of America's Pacific Northwest, the Canadian West, and Alaska, could still — and sometimes did — speak a curious jargon of mixed Indian and European words known as Chinook. One generation before them — at the most, two — this Esperanto-like frontier lingo was indispensable for communication between whites and Indians, sometimes even between whites recently arrived from linguistically divergent climes.

Today only a handful of Chinook words remain in the vocabulary of the North Pacific Coast, and even these are fading fast. For the benefit of readers unfamiliar with them, here are definitions of Chinook Jargon words used in this book.

Boston — American (because the first U.S. explorers the Indians met came from there).

Cheechako — Newcomer, tenderfoot. Actually a combination of *chee*, new, and *chako*, come.

Chuck — Water (or any other liquid) in any form. Hence *salt chuck* is the ocean, a bay, inlet, or slough, etc.

Klootchman — Woman.

Siwash — Indian (from the French, *sauvage*).

Skookum — Strong, healthy, firm, tough, etc.

Tyee — Chief, official, a very important person.

FOREWORD

I had thought to omit any sort of preface to this book — hardly anyone reads them, anyway — but I am urged to put a few words here, if only to assure the reader that this is a book of fact, not fiction.

The point is well taken. It is hard enough to believe that two great nations could come to the brink over a mere pig; the colorful specifics — before, during, and after the fact of that unlikely encounter — approach the incredible. Similarly, *inventing* the personalities involved would tax the skill of Hemingway, Gann, or Michener.

Yet, all of these things happened; all these people lived, and behaved just as they are pictured in the pages that follow.

Or, as nearly so as an exhaustive research has disclosed. (The many sources used in compiling this narrative are listed at the end of the book. So are my thanks to those who assisted me, being no less sincere for that.)

Even the occasional scene-setting vignettes which introduce parts of the book are based as closely as possible on known details of fact and dialogue; yet in deference to historical purism even these brief fictionesque passages are identified as such by the use of italics.

Let me add also, lest there be the slightest doubt, that all I have written in this book has been written in love. If its pages seem to dwell overmuch on the very human foibles of the Islands' early citizenry — many of whose descendants are my good friends today — it is not out of any gleeful wish to exploit. For, to me, each was a true hero, no matter how heroic, villainous or foolish.

This is not a matter of charity, but of perspective. Can we not perceive from the evidence — collected at this far vantage point in time — that no man then was *inherently* a good deal better or worse than his neighbor; but that circumstance and events simply cast each one in a role and then obliged him to play the part to its end? (Then the same must be true of us today, but the realization of that is unacceptable for contemporaries: it might lead us into such uncontemporary notions as Original Sin and Monism.)

So if in the telling of how it really was in the San Juans I have caused pain to someone now living, opened old wounds or recalled past hurts, I honestly regret that this is so. If the offense has been compounded by errors of fact or interpretation, I ask forgiveness — if not of perspective, then of charity.

D.R.

1

THE SAN JUAN ISLANDS

The light *June mist of a Puget* Sound *morning had clung, dead still in the dimness of dawn, about the drizzle-dulled green of island tree tops. Now, it thinned rapidly before the warming rays of a sun climbing fast and yellow from behind the distant Cascade Mountains. A brace of russet-tailed hawks awoke to the golden light and began chasing one another in an indolent fashion. Suddenly they swooped, shrieking, into a still-bedewed clearing and nearly brushed with their wings against the roof of Lyman Cutler's rude log shanty.*

It was not the cry of the hawks that roused Cutler from a profound and youthful sleep, but the clop-clop of a horse's hoofs striking the pebbled dust of the trail outside. Cutler passed a weather-tanned fist through sandy hair and hauled his lank frame from the bed, aiming as he did so a playful thwack at the inviting fanny of the Indian girl asleep beside him.

Cutler went to the window and muttered something unprintable. The passing rider, a Negro, had reined his mount to a walk and seemed to be laughing at something across the way. The tall youth followed his gaze and repeated the oath. It was that damn black boar again: it had pushed through his garden fence and was rooting up his potatoes with its ugly square snout. This was too much. Lyman Cutler seized his long, thin-barreled Kentucky rifle and threw open the door.

Jacob, the black man, whipped up his horse and disappeared down the trail. The boar — he had felt the sting of Cutler's switches before, when the tall settler discovered him similarly engaged — began a waddling retreat from the garden, a half-masticated tuber still protruding from his dirty-pink muzzle. He got a few yards away and Cutler's rifle spoke sharply. The pig fell in a heap, twitched obscenely, and died.

It is most unlikely that the sandy-haired settler from Ohio knew, that day in 1859, that he had just started a war. But it was to be an unlikely kind of war, bringing two great nations just to the brink of bloodshed, potentially to alter the course of the great American rebellion over slavery, the map of North America, perhaps even the future shape of the British empire. Yet at the end of thirteen years of confrontation England and America would part as friends, their armies retiring in peace, the entire episode passing into the dusty limbo of history, grist for the mills of Sunday supplement writers and gnome-eyed students of the past.

Most accounts of the Pig War center about the erring British-owned porker, and its sudden demise at the hands of the dead-eyed Yankee homesteader. But it was an altogether different kind of piggishness that actually brought two frontier forces eyeball-to-eyeball in a confrontation designed neither in London nor in Washington. The chief engineers were in fact an American general who wanted to be President, and a British governor who could not forget that he was a company man. At stake in their egoistic contest: a gaggle of sparsely inhabited islands, smack in the middle of a peaceful inland sea separating America's Pacific Northwest from what is now British Columbia.

14

The 170-odd San Juan Islands occupy a circular area roughly twenty-five miles across, with the center of the circle at the exact mid-point between the "little bit of olde Englande" city of Victoria, and the teachers-college town of Bellingham on the U.S. mainland. The Islands are bounded on the north by the Canadian Strait of Georgia and on the south by America's Strait of Juan de Fuca. The salt chuck lapping these insular shores ("chuck" being the old Chinook* term for water, and still in the vocabulary of Pacific Northwesterners) forms the upper extreme of the region loosely known as Puget Sound — though the latter term is most properly applied only to that arm of the inland sea which cosies Seattle, some eighty miles to the south.

Geologists tell us the San Juans are in reality the last highest mountaintops of a vanished, sunken continent, eons older than the callow land mass we know as North America. Perhaps this continental generation gap goes part way to explain other distinctions, for life has always been a very different sort of apple in these remarkable islands.

The weather may have something to do with it, too. Lying snugly in the rain shadow of Vancouver Island and its mountains, the San Juans receive remarkably less rainfall than do other parts of the drizzle-prone Pacific Northwest. While a well-nigh continual ebb and flow of marine air overhead keeps the atmosphere crisply fresh and smogless, besides maintaining summer and winter temperatures generally in the mild middle of the thermometer.

Life in the San Juans is a neighborly, unhurried sort of existence far different from the pressure-cooker ordeal of mainland city-dwellers (or "flat-landers" as island people call them, more in pity than in scorn). It is the small-town homeyness of the American mid-West, transplanted to a vastly kinder and infinitely more varied and beautiful environment. Indeed, many of the Islands' first settlers were refugees from the mid-western

* See page 9 for a glossary of Chinook Jargon words used in this book.

states, driven here by drought, or by the bankruptcy of a particular dream, or just by the siren call of the great Pacific frontier.

Take, for example, Peter Bostian and his friend David Kimple, who left Pennsylvania in the 1870's to homestead on the Kansas plains. The Kimple farm (through the middle of which passed the historic Santa Fe Trail) boasted rich, deeply black soil that should have spelled agricultural success; but son Luther recalled later that the place was flooded four times in ten years, always when the corn crop stood six inches to two feet, and was subjected as well to "chintz bugs, grasshoppers, hail, hot winds, dust storms and cyclones."

It was a cyclone that finally blew both families westward. The twister demolished the Kimples' two-story stone home in an instant, only one of the 22-inch-thick walls remaining upright. By a miracle none of the family were injured. When Pete Bostian saw the remains he shook his head gravely. "If God spares me, Davey," he told David Kimple, "I am going to get out of this country." And the next year the Bostians were on their way to Oregon.

Bostian hadn't counted on the dense stands of timber that covered the Pacific Northwest like a thick evergreen comforter — timber that took a man months or years to burn and root away until he had a respectable piece of farm ground. His search for something easier to clear brought him finally to Whatcom (now Bellingham) where someone told him about Orcas Island in the San Juans. With three other land-seeking pioneers Bostian hired a sailboat to reconnoiter the island, fell instantly in love with it and secured a homestead here.

Bostian and his new-found friends arranged for a steamer to bring over their families, furniture, and materials for home building. Ironically they arrived at the height of a February "northeaster." These fierce northeast blows of icy arctic air are the occasional exception to the Islands' general rule of mild weather, though mercifully, they rarely occur more than once every two or three years, and last only for a few days. The storm may have seemed less than auspicious to the Bostian family as they arrived in driving snow to be put ashore in lifeboats on dock-less Orcas Island; but as soon as he was settled, Bostian wrote his friend David Kimple to forget Kansas and come to Orcas, too, for he had found "as near a paradise as there is on earth."

Neither the Bostians nor the Kimples got rich on Orcas, nor has anyone else in the San Juans (with one notable exception, to be chronicled at the appropriate place in this narrative). It was not and is not the desire for wealth that brings people to the San Juan Islands. But those early pioneers did live out their lives here in a kind of contentment not measurable by the decimal system, and bequeathed to their sons and daughters riches having nothing to do with the dollar sign.

It is true no one ever starved to death — if all else failed, one could live on clams — but islanders rarely had extra cash to jingle in their homespun jeans or to spend for non-essentials. If a farmer's place produced more than his family could consume, the excess could be rowed fifteen or twenty miles to Victoria or Whatcom and traded for other items of importance. Otherwise, one resorted to makeshifts — like the coats Henry Legbandt, another Orcas pioneer, used to make for himself from empty flour sacks.

Flour-sack couture is "out" in the Islands these days, but in other ways there has been a kind of changeless quality about the San Juans. When my father left the Islands in the late twenties he first stopped in to pay his bill at the little false-fronted office of the Friday Harbor *Journal*. He returned in the early fifties and again dropped into the diminutive newsshop next to the bank. He found it exactly the way he had last seen it — the same mustachioed gentleman in what appeared to be the same ink-darkened overalls was seated at the same linotype machine amid the selfsame clutter of spilled type, soiled proofs, mountainous

17

piles of "exchange" publications and all the other typographic paraphernalia of a country newspaper. He could see nothing new — except the addition of several more portraits to the gallery of successful and unsuccessful Republican presidential candidates that graced the office's one adorable wall. From the editor-printer-publisher's mouth still protruded what appeared to be the identical unlit but well-chewed cigar butt of the earlier decade's visit, darting rapidly from side to side like the protruding tongue of an excited boa constrictor.*

Yet the years do pass, even in the San Juan Islands, and the retirement of the venerable *Journal* publisher is marked by some as a watershed event. The newspaper passed to Robert Hartzog, of Sherwood, Oregon, who updated the paper's technical equipment somewhat but stuck closely to the folksy, countrified format the *Journal* had followed for fifty-odd years. In 1969 Bob died suddenly — late on a Wednesday night, just after the weekly had been printed, folded, and readied for the mail — and the next week's paper was put together largely by townspeople who dropped in and worked for nothing but the satisfaction of helping Bob's widow, and seeing a local institution through some tough days.

For years the experts had been saying country newsshops like the *Journal*'s had become uneconomic and should give up their linotype and letterpress gear in favor of more "modern" typewriter-like composition and farmed-out printing by some large metropolitan offset enterprise. But island folk like their paper just the way it is, so in preference to a mainland outfit, the *Journal* was sold to a combine of local people who only want to continue it as long as possible in the long-established way, economic or not.

Friday Harbor is the county seat and the archipelago's only

---

* The simile is not the author's, but is borrowed from a World War Two incident. South America-based G.I.'s from the San Juans named a pet reptile after the *Journal* publisher, Virgil Frits, citing this similarity of mannerisms.

incorporated town. It has been described as a typical turn-of-the-century fishing village*, though the reader will learn that fishing was hardly the industry most associated with it then, or since. But the main drag is lined largely with false-fronted frame structures of frontier architecture, and institutions like the Moose Hall — formerly John Douglas' "Saloon Best" — take one right back to the days of hoop skirts and corset stays. A few buildings in town have been purposely remodelled to fit in with the pioneer-days décor, but most are still the real article.

A slight depression in the street is all that remains to mark the public pump and congregating point around which the town was originally built. A copious flow from this persistent fount has long since been diverted to the bay, though it still causes the street paving to settle and the basements of surrounding buildings to be flooded now and again.

Friday Harbor is located on San Juan, the island where most of the Pig War action took place. It is the second largest of the Islands, though just by a whisker, Orcas measuring 58 square miles to San Juan's 57. The principal attraction on Orcas is lofty Mt. Constitution, which rises half a mile above the level of the sea surrounding it. The 360-degree marine view from its summit is variously rated from "best in the world" to merely the most spectacular on America's west coast.

There was a time when islanders felt an almost religious compulsion to scale Constitution's heights once annually to spend a few hours exclaiming in hushed tones over perhaps 30,000 square miles of this beauteous corner of God's world. It was an all-day trek by foot or wagon then, but considered well worth the day or two of resulting soreness in the legs (or elsewhere, depending upon the means of locomotion).

In 1912 Karl Rilling tried driving one of the first automobiles on the island up to the summit and back. The grade was so steep

* Friday Harbor was chosen as the fishing village locale for shooting a 1966 United Artists motion picture, "Namu the Killer Whale."

19

the two-year-old Model T Ford's gravity-fed carburetor kept starving, so Charlie's passenger had to run alongside with an oil-can filled with gas in order to squirt fuel into it from time to time. They made it to the top, cutting trees from the path and defying precipices and rock slides, but there wasn't much left of the tin lizzie when they got her back down again.

Nowadays motorized tourists zip up the switch-backed, black-top mountain road in a quarter hour or less, climb the stone observation tower built by federal money as a make-work project during the Depression, and spend as much time as they like or as little, ooh-ing and ah-ing and snapping pictures, without missing a single meal or ferry connection.

Modern ferries (augmented by some not-so-modern holdovers that once plied the San Francisco-Oakland run) connect San Juan, Orcas, Shaw and Lopez Islands with Vancouver Island in Canada, and with the U.S. mainland via the terminal at Anacortes. Billed — with considerable justification — as "America's most beautiful water trip," the route through the San Juans is a unique visual delight that can only be described in press-agentry terms, but they happen to be true: madrona and fir-lined shores rise now steeply, now gently from fjord-like waters; kelp-flagged reefs and shallows and bubbling, foam-flecked tide rips vary the sea's tamed surface; snug summer or year-around cabins hug the beach or peep suddenly from the midst of a bosky knoll above it, or rise picturesquely from a low, low spit of land. You have to look sharp to spot some of them, like the cozy dream cottage Lew and Tibbie Dodd built entirely of flotsam that washed ashore over the years. It is located on little Yellow Island, just where the ferry wheels hard over for Friday Harbor after negotiating narrow Wasp Pass between Shaw and Crane.

Most of the land and seascapes appear little differently today than they did in 1791 when the Spanish explorer Francisco Eliza sent the schooner *Santa Saturnina* into the area for the first look-see by Western man. Under the command of First Pilot Juan Pantoja y Arriaga, the little ship proceeded from Esquimalt (presently a Canadian naval base at Victoria) at 9 in the morning and was soon sailing, urged by a fresh June breeze, northward up Haro Strait. There was an accompanying long-boat, armed and manned by soldiers against the possibility of attack by Indians.

The two vessels soon found themselves, Pantoja wrote, "in an indescribable archipelago of islands, keys, rocks, and big and little inlets," so that the four days allotted for the reconnoiter would obviously be insufficient.

Toward noon Pantoja, in the longboat, ordered the sails furled as the breeze strengthened gradually into a stiff sou'west blow. At the moment, this was no pleasure cruise. The skipper put his men to working at the oars in water so choppy it kept pouring over the gunwale. In the schooner as well, sailors worked fever-ishly to keep that vessel on its northwestward course.

But by dark the wind had subsided until only an occasional desultory puff pushed at the vessels' slack canvas. Pantoja ordered the schooner to anchor for the night, probably in wedge-shaped Fulford Harbour on Saltspring Island. By fading light the pilot himself set out in the longboat to examine the northern reaches of the channel.

Pantoja's spellbinding twilight row took him up into the Canadian Gulf Islands, near-neighbors of the San Juans, where the Spaniards got their first close look at these isles — particularly the two Penders, petite Prevost Island, and parts of sprawling, mountainous Saltspring.

Perhaps the explorers noticed a characteristic northwest-to-southeast striated appearance common to all these northern islands. It is as though the ice-age glaciers of a past eon, reluctant to withdraw, dug into the earth's surface with giant scooping fingers as they inched home to the Alaskan arctic and left behind bays, channels, reefs and islands all trending northwestward. In the San Juans, only Patos, Sucia, and Matia, on the northern periphery, show the same unguicular corduroying.

At three the next morning the two Spanish vessels set out eastward toward Georgia Strait by starlight. The wind was contrary again, so they proceeded slowly, pulling at the oars. With the dawn came a freshening of the east wind and they decided to again seek an anchorage, finding it in long, narrow Bedwell Harbour, which separates North and South Pender Islands.

At mid-morning Pantoja, impatient, gave the order to move on. With great exertion the sailors were able to round East Point on Saturna at seven that evening, and were suddenly caught up by a spanking northwest blow sweeping down the Strait of Georgia. Quartering this they sailed briskly toward Patos Island, close on the lee of which they dropped anchor for the night. The sailors were impressed with the great number of gulls, seals, whales and "tunny" near the island which is named for another variety of sea-creature, "patos" being the Spanish for ducks.

Two calm days enabled Pantoja to move slowly eastward toward Rosario Strait, but on the third day a severe storm broke from the southeast, bringing forty-eight hours of drenching rain and gale-force winds. Running short of food and far over-schedule, Pantoja at last turned back and reported to Eliza what he had seen.

The commander was greatly excited and proposed to resume the exploration in the packet boat *San Carlos*; but Pantoja convinced him the area was too dangerous for the larger vessel to navigate. Instead the Spaniards moved their base of operations to Port Discovery, across the Strait of Juan de Fuca, from where the second pilot, Don José Maria Narvaez, made a brief inspection of the southern perimeter of the Islands.

Narvaez actually discovered Admiralty Inlet on this circuit, and intended to enter and explore it, and probably would have — and so would have discovered Puget Sound, a year before England's Captain Vancouver — if it hadn't been for a school of whales. Few had been seen in the Strait of Juan de Fuca, but a number of them had appeared in the Gulf of Georgia. Narvaez rightly concluded there must be another ocean entrance to the latter, and concentrated on the quest for it, for the explorers of that day were still preoccupied with rediscovering the fabled Northwest Passage — that mythical short-cut to the Atlantic which would vastly shorten the sailing time between Europe and Asia.

Taken together, the sorties of Pantoja and Narvaez amounted to a circumnavigation of the San Juans, but at no time did the Spaniards actually enter the archipelago or — so far as the records indicate — land on any of them, until the following year. At this time the Spanish launched another expedition, this one equipped with the very latest in navigational devices, and headed by officers loaned for the occasion by the well-known Italian explorer-astronomer, Alejandro Malaspina. Two brand new 47-foot brigantines, each with a crew of 24, including artists, carpenters and chaplains, were supplied. They were the *Sutil,* under the command of Dionisio Alcalá-Galiano; and the *Mexicana,* commanded by Cayetano Valdés.

Galiano and Valdés had no notion, when they arrived at Esquimalt on June 9, that a British exploring party under Captain George Vancouver was already deep in the Puget Sound country — in fact, were using as their base the same large bay at Port Discovery which Eliza had used for the purpose the year before. Vancouver was also unaware of the approaching Spanish expedition, though he had heard a rumor that some Spanish ships had been inside the strait the previous year.

Meanwhile, on May 18, Vancouver's vessels *Discovery* and *Chatham* had landed the good captain on the eastern end of Protection Island where he viewed his surroundings from a jut of high ground. The weather was fair and the air clear, and Vancouver noted to the north "an archipelago of islands of various sizes." Returning on board the *Discovery,* he ordered a lieutenant, William Broughton, to make a reconnaissance of those islands in the *Chatham,* an armed tender. Vancouver himself turned south, in the well-named command ship, toward his historic explorations of the Puget Sound country.

Lt. Broughton (who, as a midshipman, had participated in the British attack on Bunker Hill) left at noon on a course for the southern tip of Lopez Island, steering for some "Peaked Hills" — probably Chadwick Hill above Watmough Head. By mid-afternoon he had weathered Smith Island and, spotting the southern entrance to San Juan Channel, made for this opening. Threading gingerly between rocks off San Juan Island's Cattle Point and the reefy instep of Lopez, Broughton passed into the interior of the archipelago, which he described as "rocky isles . . . well cloath'd with wood."

The Englishmen were on the point of anchoring in Griffin Bay for the night — all unaware, of course, of the dramatic confrontation to take place between their own naval successors and American forces in these waters 67 years after — but on seeing an opening to the northeast (Upright Channel, between Shaw and Lopez) and another to the northwest (San Juan Channel) Broughton decided to investigate both passages. He anchored in twelve fathoms where the two waterways join, off the southern tip of Shaw.

Early next morning Broughton sent a cutter to reconnoiter Upright Channel. Its crew returned before breakfast to report that after a short distance they had encountered a bay, from which half a dozen small and large channels were found leading off in as many different directions. Broughton decided to examine this area in the *Chatham* and sent two small boats for a look at the western passage.

The diminutive brig-rigged *Chatham* worked slowly against a strong ebb tide, anchoring for a time off Lopez' Flat Point for astronomical observations. The crew enjoyed fishing in the fine spring weather but didn't catch much. At 8 o'clock the two small boats returned with a report of more islands, more channels,

24

and one wide expanse (Haro Strait) to the north and west.

Next morning, a Sunday, the brig proceeded under tow at slack tide as far as Harney Channel before Broughton sent out the small boats again, one toward the northwest and the other southeastward into Lopez Sound. Somewhere around Blind Bay, the crew of the former boat found a camp of Indians for the first time. Two canoes, each carrying three persons, had come out to meet them. With broad smiles, the short-statured benign natives held up several small, newly killed deer which they offered to trade. The Englishmen bought three of these, and obtained a live fawn as well. The party continued, then, about as far as Wasp Pass before returning to the *Chatham*.

The next morning Broughton had the brig towed toward Obstruction Pass, where he correctly guessed he would find a passage to Rosario Strait. Shortly after noon the *Chatham* entered "a spacious Sound containing several Islands and openings in all directions." The islands were no doubt Cypress, Sinclair, and Lummi.

No sooner had the party entered the Strait than they were caught up by a strong tide and carried rapidly toward the rocks on the southeast coast of Orcas. The small boats worked to pull the brig away from the danger, but one of the tow ropes broke, and before the slack could be taken up in the other one, the *Chatham*'s bow swung inshore and just brushed against a rock. A crewman who kept an unofficial — and illegal — diary on the trip recorded their amazement at striking the rocky coast on one side, while at the same moment the leadsman on the other side called twenty-two fathoms!

In the feverish business of getting the brig off the rocks and into the open channel again, the sounding line was fouled, and Broughton reported losing the lead and about 120 feet of line. As lead does not deteriorate in salt water, it is presumably still there, should some enterprising skin-diver care to look for an interesting souvenir.

25

Broughton anchored his ship in a safe depth and, after dispatching a boat to look over the various arms to the north and east, put the men on the *Chatham* to fishing.

At eight the following morning the party got underway again, the boats towing to the east, while the tide set them rapidly toward the south. By two-thirty they were off the shore of a rugged island, where Broughton came to anchor in "a fine Bay on the North shore within a small Island in 11 fa^{ms}." The crewmen delightedly picked wild strawberries they found growing there, and drew sparkling clear fresh water from springs near the beach. Broughton, mistaking a fine stand of evergreens for cypress trees, called the island Cypress and the little cove Strawberry Bay. His men spent another afternoon with net and lure, and in the evening sat out a southeast storm which was accompanied by heavy rain and much thunder.

It was still raining the morning of May 23 when the party left Cypress on a southward course to rendezvous with Vancouver, whom they met two days later just opposite Seattle's Alki Point. Vancouver's busy investigation of Puget Sound had coincided exactly with Broughton's rather more leisurely examination of the San Juans.

It also concurred with the final preparations of Galiano and Valdés for their expedition. The *Sutil* and the *Mexicana* were at Nootka, the Spanish base on Vancouver Island, having their bottoms pitched and their crews brought up to strength. They departed the morning of June 5, arriving at Esquimalt on the 9th. Meanwhile Vancouver's two vessels emerged from Admiralty Inlet on the 6th, but were forced to anchor off Partridge Point because of contrary currents and little wind. The small boats were sent ahead to Strawberry Bay, where the larger vessels were able to join them at last on the 8th.

It was three in the afternoon when the *Discovery* succeeded in riding a flood tide into Strawberry Bay with the help of a light breeze. Just as the sloop hove to in the lee of the little island, however, the wind failed and the *Chatham*, some distance behind, was caught in a cross-current. In seconds she had drifted so far eastward that she was obliged to anchor hurriedly among the rocks off the south shore of Cypress. There the booming tide severed the stream anchor from its cable and Broughton, his vessel straining at the larger bower anchor, spent the better part of a day in a futile attempt to recover his lost hook. At last Vancouver told him to come on without it and the anchor is, presumably, still there.

Vancouver's men, eagerly looking forward to the strawberries Broughton reported, were dismayed to discover the luscious fruit was now out of season. Captain George set them instead to collecting some small, wild onions they found growing on the island, and encouraged them to brew up some "spruce beer" — a drink the English had found to be a protection against scurvy, if not a sailor's thirst.

At this moment the *Sutil* and the *Mexicana* were entering the Strait of Juan de Fuca. Their crews spent the night at Esquimalt, and on the tenth set sail for the southern tip of Lopez Island, arriving there in a few hours, still totally unaware of the presence of the English explorers a few miles to the northeast. The Spaniards set up an observatory and corrected their timepieces by clocking the transit of one of Jupiter's moons. Next day they rounded Watmough Head and proceeded up Rosario Strait, practically in the wake of the English vessels which were just disappearing behind Point Lawrence on Orcas Island.

Galiano and Valdés rounded Fidalgo Head and sailed through Guemes Channel, up into Bellingham Bay, and on through Hale's Passage to the north. Unaware that Vancouver's small boats had just reconnoitered the same route, the Spaniards were still hoping to find a "Northwest Passage" to the east.

But later in the day the Spanish lookouts spotted two small sail-rigged craft following the shoreline of Lummi Bay, and toward midnight lights were seen glowing in Birch Bay, where the *Discovery* and *Chatham* were at anchor. Dismayed at this evidence of other Europeans engaged at the same errand as themselves, Galiano and Valdés ignored their English confreres and continued north to the vicinity of present-day Vancouver, B.C. There they were met at 7 the next morning by a small boat bearing Lt. Broughton, who boarded the *Sutil* to present Capt. Vancouver's compliments and to offer assistance. The British were irked to learn so much of the area had been visited the previous year by the Spanish.

Reluctantly Galiano and Valdés acceded to Vancouver's suggestion to join forces in further explorations which took them through Georgia Strait and the narrow passages separating Vancouver Island from the mainland, and finally out through Queen Charlotte Strait into the Pacific Ocean.

Today the predominantly Spanish names by which we know so many of the islands, channels and other features north of Juan de Fuca's strait are our token of the area's first visitors. The American islands of San Juan, Orcas, Lopez, Patos, Sucia, Matia, Guemes, Fidalgo, etc. owe their names to His Catholic Majesty's explorers; as do Galiano, Gabriola, Saturna, and others of the Canadian isles.

But other names bestowed by the Spanish have fared less well. British and American surveying expeditions in the following decades sprinkled their charts instead with such imaginative monikers as Jones and Smith, along with other names honoring a miscellany of obscure historical — largely naval — figures. The result is a colorful admixture of Hispano-Anglo-American appellations, though from the contemporary local tongue each one rolls in the same precisely careless North American accents.

Some names on today's maps and charts date from an even later era, and commemorate men and ships which played a part in the region's unique contribution to world history, the celebrated Pig War. To this we shall now turn our full attention.

28

2

"OLD SQUARE TOES"

Governor James Douglas of
the Crown Colony of Vancouver Island was the tall, broad-
shouldered, resourceful and illegitimate son of a Scottish merchant and a Creole charmer. Educated in Scotland to the
niceties of the Britannic way of life, he had entered the service
of the all-powerful Hudson's Bay Company at the age of sixteen
and for a quarter-century pursued the storied life of the Canadian
fur-trader. His self-avowed maxim was to be "the bold, resolute,
strong, self-reliant man, who fights his own way, through every
obstacle," while screening any personal feelings or emotions
behind a perpetual mask of British reserve. His long service and
unflagging loyalty to Hudson's Bay led to his assuming the
administration of all the Company's affairs in Western Canada
by 1851, while his devotion to empire and manifest managerial
abilities later gained him the governorship of that new nation's
most westerly outpost.

From the Colony's bastion at Victoria, Douglas — who would
be knighted later on — looked with disdain on the small but
growing army of American adventurers and gold-seekers who

drifted into the northern Puget Sound country in the 1850's — men who made up in two-fisted resourcefulness and sheer guts what they lacked in education and refinement. He agreed whole-heartedly with the Englishman of that same period who wrote: "The mode in which the far [American] West is prepared for civilization is familiar to all readers of [James Fenimore] Cooper's novels, which, although overdrawn, afford some idea of it. How the hardy squatter penetrates, rifle and axe on shoulder, into the recesses of the forests, how he builds his bark huts, and makes the little clearing in which he plants a few potatoes and sows a little Indian maize; how, when civilization presses upon him, he sells his hut and clearing, and disappears again into the forest. . . . Men of this stamp would appear to be eminently unfitted for life in a respectable and civilized colony, and might be most unpleasant neighbours."

But the influx of Yankee "squatters" had not yet begun back in 1846, when the United States and Great Britain concluded their treaty fixing the boundary between their western territories at the 49th parallel of north latitude. Britain seemed glad, simply to get the boundary question settled. Her own team of explorers, just returned from the Puget Sound country, termed the whole area north of the Columbia River "worthless." The British were asking only that the line be deflected slightly at its western end, bending around the lower part of Vancouver Island.

To Hudson's Bay, however, whose fur trade extended all the way to the Columbia, the area was anything but worthless, and the Company was in no rapture over being compelled to withdraw several hundred miles to the north. While London was not even well informed of the geography of the area, Hudson's Bay officials were, and even as the treaty was being negotiated, they urged the home government to lay claim to the islands lying between the mainland and Vancouver Island. To add what force they could to the claim, it was hinted that a British settlement was about to be made on "Whitbey's Island," an indication that when Hudson's Bay said they wanted islands, they meant *all* of them, as Whidbey lies far to the south and east of the most extreme point Britain ever felt justified in claiming.

From the American point of view, the real hero of the piece proved to be that grand old historian and diplomat, George Bancroft, who isn't even mentioned in most accounts of the pig war. Bancroft was Secretary of the Navy in 1845, while the treaty was being negotiated, and he had a tracing made of an early chart of lower Puget Sound waters, the most detailed then in existence, for the guidance of our negotiators. But Britain was still using Captain Vancouver's 50-year-old chart, though primitive as it was, even his drawing indicated that the waters between the mainland and Vancouver Island are thickly dotted with islands, separated by a variety of channels. Yet for some reason the treaty language ignored this fact. It said:

"*...From the point on the forty-ninth parallel of north latitude, where the boundary laid down in existing treaties and conventions between the United States and Great Britain terminates, the line of boundary between the territories of the United States and those of her Britannic Majesty shall be continued westward along the said forty-ninth parallel of north latitude, to the middle of the channel which separates the continent from Vancouver's Island, and thence southerly through the middle of the said channel, and of Fuca's Straits, to the Pacific Ocean:* Provided, however, *that the navigation of the whole of the said channel and straits, south of the forty-ninth parallel of north latitude, remain free and open to both parties.*"

It was that ambiguous "the channel" which caused all the later difficulty. At least *three* channels "separate the continent from Vancouver's Island": one to the west, one to the east, and one running right down the middle of the San Juans. Nothing in the treaty spelled out just which channel was to be the boundary.

The then minister to England, J. McHenry Boyd, had got wind of Hudson's Bay Company designs on the "Arro Islands," as they called them then. He tipped Washington off; but his warning went unheeded. After the treaty was signed, Bancroft himself was sent to London as U.S. minister, and he soon was renewing the warning that Britain, at H.B.C. urging, would try to claim the San Juans. To forestall just such a move, he gathered evidence showing that diplomats on both sides had only meant to deflect the boundary enough to avoid cutting off the tip of Vancouver Island, and that this was all Britain was entitled to have south of the 49th parallel.

In 1848 the British government published a chart of the area on which the boundary was shown to pass through Rosario Strait, thus giving the "Arro Islands" to Great Britain. Bancroft protested; the British were noncommittal.

On January 13, 1849, Vancouver Island was handed over to the Hudson's Bay Company by royal grant, on condition the Company promote colonization of the island. Douglas was in practical charge, though a young, unpaid, sickly Britisher named Richard Blanshard was nominal governor for the first couple of years. Nothing was said in the Grant about the offshore islands, but Douglas was soon claiming them as part of the Hudson's Bay empire. Later he was to insist that San Juan Island had been "taken possession of" by Hudson's Bay people as far back as 1845, but admitted there were no written records of this.

In the summer of 1850, Douglas sent one of the company's clerks, a man by the name of Simpson, over to San Juan with instructions to set up a fishing station. Camp was established for a few weeks at Eagle Cove, where Indians showed him their techniques of salmon fishing with reef nets.

In June of the following year another clerk, William John Macdonald, left Victoria in one of the long, graceful Indian canoes then so common on the Sound. With him as "pilot and locator of a site" was Joseph W. McKay, also a crew of native

32

Washington State Ferries' *Evergreen State* threads its way through Wasp Pass in the San Juans.

DRAWING BY F. P. THURSBY

The schooner *Santa Saturnina*, under the command of Spanish explorer Juan Pantoja y Arriaga, reconnoitred the San Juans in 1791. *Vancouver City Archives.*

Waters off Saltspring Island — probable site of Juan Pantoja's nighttime reconnaissance — today. Vessel in foreground is a replica of the historic Hudson's Bay Company steamer *Beaver*.

B.C. Government Photo.

The diminutive brigantines *Sutil* and *Mexicana* used by the Spanish for exploring the San Juans in June 1792. *Provincial Archives, Victoria.*

Captain George Vancouver, R.N.
Vancouver City Archives.

William Robert Broughton, R.N.
Provincial Archives, Victoria.

PAINTING BY F. P. THURSBY
The British sailing ships *Discovery* and *Chatham* explored
the San Juans in 1792. *Vancouver City Archives.*

British survey crew made this pre-Pig War sketch of West Sound, from Ship Peak, Orcas Island. *Courtesy Mr. Cecil Clark, Victoria.*

The Hudson's Bay Company farm on San Juan Island in Pig War days.
Sketch by James Alden, U.S.N.
Washington State Historical Society.

Sir James Douglas, governor of Vancouver Island 1851-1858,
and of British Columbia 1858-1863.
Provincial Archives, Victoria.

paddlers, and four French Canadian workmen. Crossing over to San Juan they selected a small, sheltered bay and erected a rough shed for the large-scale brining and barreling of salmon. Indians were paid one blanket — worth $4 — for every 60 fish. They put up 2,000 to 3,000 barrels a year during the time the enterprise stayed in operation.

Macdonald's memoirs relate that "The first month on this Island I lived under a very primitive rough shelter, four posts stuck in the ground with a ceder [*sic*] bark roof, and wolves used to prowl round us all night. My men soon built a house for me of rough logs, with bedstead and table of the same, and as the Hudson's Bay Company always furnished plenty of blankets, I had a very comfortable bed. Soon the old schooner Cadboro, Captain Dixon, came into our little bay with different kinds of supplies. I removed my quarters to her, and after a month we came back to Victoria, and I went back to office work."

Macdonald recalled that he had no trouble with Indians during his stay on the island. It is remarkable that the Hudson's Bay people generally did not, even when Americans were being methodically slaughtered. The British were known for their reasonably fair dealings with the natives, and for the immediate, stern retribution which followed any wrongdoings. Hudson's Bay had dealt with the Indians long enough to have formulated an Indian policy that was as successful as it was inflexible; while Americans were largely disorganized, inconsistent, and oftentimes unjust in their Indian dealings, the results being predictably tragic in many cases.

But Macdonald was able to leave San Juan in the fall of 1851, leaving all his horses behind, and to find them there undisturbed when he returned the next spring.

Meantime Douglas' position was strengthened all the more when the unhappy Blanshard, who was totally unprepared for frontier life and unsupported by his home government, threw in the towel and returned to England. No one was surprised

33

when Douglas himself was named governor to replace him. In this capacity, one of the wilful Scot's first acts was to grant a license to one William Pattle, a Hudson's Bay employe, to cut timber and carry on trade with the Indians on the southwest side of Lopez Island. Pattle erected a couple of log huts and began cutting spars for export to San Francisco, but left the island in 1852 to investigate Indian tales of "black fire dirt" — coal — over Bellingham way. Finding the stories true, Pattle abandoned his Lopez Island layout to pioneer Bellingham's coal mining industry.

Pattle's camp was taken over by an American, Richard W. Cussans (or Cousins), who had made some $1500 worth of improvements before Douglas got wind of it. Cussans was curtly informed that he and his companions were trespassing on British property, that the spot they were occupying was reserved for Her Majesty's government, and that if they persisted in building there, they "would in all probability lose their labour and improvements." Cussans, by Douglas' account, then maintained that he was a British-born subject and intended to settle in the Colony. Douglas doubted his story, but issued him a license to cut timber, and waited until he had felled and squared some 30,000 feet of it to inform him the vessel taking it away would have to clear the Victoria customs house and a stiff duty would need to be paid.

Cussans told his sad tale to Lieutenant James Alden whose ship *Active* nosed into Lopez waters in October 1853, on a U.S. surveying mission. As Alden's orders were to stick to his chart-making and not to provoke trouble, he was unable to offer Cussans' party more than sympathy. Cussans' license was to expire, moreover, at the end of 1853, so he decided to close up shop. Upon his departure Douglas sent a canoe party to Lopez with instructions to take possession of the island formally and "mark that act by some permanent improvements."

By this time Douglas, thoroughly alarmed at the prospect of

more and more Americans' "encroaching" on land he considered Company property, decided the best counter was to encourage some of that British settlement his Royal Grant talked about. There was this problem, though: no prospective British settlers were to be found who had the capital — much less the inclination — to go off pioneering in these remote, Indian-infested islands whose very nationality was open to question. Accordingly, he decided the Company should start up a colony of their own on San Juan, which was renamed "Bellevue." William Macdonald — the salmon packing pioneer — was at first designated to head it up, but was passed over in favor of a new arrival from Fort Simpson named Charles J. Griffin.

Griffin, together with 1300 sheep and a band of Hawaiian shepherds, landed on the south shores of San Juan Island from the historic steam side-wheeler *Beaver* on the night of December 13, 1853.

Now events began to move rapidly. Colonel Isaac E. Ebey, who later lost his head — literally — in an Indian uprising at Port Townsend, had recently been named Collector of Customs for the Puget Sound district. Learning of the landing of livestock on San Juan, Ebey sent word to Governor Douglas that the sheep were liable to seizure for being unlawfully imported without a customs clearance. (They weren't; the sheep had been enshipped at Nisqually, in Washington Territory.) Douglas promptly appointed Griffin to be Justice of the Peace for San Juan District and told him to arrest Ebey, if he came around, "as a common offender."

Ebey — a man given to stuttering when excited — did indeed come to San Juan on May 2, 1854, on board the chartered schooner *Sarah Stone*. With him as quartermaster was good-natured, easy-going Henry Webber, a friend who was pioneering on the Lummi River. Landing at Griffin Bay, they pitched their tent at the spot which later became San Juan Town. Ebey summoned Griffin to the camp and told him he had come to seize his sheep for violating the U.S. revenue laws. Griffin, who had already sent off a message to Victoria telling of Ebey's arrival, was content to temporize.

Next day Governor Douglas himself steamed over to San Juan in the *Otter*, bringing with him James Sangster, the British Collector of Customs at Victoria. Ebey, when he saw the *Otter* coming, had his men raise the U.S. flag atop the nearest hill. The British countered by bringing ashore the ship's Union Jack and hoisting it at Griffin's farm.

Sangster landed in a small boat while Douglas rather grandly stayed aboard the *Otter*. Ebey and Webber greeted Sangster, whom they knew, but considered it rather ominous when the British officer declined the drink of whisky they offered him, contrary to his usual nature.

Coming to the point, Sangster asked Ebey what he thought he was doing on British soil, and Colonel Ebey replied that he was an American officer on American soil, and not bound to answer, but that as a matter of fact he was there to confiscate some contraband livestock.

Sangster reddened. Ebey, enjoying the situation, remarked as coolly as possible that Sangster appeared a bit overwrought, advised him to calm down a bit, and turned the conversation to less apoplectic subjects.

Douglas was invited to come ashore for a conference but he declined, sending his respects and an invitation to come aboard the *Otter* instead. Ebey, fearing a trap, refused.

The next morning Ebey and Webber met with Captain Sangster and Justice Griffin, and after some polite socializing, the colonel announced that he had decided not to seize the sheep just then, but that he intended leaving an American officer on the island.

"Who is he?" Sangster demanded to know.

"Mr. Webber," Ebey told him.

36

"Then I arrest him in the name of the Queen!" was Sangster's reply.

Now it was Ebey's turn to become excited. "S-s-stop, you're t-t-too f-f-fast," he stuttered. "He has n-n-no c-c-c-commission yet!"

Later in the afternoon Ebey gave Webber that document, and swore him in as U.S. Deputy Collector of Customs. Douglas and the *Otter* steamed off to Victoria, leaving Sangster and six men on the island. Ebey advised Webber to move his tent nearer to Griffin's farm "for the sake of company," but Sangster snorted that it would be a waste of time, as he planned to arrest Webber as soon as Ebey left.

Colonel Ebey returned to Port Townsend where he penned a report of his adventures to the Treasury Department, adding:

"I have no doubt but Mr Webber, the Inspector, has been arrested and taken to Van Couver's Island a prisoner. I shall visit San Juan Island in a few days and assertain his fate. Should I find that Mr Webber has been Kidnapped I shall place another Inspector on the Island and call upon the Executive of this Territory to protect him."

Meanwhile, Sangster was once again presenting himself at the Inspector's tent trying to arrest Webber in the name of the Queen. When Webber demanded to see his process, Sangster admitted he didn't have one, and went back to confer with Griffin. The latter thereupon drew up a paper Webber later described as "a most remarkable document . . . . I'm sorry I did not save it, for it was a literary and legal curiosity."

Armed with this unconventional writ and backed up by a hastily appointed constable, Sangster clapped his hand on Webber's shoulder for the third time. When Webber had read the process he said, "Now do your duty; don't flinch." But the constable had detected something ominous in Webber's eye and decided to collect some moral support first. After rounding up a group of six stalwarts, he advanced toward Webber.

37

At three paces, the American produced four six-barreled revolvers and aimed one of them directly at the constable's head. "One more foot and you are a dead man," he said calmly. "I have no ill will toward you; on the other hand, the first one who steps toward me I will blow his brains out."

The constable retreated a pace or two, then ordered his men to advance and disarm the "prisoner." When they refused, he repeated the order to a Negro servant, who similarly declined.

Finding himself master of the situation, Webber seated himself on a convenient stump. The constable sat down on another, a few feet distant, while they talked. Then the constable withdrew with his posse for further instructions.

Two hours later the constable returned alone, shouting from a distance: "Don't shoot! I'm on a peaceful mission." Nothing more would be done, he said, until Governor Douglas' return; and just to show their hearts were in the right place, here was a leg of mutton for Webber's supper.

Griffin himself offered to give Webber supplies for his camp, but the American planned to return home the next day for his own gear.

When Webber got back to San Juan four days later, he sent word to Griffin that he was now ready to be arrested, as he had some business to transact in Victoria and would appreciate the free transportation. He was disappointed when Griffin informed him that Governor Douglas no longer wanted him apprehended. Paying for his ride to Vancouver Island, Webber was seen at Victoria by a correspondent of the Washington paper, *Pioneer and Democrat*, which reported the fact and speculated whether he was a prisoner there. "We have a rod in pickle for the H. B. Co.," said the paper, "and we will make use of it ere long."

Webber spent a year on the island, during which time he and Charles Griffin became fast friends. When belligerent Indians raided his camp, he went to Griffin's farm for protection. But as the raids became more frequent and more savage he lost his former *sang-froid*, resigned his inspectorship, and left the island.

Meanwhile the first session of the new Washington Territorial Legislature was held in 1854 in Olympia, and the county of Whatcom was formed, with boundaries which included the San Juan Islands. Early the following year the Whatcom County commissioners instructed their new sheriff, Ellis "Yankee" Barnes, to assess the property of Hudson's Bay on San Juan, and levy taxes on it. Barnes visited Griffin's layout and figured the tax at around $80, which Griffin resolutely refused to pay.

Barnes returned to Whatcom and advertised a sheriff's sale to satisfy the delinquent taxes. When no bidders showed up on the appointed day, Barnes rounded up six or seven men — most of them county officials — and they set off for San Juan in two small boats.* Arriving about noon on March 30, after almost twenty hours at the oars, Barnes' party hunted up Griffin and asked where the sheep were.

"At the other end of the island," Griffin replied, and the party took to the boats once again for a fruitless row up to Roche Harbor and back.

Returning to Griffin's place about 3 in the morning, the men poked about on a hill-top and located a pen containing several dozen breeding rams about a mile from Griffin's house. Barnes left a guard at the enclosure until daylight, when the sale commenced.

The rams were knocked down for fifty cents to a dollar a head (according to the Hudson's Bay Company they were worth more like fifty to a hundred dollars each) and when they all had been auctioned and the amount paid still did not equal the taxes due, sheep running at large on the island were sold unseen for one or two cents apiece.

* They included Edmund Fitzhugh, auditor; William Cullen, chairman of the county commissioners; W. A. Carpenter, coroner; Alonzo Poe, Whatcom County representative to the Legislature; Dominic Mahoney; Charles Vail; and Barnes.

The taxes being thus satisfied, Barnes and his companions began the not inconsiderable chore of hauling their purchases down to the water and into the boats. They were about half through the job when there was a whoop from the hill and Griffin, together with some twenty Kanakas brandishing knives, were seen charging down toward them. Rising grandly to the occasion, Barnes ordered his party to draw the revolvers with which they had the foresight to arm themselves, and to protect their property "in the name of the United States." Griffin, unable to recapture his livestock, called his men off and sent a party of six in a canoe to Victoria to get help.

Barnes' group had carelessly let their boats get aground and it took several hours' work to get them water-borne again. When they had done so, a wisp of smoke in the southwest convinced them that the *Beaver* was on its way, and as one of the party later put it, "We did not wish to be taken prisoners and lie in jail until the boundary question could be settled by the two governments; we loaded about one half of the sheep into our boats and 'lit out'. We were all worn out from loss of sleep and hard work, the tide was running strong against us, our boats were heavily loaded, but we bent to the oars and like Wellington at Waterloo, prayed for 'night or Blucher' to come to our relief."

When Barnes and his crew arrived back at Whatcom they had only 34 of the rams with them. But the Hudson's Bay people could scarcely contain their indignation. Against the United States they filed a claim through the British government, asking for the "outrage" 2,990 pounds and 13 shillings — roughly $15,000. Besides the rams, Hudson's Bay asked damages for 409 sheep lost in the woods (Griffin had driven them off as the group approached); hire of 18 men for eight days at about three dollars a day; $2500 for hire of the *Beaver* for protection of the Company's property; and a nice, round $5,000 for "Incidental losses through the derangement and suspension of business in consequence of Sheriff Barnes' violent acts."

This claim — which was never paid — was met with derision by Americans who knew better. The *Pioneer and Democrat* at Olympia observed, among other things, that so far from paying their help $3 a day, Hudson's Bay paid around $7 a month for shepherds, and two to three blankets for Indians; that the *Beaver* could scarcely be "hired" when it was the Company's own vessel; and that the claim of 1000 pounds for "incidentals" was a downright case of bill-padding.

News of these goings-on reached Washington, D.C. and caused President Franklin Pierce considerable anxiety. He had his Secretary of State, William L. Marcy (who secured his place in history by coining the phrase "to the victors belong the spoils") instruct Washington Governor Isaac Stevens to have his territorial officers "abstain from all acts on the disputed grounds which are calculated to provoke any conflicts," but without conceding to Great Britain "exclusive right over the premises." A copy was sent to the British Foreign Office with the suggestion that authorities at Victoria be similarly instructed.

Meanwhile, back at the disputed grounds, Colonel Ebey had found a replacement for Henry Webber: Oscar Olney, a hard-drinking two-fisted frontiersman, was sworn in and set up in business as Customs Inspector. He occupied the building Webber had lived in but, like his predecessor, found he spent much of the time hiding out in the Hudson's Bay settlement while Indians prowled his premises.

It was a time of growing Indian difficulties all over the Puget Sound country; raids by the feared Northern tribes were becoming more frequent; even the generally docile local Indians were beginning to rebel at one-sided "white man's justice." Alarmed, settlers all along the Sound were forming volunteer armies and sheltering their women and children into stockades. In isolated places people left their homes behind for the protection of the nearest town. Seattle came under siege and was attacked.

The U.S. Army was slow to respond to Governor Stevens' plea

for more protection; but it must be stated here that Governor Douglas, to whom Stevens turned next, was almost lavish in his assistance. On his own responsibility he sent $5,000 worth of supplies; ordered the *Beaver* and *Otter* to patrol Territorial waters and repel any incursions of hostile Indians; and arranged for Hudson's Bay posts to furnish arms and ammunition worth over $25,000.

Douglas' instant decision to make common cause with his white brethren below the border was an enormous factor in containing the rebellion. If some of the Indians expected the British to side with them against the "boston men," they were quickly disabused of the notion.

James Douglas had been dealing with Indians most of his life. In his prime he once faced down a mob of them, armed and screaming, intent on avenging a convicted tribesman he had ordered executed. Standing firm-footed and unflinching he cowed them with nothing deadlier than his cool, resolute stare and firm speech. It was startling to contrast this bold, self-reliant man of action with the prim, dandified Douglas who walked the streets of Victoria attended by aides in gaudy uniform. The fort town's society — stratified, as one resident put it, as to "nobs, snobs and flunkies" — generally applauded the one Douglas and sneered behind the back of the other. "When the prayer for the Governor and Council is made in Church," observed one young Englishman, "old Square-toes looks as if his health was being drunk at dinner, and doubting whether or not to rise and return thanks."

Eventually, in mid-1856, the U.S. Army sent two companies to protect settlers in the northwest corner of the Territory. To Port Townsend came I company, Fourth Infantry, under Brevet Major Granville O. Haller.* To help guard the entrance to

---

* A brevet was an advance in rank awarded for meritorious service, especially in war time.

Admiralty Inlet, Haller was given the diminutive Revenue Cutter, *Jefferson Davis*. Company D, Ninth Infantry, was dispatched to Bellingham Bay, under the command of a young West Point captain named George E. Pickett. The orders were signed by the commander of the Department of Oregon, Brigadier General William S. Harney.

In November the Navy sent the U.S. Steamer *Massachusetts,* Captain Swartwout, into the area with instructions to clear Northern Indians out of American waters altogether. Swartwout took his orders seriously and in a short time had engaged a party of around a hundred Stikines at Port Gamble. When the smoke of the wholly one-sided battle cleared, the *Massachusetts'* cannon had taken the lives of twenty-seven Indians — including one woman — and destroyed their camp. Ten Indians were missing, and the tribal chief was writhing with the pain of two broken legs. U.S. casualties: one marine was killed and another sustained a wounded thumb.

Anyone who knew the Northern Indians knew there would be reprisals. In December, rumors trickled down from the North that they were out for Yankee blood, but out of consideration for the *Massachusetts'* 32-pounders, planned to take their revenge as close to home as possible. Their target proved to be that *boston tyee* on San Juan Island, the elusive Oscar Olney.

Griffin heard the rumor and warned Olney, who cleared out just in time. The coals of his cook fire were hardly cold when the party of half-a-hundred determined Stikines descended on the island for the express purpose of relieving him of his head.

(Olney, doubling as a private in the territorial volunteers, had already lost part of his scalp and some fingers the year before, when a cannon burst near him while firing a ceremonial salute.)

In the spring Governor Douglas sent word that 300 Northern Indians had appeared in Victoria, and another 300 in Nanaimo, apparently on their way to northern Puget Sound. Oscar Olney decided enough was enough; slipping down to Port Townsend

43

on the next tide he handed his resignation to Major Jacobus Jan Hogerworth Van Bokkelen, who had just succeeded Ebey as Collector of Customs.*

Van Bokkelen cast about in his mind for a replacement for Olney and came up with the name of Paul K. Hubbs, Jr. Hubbs had been a scout for Van Bokkelen in the Indian wars east of the Cascade Mountains; small but wiry, traveled and well educated, yet tough and resourceful, Hubbs had been in the Northwest for years and had lived among the Indians. Van Bokkelen thought Hubbs could handle the situation and sent Olney to find him.

Hubbs received his commission April 29, 1857. Olney took him to San Juan and turned over to him what government property there was, including the little log dwelling some 100 yards from the Hudson's Bay spread. Then he hastily wished Hubbs well, and saying a last good-bye to San Juan Island, rowed off as energetically as he could.

No one told Hubbs why Webber and Olney had each quit the post on short notice, but he was not long in finding out for himself. Between Indian troubles and strained relations with Hudson's Bay, life proved to be anything but monotonous for him.

In April 1858, a large party of hostile Clallams landed on the island for one of their periodic attempts on the American's life. Firing into Hubbs' cabin at night they would have succeeded in their murderous purpose but for Charles Griffin, who heard the shots and sent help. Thus thwarted in their original design, the Indians contented themselves with garroting two luckless white men who chose this inopportune moment to land some 200 yards from the scene of action.

Next morning Hubbs sent word of the murders to Port

---

* Van Bokkelen had had his own run-in with the British who, following the accidental damaging of some H.B.C. machinery, put the Dutchman in jail and threatened to send him to London for trial.

44

Townsend. A guard of soldiers was dispatched on the *Jefferson Davis*, and were welcomed by Hubbs and Griffin alike.* The Clallams quickly broke camp and left the island.

The two unfortunate whites are not identified in any of the historical accounts but they were most likely in the vanguard of a growing army of gold-seekers who streamed through the Puget Sound country on their way to the Thompson and Fraser Rivers, scenes of the latest gold discoveries. Estimates are that upwards of 100,000 hopeful argonauts came north in that summer of 1858. Most traveled by ship to Victoria or to Bellingham Bay, hoping to make their way overland to the Canadian "diggings." Thousands more poured into Port Townsend and other settlements along the Sound; hundreds of these traveled northward in small boats, passing among the San Juans and camping there when overtaken by nightfall.

Many were overtaken by Indians as well, and were unburdened by them of their money, firearms, food supplies, and sometimes their lives. Bullet-ridden white bodies were regularly washing ashore, sometimes with cotton cords tied tight around their necks, or floating aimlessly in their frail boats. One large party of miners was attacked by 130 Coghole Indians on Orcas in June, the men fleeing into the brush until rescued by Hubbs and two boatloads of marines sent from Victoria.†

In a few months the gold rush of 1858 proved a fizzle and traffic through the islands began flowing southward again; and Indians or no, some who drifted down to the San Juans, grumbling over the "Frazer River humbug," decided to stay — either because they were genuinely attracted to the islands, or because they were too discouraged, or broke, to go further. The first to settle in the fall of 1858 were John Hunter MacKay and John

* Thus Pickett's men were not the first U.S. soldiers to land on San Juan, as is usually assumed.

† This landing of British red-coats, overlooked by most histories of the affair, predates the 1859 Pig War confrontation by a year.

Mills, both of whom took ranches in the rolling open ground of San Juan Valley. MacKay, who was from Glasgow, Scotland, stayed until 1860 and then left to go silver-mining in New Zealand. Mills was killed by Indians within the year.

Others who settled on San Juan in 1858 or early 1859 included John Witty, William Smith, Daniel W. Oakes, Charles McCoy, and the brash, good-humored young fellow by the name of Lyman A. Cutler. Cutler already had a well-deserved reputation as a dead shot with a rifle who "didn't scare worth a cent"; but his permanent place in history was to be won in the unlikely confrontation with Charles Griffin's pig.

3

MAKING A BUNKER HILL OF IT

BRIGADIER GENERAL WILLIAM
Selby Harney, U.S. Army, believed it was a soldier's business to
fight. From the moment he entered the service as a second
lieutenant in 1818, his was a career which generally found him
in the thick of some battle, somewhere. His Indian-fighting expeditions in Florida paralleled those of his idol, Andrew Jackson, and
led to rapid promotions which found him a full colonel at 46. In
the Mexican War he was ranking cavalry officer under General
Winfield Scott, whose concept of soldiering was somewhat
broader: Scott considered Harney's exploits in Florida as over-
zealous — he had hung some Indians there on rather flimsy
grounds — and suspected him of emulating Jackson's expansionist as well as his military traits.* He also considered Harney
impetuous and unmanageable, and had him relieved.

Harney at first complied, then defied Scott and resumed
command on his own orders. Scott had Harney court-martialed,

---

* Nor was Scott any admirer of Jackson, who once challenged him to a
duel — declined by Scott, on grounds the nation could "spare" neither of
them.

47

but Harney pulled some political strings and it was Scott who drew a mild reprimand.

Restored to command, Colonel Harney fought brilliantly under Scott and opened for him the road to Mexico City with his decisive victory at Cerro Gordo, personally leading his men in hand-to-hand battle to take El Telégrafo hill.

Harney's next exploits were in the Platte country where he defeated the Sioux in the battle of Sand Hill, and in the Utah "Mormon War" of 1857-8. It was Harney who, faced with superior forces and being implored to withdraw, replied, "Gentlemen, I have orders to winter in Utah, and I'm going to winter there or in Hell." And Harney was on the point of hanging Brigham Young, together with a number of the latter's fellow apostles, when removed from command of this campaign — which his superiors felt should have been waged with more tact and less vigor.

Such was the man selected to command the newly created Department of Oregon. He arrived at Fort Vancouver on the Columbia River in October 1858.

Meanwhile Governor Douglas' anxiety over the burgeoning invasion of San Juan Island by Yankee "squatters" continued. In February, several Americans came to the island from Victoria with a surveyor, Edward C. Gillette, and began staking claims to land; by making a few minimal improvements they hoped to qualify for preemption claims later on.* Hudson's Bay agent Griffin reported this to his superiors, whereupon some Vancouver Island politicians proposed forestalling American settlement by banishing the more troublesome of their Indian population to San Juan.

---

* Americans who showed they had lived on and made improvements to government land had first chance to buy, and at cheap rates, when the land was released to public sale. Under the Oregon Land Bill "donation law" of 1850, which was in effect through 1855, Henry Webber had already filed a claim — comprising the choicest parts of the Hudson's Bay Farm on San Juan Island.

48

In April, Lyman Cutler arrived and began looking around for a place to settle on. The tall, light-haired Ohioan was not known for an overly industrious nature. Hoping to avoid the manual labor entailed in clearing the giant firs which grew "thick as hairs on the back of a dog"* over most of the island, he made his choice on a bit of rolling, sparsely timbered prairie a mile to the north and west of Bellevue Farm. That this spot was exactly in the middle of Charles Griffin's best sheep run did not bother him in the slightest.

Cutler threw together a log shack and selected a winsome copper-skinned lass to share it with him, after the custom of the country. He spaded up a third of an acre of garden, around which he built a half-hearted fence. Then, rowing twenty miles across the Strait to Dungeness, he paid ten dollars for a peck of seed potatoes and planted them in his modest plot. At such prices, a neighbor of Cutler's liked to point out, "spuds is spuds."

Before long Agent Griffin could count upwards of sixteen American settlers on or near his premises. Alarmed, he reported to Douglas the newcomers were assuring him the island was considered U.S. soil by their government, that it was about to be officially surveyed, and that land claims were soon to be recognized.

Paul Hubbs was worrying too. Northern Indians were still making periodic forays and it was hard to say how long the British would continue to protect the unwelcome settlers. It appears that Hubbs wrote to General Harney about May 1859, asking that a guard of around twenty soldiers be stationed on San Juan for protection against Indians. Harney was also invited to visit the island and "view its resources and its commanding position."

The invitation may or may not have influenced Harney's decision to make an inspection trip of the northern Puget Sound area the following July.

* The phrase is from "The Old Settler," a popular pioneer song by Francis Henry.

The spring rains that year melted into an early, warm summer. By mid-June Cutler's potato patch was sending up a thick matting of green. He was setting great store by those spuds; although he had a few pigs on the island, like the rest of the settlers he was counting on potatoes and venison for staple edibles. But Cutler found his maturing tubers were also becoming staples for a certain black breeding boar from Bellevue Farm. More than once, he found the impudent porker rooting among his precious spuds. Each time he would have to stop what he was doing, cut a switch, and shoo the animal down the road to the Farm — to the accompaniment of some highly colorful frontier language.

Finally Cutler went to Agent Griffin and, so the local legend goes, asked Griffin to keep his (Griffin's) pig out of his (Cutler's) potatoes. To which Griffin, pointing out the imperfections of Cutler's fence, blandly suggested it was up to him (Cutler) to keep his potatoes out of his (Griffin's) pig.

It was not many days afterward that Cutler was awakened in the early morning by the sound of a horse's hoofs outside his cabin, and going to the door saw Griffin's black servant, Jacob, riding by. Cutler's eyes drifted to the potato patch, led by Jacob's gaze, and there he saw the Hudson's Bay hog again busily gorging himself on the fruits of his agricultural endeavors. Cutler said later it was the "independence" of the Negro at seeing his loss and not restraining the boar which enraged him most, and "upon the impulse of the moment I seazed my rifle and shot the hog."

If the shot was not heard round the world its repercussions would encircle a good portion of it. But Cutler had no notion of this when he rode over to Griffin's place and 'fessed up that he had felled the roving porker. Cutler offered to replace the animal with one of his own, but Agent Griffin flew into a passion.

"It's no more than I expected," he stormed, as Cutler later recalled it. "You Americans are nothing but a nuisance on the island and you have no business here." He would write to Governor Douglas, he said, and have the Americans removed; he only regretted he hadn't done it before.

Cutler replied he wasn't there to discuss international politics but to settle up for shooting the hog, and how much did Griffin figure it was worth? The farmer informed him the price would be a round one hundred dollars. The Ohioan's indignant answer was that Griffin was more likely to be struck by lightning than to get that kind of money for his hog, "for I can buy one like it on the sound for ten dollars."

Griffin turned down a proposal to have three neighbors set the price by arbitration, stating that he had his own resources for dealing with the matter, whereupon (Griffin claimed) Cutler told him he would "as soon shoot me as he would a hog if I trespassed on his claim." This ended the interview.

The same afternoon the Hudson's Bay vessel *Beaver* chanced to steam over to San Juan where it landed several officials, including Alexander Grant Dallas, who was a director of the company and president of their council in North America, and also a son-in-law of Governor Douglas. The trip was probably a junket to show the islands to one of their number, Dr. William F. Tolmie, a new arrival. It is uncertain whether they had already heard anything of the pig episode, but surely Griffin — who had been composing a furious report of the matter for Douglas — was quick to tell them his troubles.

Later the men were making a horseback tour of the island and found themselves in front of Cutler's place. They stopped, and Griffin called to the American to step outside for a chat. When he appeared, Dallas demanded whether it was he who shot the pig. The tall settler allowed that it was, and a moderately heated discussion ensued. Dallas, as Cutler afterward reported, threatened to have the American taken to Victoria for trial, whereupon Cutler fingered the Kentucky rifle with which he had shot the pig and said he'd like to see them try it.

"You had better be careful how you talk," said Dallas, pointing

51

in the direction of the *Beaver* which lay with steam up and a crew aboard to serve as a posse.

Cutler said he told Dallas to "crack his whip" and, turning on his heel, went inside and slammed the door.*

Cutler was soon telling Paul K. Hubbs, as the one representative of American government on the island, about his day. Within the week Hubbs drafted a letter to Collector of Customs Morris Frost summarizing the strained situation on San Juan Island. "Collision is imminent," he said, "and that of such a character as may produce the most serious result to the two governments." He warned that the threatened difficulties "can only be avoided by a settlement of the Boundary question," or by "placing immediately a large military force to protect the American Settlers from being carried off at will of the Hudson Bay Co. and shut up in the prison of the British Columbia," adding darkly that this was no doubt "somewhat worse than the Dartmoor was in 1813."

To post this letter Hubbs had to go by canoe to the mainland and it was likely on this same trip that he paddled into Bellingham Bay to look up a friend. Hubbs had known Captain George Pickett since Indian War days when both were in the White River fracas of 1856. He found Pickett and his men perfunctorily engaged in running a large truck farm for the Army, Indian troubles in that area having become a rarity. Hubbs gave his old friend a run-down on affairs on San Juan and received a promise

---

* Of those present, only Cutler and Dallas wrote down their versions of the confrontation. The most disinterested witness, Dr. Tolmie, though a voluminous diary-keeper, was not diary-keeping that day. Dallas denied he threatened to take Cutler to Victoria. His version, however — written to General Harney on May 10, 1860, to refute charges made by Americans against the H.B.C. — is very cleverly worded so that while its statements are perhaps literally true, what they seem to say is not always so. Paul Hubbs' father, a Port Townsend attorney, called the letter "a quibble." The author has leaned toward Cutler's sworn affidavit of September 7, 1859, and a statement written out by him for Paul Hubbs on June 23 of that year. Both were written shortly after the interview took place, and are, in the main, consistent with the known facts and with later events.

to pass the word along to General Harney, whose tour of inspection would bring him to Fort Bellingham in a matter of days.

Hubbs had brought with him another settler, and the two had been commissioned by the American colony on the island to purchase "the largest American flag they could find" and a good supply of ammunition. The Fourth of July was approaching, and the settlers had determined the celebration would be a humdinger.

It was. Fifteen to twenty Americans gathered on the morning of the Fourth at Hubbs' cabin, in front of which a flag pole no less than fifty-five feet high had been erected. There, almost within spitting distance of the Hudson's Bay compound, the big, powerful ex-miner named Charles McCoy hoisted Old Glory to the breeze amid a chorus of cheers and a volley of gunfire. One of the bullets pierced the flag's star-studded field but, in Hubbs' words, it "got there all the same." Afterward it was agreed each person present must make a speech. They must have been dandies; by evening the patriotic fervor was such the settlers were ready to take on the whole British Empire then and there. Completely carried away, one orator — a Welshman — suggested they declare their independence not only of Great Britain, but of the United States as well, and start a country of their own on such a beautiful island.

About the time Hubbs was jawing with Captain Pickett, General Harney was crossing the bar of the Columbia River on board the *Massachusetts,* and in another twenty-four hours had entered the wide mouth of the Strait of Juan de Fuca. Deeply impressed with the vision of the placid islands and lazy waters gleaming in the July sunshine, Harney would soon be writing his superiors glowingly:

Puget's Sound is a most remarkable sheet of water, and is destined to be eminent in the annals of commerce from its great advantages. ... Its entrance is fifteen miles wide and as deep as the sea from

53

shore to shore, yet so sheltered by the high mountains on its islands and shores that its waters are as smooth as those of a river or lake.

Harney's tour over this remarkable sea took him first to Steilacoom, near present-day Tacoma, headquarters of the Army's Puget Sound District under the command of another Mexican War alumnus, Lt. Colonel Silas Casey; then north to Port Townsend, and from there through Rosario Strait to Fort Bellingham, which he reached on the evening of July 6. Harney's aides, Captains Ingalls and Pleasanton, were old West Point classmates of Pickett's, and the three spent the night at the latter's home. Harney was the guest of Edmund Fitzhugh, erstwhile member of Sheriff Barnes' sheep-raiding party, now the biggest name on Bellingham Bay. Later, some historians would make much of the fact that Harney, Pickett, Fitzhugh, Hubbs and some of the other actors in the San Juan drama, were Southerners.

Undoubtedly Pickett kept his promise to report the recent events on San Juan to his commander. It is less certain, though most probable, that Harney at this time made the decision to occupy the island. He may well have given Pickett verbal orders on how the operation was to be carried out.

The next morning, July 7, Harney left Bellingham Bay for Semiahmoo, near present-day Blaine, where a joint British and American team of surveyors was engaged in placing monuments to mark the land border. This commission was also charged with coming to an agreement, if possible, on the water boundary from Semiahmoo to the Pacific; but of course this was not possible, for neither side was prepared to accept any boundary but the one favorable to its own interests. Harney consulted with the American commissioner, Archibald Campbell, who struck the general as a wordy, somewhat pompous, wholly indecisive individual, to whom he decided not to divulge his plans. His staff officers, however, confided to Campbell's secretary that Harney was planning to send Pickett's company to occupy San Juan Island.

On July 8, Harney's party left Semiahmoo, passed through Haro Strait and entered Victoria Harbor, where Harney wanted to meet Governor Douglas and see how the wind blew in the enemy camp. He was received with a salute of guns from the Hudson's Bay Company fort. Douglas treated him courteously and invited him to dinner, where he freely answered the general's questions about affairs on Vancouver Island. Harney summed up what he learned in a significant paragraph dispatched to General Winfield Scott, who had now become commanding general of the entire U.S. Army:

The population of British Columbia is largely American and foreigners [he wrote]; comparatively few persons from the British Isles emigrate to this region.* The English cannot colonize successfully so near our people; they are too exacting. This, with the pressing necessities of our commerce on this coast, *will induce them to yield, eventually, Vancouver's Island to our government. It is as important to the Pacific States as Cuba is to those on the Atlantic.*†

It is not hard to imagine the trend of Harney's thoughts as he steamed out of Victoria Harbor next morning and crossed over for his first look at San Juan. When he had seen the island, he would say in his report to Washington City that it

contains fine timber, good water and grass, and is the most commanding position we possess on the Sound; ... at the southeastern extremity one of the finest harbors on this coast is to be found, completely sheltered, offering the best location for a naval station on the Pacific Coast.

About one o'clock that afternoon the *Massachusetts* dropped her hook in that very harbor — Griffin Bay — soon after rounding the point where the Stars and Stripes were still majestically flying over Hubbs' cabin. Harney came ashore, met Hubbs, dismissed

* Actually it was the gold rush which brought this swell of population to Victoria and most of the newcomers were, indeed, American by nationality or sympathy.

† Italics added.

his staff officers and (according to Hubbs' memoirs) had a long private discussion with the diminutive customs inspector. Here the arrangements were made which led to the occupation by American troops and, in Hubbs' revealing words, "hastened the long-delayed question of sovereignty which took a Jackson or a Harney to consummate."

Harney asked Hubbs to draw up a petition and have all the settlers sign it, asking protection against marauding Indians. The petition was to be justification for landing troops. Nothing was to be said about the pig, Cutler's potatoes, or friction with the Hudson's Bay people. Hubbs drafted the petition himself and had it signed by all the Americans living on the island (and, for good measure, a few non-residents as well).

Harney did not wait for this document (in fact, did not receive it until after troops were already esconced on the disputed island). Taking his leave of Hubbs, he had the *Massachusetts* make for Fort Townsend, which he inspected, then continued up-Sound to Olympia, where he went into a huddle with Isaac Stevens, now ex-governor of the territory, and Richard D. Gholson, who had just arrived to replace him.

After meeting with these officials Harney determined to return to his headquarters the quickest — though most inconvenient — way: travelling overland and by Indian canoe to the Columbia. The next three days were spent furiously drawing up orders for a redisposition of the troops under his command: Townsend was to be evacuated as too "expensive" and "out of position" for the economy of the service; Bellingham was to be abandoned as having "no military advantages whatever"; and Lt. Colonel Silas Casey, commanding at Fort Steilacoom, was to place the steamer *Massachusetts* at George Pickett's disposal in a remarkable order which had the effect of bypassing Casey altogether. Harney figured this level-headed commander lacked the needed spirit of do-or-die recklessness the operation would demand.

In the late evening of July 26, 1859, Paul K. Hubbs was peacefully snoozing in his log cabin, when a persistent rapping worked its way into his consciousness and finally aroused him. Stumbling sleepily to the door, he opened it a crack and peered into the darkness. There in full Army uniform stood an orderly sergeant by the name of William Smith who saluted and informed Hubbs that Captain Pickett was down on the beach and wished a word with him. Dressing quickly, Hubbs followed the orderly down to the shore of Griffin Bay, where he could see by the moon's light the dim hulk of the *Massachusetts* riding at anchor. Pickett greeted him warmly and after introducing him to his officers asked Hubbs' advice about locating a temporary camp. A gravel spit close to the Hudson's Bay wharf was selected and preparations were made to land the troops there early next morning. Hubbs, Pickett, and the latter's aide, Lieutenant Howard — another Southerner — then broke out a decanter of brandy and toasted the success of their venture.

On the same night, ostensibly by a coincidence, Her Britannic Majesty's steam corvette *Satellite* arrived in Griffin Bay from Victoria. On board was Major John Fitzroy de Courcy, who indicated surprise at seeing the *Massachusetts* at anchor, her decks thronged with Yankee soldiers. Actually he had been tipped off about the landing of U.S. troops earlier in the day by Douglas himself, whose contacts on the American side had learned of the pending movement of troops. (Boundary Commissioner Campbell, too, "happened" to be on hand aboard the side-wheel steamer *Shubrick* when the *Massachusetts* arrived at San Juan.)

De Courcy had been hastily appointed stipendiary magistrate (justice of the peace) for the island and Hubbs and Pickett supposed his true mission was to apprehend Lyman Cutler. Hubbs was hurriedly commissioned to beat him to it, and just as the sun was rising from behind the Lopez hills he strode up in front of the settler's cabin. When Cutler came outside to wash, Hubbs placed him under arrest.

57

"I surrender," replied the Ohioan, laughing, after Hubbs explained the situation. He drew on a shirt, strapped a six-shooter around himself, and the two started down the trail. It was a mile and a half to Pickett's camp, and when they had gone about half way they met de Courcy and three British officers coming from the opposite direction. For a minute it looked as if there might be a fight. Cutler and Hubbs stuck obstinately to the middle of the narrow path, while the Englishmen as adamantly advanced towards them. At the last moment (as Hubbs was to claim later) the British gave way and let Hubbs march his "prisoner" past them. Pickett kept the hog-slayer around camp for a day or so, after which the American settlers persuaded him to go into hiding.

Pickett landed the bulk of his troops — about sixty in all — the morning of July 27 and before long he was tacking up a proclamation near the beach. Entitled "Orders, No. 1" it read:

Military Post, San Juan Island
Washington Territory, July 27, 1859

I. In compliance with orders and instructions from the general commanding, a military post will be established on this island, on whatever site the commanding officer may select.

II. All the inhabitants of the island are requested to report at once to the commanding officer in case of any incursion of the northern Indians, so that he may take such steps as are necessary to prevent any future occurrence of same.

Then came the snapper:

III. This being United States territory, no laws, other than those of the United States, nor courts, except such as are held by virtue of said laws, will be recognized or allowed on this island.

When the British read this document it was not long before the *Satellite* had turned about and was making for Victoria at top speed. About 4 o'clock the next afternoon the stately British frigate *Tribune*, its decks bristling with cannon, entered Griffin

Bay and swinging broadside to bring its guns to bear on Pickett's little camp, came ominously to anchor.

Paul Hubbs and Pickett were having a smoke together when the *Tribune* showed up. Hubbs observed that the situation had turned a bit uncomfortable.

"Not in the least," replied Pickett coolly — but his real thoughts may have been something else.

Next morning the U.S.S. *Massachusetts* lumbered into the bay again, bringing the Whatcom County coroner, Henry Roberjot Crosbie, who had been summoned to hold an inquest on a body found murdered on Lopez Island. Crosbie sized up the San Juan situation and decided to stay awhile as representative of the local civil authority. On learning that Cutler was still in hiding, and that his cabin had been reportedly visited several times by Magistrate de Courcy and a constable, Crosbie had Cutler brought from hiding and placed him once again under Pickett's protection. An able frontier lawyer, Crosbie assumed the role of justice of the peace and swore in two constables of his own, settlers William Smith and Isaac Higgins. Court was held and Cutler was tried, convicted and fined for shooting the Hudson's Bay boar; or so the British were informed, though no formal record of the proceeding has come to light and Paul Hubbs always insisted Cutler never came to trial.

Meanwhile, Agent Griffin and Captain Pickett were exchanging notes in the formal diplomatic language of the time. On Saturday, July 30, Griffin wrote Pickett:

Sir: I have the honor to inform you that the island of San Juan, on which your camp is pitched, is the property and in the occupation of the Hudson's Bay Company, and to request that you and the whole of the party who have landed from the American vessels will immediately cease to occupy the same. Should you be unwilling to comply with my request, I feel bound to apply to the civil authorities. Awaiting your reply, I have the honor to be, sir, your obedient servant,

CHAS. JNO. GRIFFIN

Pickett replied the same day in equally polite but forceful language:

Sir: Your communication of this instant has been received. I have to state in reply that I do not acknowledge the right of the Hudson's Bay Company to dictate my course of action. I am here by virtue of an order from my government, and shall remain till recalled by the same authority.

I am, Sir, very respectfully, your obedient servant.

GEORGE E. PICKETT

To Colonel Casey, Pickett was soon writing a brusque note — hardly the sort a subordinate normally sends his commanding officer — "requesting" the assistance of the *Massachusetts*. As Harney had already directed Casey to accede to just such a request, the venerable old tub — with Major Haller's infantry company on board as crew — was dispatched to San Juan the next day. Casey in turn wrote to General Harney's headquarters informing him of the events reported by Pickett. More plaintively than subtly, Casey pointed out that "Not having been informed of the tenor of Captain Pickett's instructions, I could not, of course, advise him with regard to them." So far this show was all Pickett's and Harney's, and Casey was sore as a hungry hornet about the whole thing, and getting sorer every minute.

Governor Douglas' humor was not improving any either. In Victoria he was composing a proclamation protesting the landing of U.S. troops, stating that "The sovereignty of the island of San Juan and of the whole of the Haro Archipelago has always been undeviatingly claimed to be in the Crown of Great Britain" and again that "the sovereignty thereof by right now is and always hath been in Her Majesty Queen Victoria, and her predecessors, kings of Great Britain." He then proceeded to order H.M. *Plumper* to embark a detachment of royal engineers and light infantry from the mainland of British Columbia, and land them on San Juan Island. For Victoria was now the headquarters of Her Majesty's naval forces on the Pacific and, in the absence of their commander, Rear Admiral R. L. Baynes, the ex-officio rank of Vice Admiral held by Douglas placed him in technical command.

By August 3 excitement in Victoria was intense. Douglas sent a special message to the colony's legislative assembly; vessels of all kinds came and went, carrying curious civilians between Victoria and what the Victoria *Gazette* was calling the "seat of war"; Pickett reported that upwards of 500 persons had visited his camp. Both the *Plumper* and H.M. *Satellite* arrived and, like the *Tribune*, anchored in Griffin Bay with their guns run out. Shrill repeated commands signalled by the boatswains' whistles, a continual movement by the troops aboard, and preparations to launch landing boats caused understandable alarm among the Americans on shore. In the face of 61 heavy naval guns, and a force of some 775 men, Pickett prepared to obey his orders to resist a landing. His force: sixty-some men and three brass field pieces, one of which was in use as a flag standard. The settlers ruefully observed that the British had one heavy gun for each American soldier.

Major Haller had meanwhile arrived on the *Massachusetts*; but Pickett now declined his help — presumably because Haller, who outranked him, would have taken command — and Haller sailed on to Semiahmoo at noon the same day.

It happened that the senior British officer then present at San Juan was Captain Geoffrey Phipps Hornby, slight, chestnut-haired, cool-headed commander of the *Tribune*. Hornby and Pickett had met the evening of July 31, when the former called at Pickett's camp to acquaint him with his strongly-worded orders from Douglas. Fortunately Pickett was absent on Hornby's first visit, for by the time the two got together Hornby had received fresh orders in a more cautious vein. The Britisher was well impressed with the 34-year-old officer from Virginia who, he wrote his wife, "speaks more like a Devonshire man than a Yankee."

On this climactic August 3 Hornby called on Pickett again. He had been ordered, he informed the captain, to land his troops by nightfall and occupy San Juan Island "concurrently" with the Americans. Pickett replied that he had most positively been ordered to resist a landing under any circumstances. When Hornby pointed out the superiority of his forces, Pickett assured him that he would follow orders nonetheless, and fight "as long as I have a man."

"Very well," replied Hornby; "I shall land at once."

Pickett then asked whether, off-the-record, he could not have forty-eight hours to communicate with General Harney — perhaps his orders would be countermanded.

"Not one minute," replied Hornby, and stomped off, apparently to give the fatal command.

Pickett dictated a fast letter telling Harney what had happened, pointing out that the British "have a force so much superior to mine that it will be merely a mouthful for them" and begging further instructions "at such an early hour as to prevent a collision.... I do not think there are any moments to waste...."

Having sent off the steamer *Shubrick* with this missive, Pickett looked to his defenses. He stationed his troops in the edge of the woods overlooking the bay, giving each man sixty rounds of ammunition and three days' rations. Hubbs was put in charge of the settlers, each of whom volunteered to fight. They were all crack rifle shots, and their assignment was to pick off the British officers in the boats as they landed, and then fall back to a rendezvous point in the woods. Pickett put them in line, six paces apart, near the shore.

"Don't be afraid of their big guns," Pickett told the settlers. "We will make a Bunker Hill of it."

Nervously the men waited for the British to commence the

landing operation. But on board the *Tribune* Hornby was deep in thought. His orders were clear enough; he was to land; he had not been bluffing. Yet he was convinced Pickett wasn't bluffing either, and he was greatly distressed to think of the bloodletting that was about to take place.

Hornby examined again his orders from Douglas. They directed him to land — while at the same time placing on him (a bit too cleverly, he felt) the responsibility for avoiding a shooting conflict with the American forces. Yet Hornby shrewdly guessed that a shooting conflict was precisely what General Harney was angling for. Reflecting that the British presence in overpowering numbers clearly demonstrated their *power* to come ashore at will, the English captain decided that Britain's honor would suffer no tarnish if the landing were delayed a bit.

When the sun went down that evening without a shot's having been fired, Pickett ordered his men in the darkness to new positions on higher ground farther from the beach, out of the range of the British guns. The next day a lone sentry paced the top of the hill to give warning if the attack came; but there was none.

At Fort Vancouver, Harney, having received Pickett's S-O-S, was swinging into action. In his element now, he penned an insolent letter to Douglas, stating that he had sent troops to San Juan to protect Americans there "from the insults and indignities" of the British and Hudson's Bay authorities. Next, he commended Pickett for his actions and directed him to allow neither a military occupation jointly with British forces (such as Douglas had tried to effect by ordering Hornby to land his troops) nor any civil jurisdiction by Britishers. Further, he now ordered Lt. Colonel Casey to reinforce Pickett with his command — in other words, with every available soldier on the Sound.*

---

* It is tempting to speculate that Harney aimed to have Casey arrive — and take command of the fighting — *after* the opening of hostilities had committed both sides to serious battle.

In addition, Harney wrote the senior officer of the U.S. Navy on the Pacific Coast requesting a few warships. And lastly, to Washington Territorial Governor Gholson, Harney wrote asking authority to call up volunteers if the situation should worsen. Gholson assented almost with enthusiasm, and Captain William Dall, of the mail steamer *Northerner*, volunteered to bring them to San Juan whenever Pickett requested them.

Meanwhile Major Haller, still aboard the *Massachusetts* with his company of forty-four men, and still fuming at being passed over for the San Juan command, was cruising among the islands, perfunctorily patrolling for Indians. Periodically he would land in Griffin Bay to take on water, fuel, and news. But it was painfully apparent that Pickett didn't want him around.

Lt. Colonel Silas E. Casey had been itching to get his fingers into things, too. Now, at last, he was going to get that chance.

4

COLONEL CASEY TAKES A HAND

When the british failed to attack, the Americans suspected but could not know the anxiety Captain Hornby was suffering. He had disobeyed a direct order, pinning his hopes — perhaps his career — on what Admiral Baynes would do upon his return. And Baynes was expected back at any moment, now, from his Pacific cruise.

In the meantime, there was a week of agitated truce. Only the *Tribune* stayed at anchor in Griffin Bay to keep an eye on things: *Plumper* — after transferring its two hundred troops to the already crowded decks of the *Tribune* — went back to its regular job of surveying lighthouse sites in the Strait; while *Satellite* was employed in ferrying a profuse correspondence between Captain Prevost, the British boundary commissioner, and his opposite American number, Archibald Campbell. The polemics exchanged by these two officials were becoming more and more spirited but not, of course, any more fruitful.

Officials, journalists, and curious civilians from both sides came in an endless stream. The publicity brought permanent newcomers, too; by August 8, the Victoria *Gazette* reported, the number of American settlers on San Juan had grown to between thirty and forty, and most of the good land had been spoken for.

Captain Pickett, who obviously expected to stay awhile, sent a detail to dismantle the buildings at Fort Bellingham and was soon reerecting them at his Griffin Bay camp. (Promptly there was an outbreak of Indian trouble on Bellingham Bay but Major Haller's company went after the raiders, pursued them all the way to Point Roberts, and put a summary end to the disturbance.) The rude structures clustered just east of a small tidal basin were to become the village known as San Juan Town then, and "Old Town" in later years.

Hardly had the first building gone up when there occurred an incident highly prophetic of a kind of trouble that would plague the settlement for years. Three or four enterprising individuals had imported supplies of "red eye" and other intoxicants which they were dispensing from nearby tent groggeries at highly profitable prices. As a predictable result, a number of the local citizenry were soon seen disporting themselves in ways which raised grave questions as to their sobriety. Justice Crosbie, who had chosen to remain on the island for the time being, promptly visited each of the establishments and served notice that liquor was not to be sold without a license; and further, he said, "in the prevailing state of affairs," no licenses would be issued by American authorities. Crosbie ordered Constable Higgins to inventory the "contraband" and have it packed up.

One of the outraged dispensers of fire-water went directly to Crosbie's counterpart, Magistrate de Courcy, and applied for a *British* license to carry on his trade. De Courcy coldly informed him no such permit would be issued, and threatened to arrest him for violation of the British license law.

Crosbie and de Courcy discussed the matter and, while neither would recognize the other's authority officially, they agreed to cooperate to suppress the sale of intoxicants on San Juan; con-

66

sidering the powder-keg that had been created by individuals who were sober, they shuddered to think what might be accomplished by drunks.

Thus the island went dry — but not for long. Next morning, one of the hooch merchants was again doing business at the same stand, whereupon Crosbie had him arrested and thrown into the camp pokey. Thus began the long, and not always successful, campaign against San Juan Town's liquor sellers.

Meanwhile Lt. Colonel Casey had finally gotten the order to reinforce Pickett. Probably he had never received instructions with which he was so impatient to comply. His men were ready to move in a moment, but the Army's steamer *Massachusetts* wasn't on hand to transport them. Casey elected to crowd the three infantry companies aboard the waiting stern-wheel mail steamer *Julia*, hoping this unusual conveyance would also afford some secrecy to the move.

Departing from Steilacoom early the next morning — August 9 — the party was met and hailed along the way by the surveying steamer *Active*, Captain Alden, who was bringing Casey the latest dispatches from the scene of action. Alden, in obvious distress, gave it as his opinion that the British "steamship-of-war" *Tribune*, whose big guns were being kept constantly ready, would prevent reinforcements from landing. He urged Casey "strongly and solemnly" not to attempt the landing, "in view of the momentous consequences that might arise."

Much agitated, no doubt, Casey nevertheless proceeded toward San Juan to carry out his orders by landing — as honor demanded — in full view of the enemy. When the *Julia* stopped at Port Townsend for fuel, he met Commissioner Campbell there and hoped to get some late inside information from him; but Campbell was not the man to get this from.

Archibald Campbell deserves an extra portion of sympathy for his part in the San Juan business. As official head of the United

67

States Boundary Commission, appointed by the President, he was the government's top representative on the scene. Anything concerning the boundary question was his proper concern; and yet all this was happening without his counsel having been sought or given — in fact, without his even having been informed of it officially. General Harney had simply bypassed Campbell on the pretext that the Commissioner was rumored to be on his way to Washington City. And while he was being addressed the most forceful diplomatic messages of protest by the British, to which he was obliged to reply formally on behalf of the United States government, Archibald Campbell was reduced to getting his information by his own hook or crook. He was forever jumping from place to place on the Sound, buttonholing anyone who might know something; writing letters to everyone and getting little satisfaction from anyone; forever missing steamers, not receiving his mail, being in the wrong place at the right time. Campbell is one of those pitifully comic characters who enliven the pages of history but really deserve to have been cast in better roles.

Still, Casey learned enough to make him jittery. He decided to wait for evening before crossing the Strait, in order to arrive at San Juan during the dark of the night. Accordingly the *Julia*, bulging with its load of arms and men, steamed out of Port Townsend at midnight, expecting to make Griffin Bay in the early hours of the morning.

Casey got more cover for his movement than he bargained for. Silently, almost imperceptibly, a thickening shroud of white fell over the Puget Sound country that night. Summer was ending — everyone had noticed the early chill in the air of an evening — the change of season heralded as always by the fog, which does not creep in on cats' feet in this country, but simply materializes out of the damp, grey gloom that is fall's uniform. It descends, one huge all-encompassing white cloud, reducing visibility to nil, slowing water traffic to a crawl, putting boatsmen to the

68

test. At 6 o'clock the sun began to rise — somewhere beyond the thick curtain of fluff — and found the little stern-wheeler still well out in the Strait, her navigator still groping warily by aid of compass, lead line and chart. By the time the *Julia* found the south shore of San Juan Island, it was 7 in the morning and full daylight. By then, her captain informed an agitated Colonel Casey, the tide was too far out to allow landing at the Griffin Bay wharf.

Honor obliged Casey to land his men under the guns of the British vessels while prudence tempted him to land them almost anywhere else; the fog and low tide gave him all the excuse he needed to follow prudence. Locating a stretch of low beach on the south shore, just over a ridge from Pickett's camp, Casey put his men and field guns ashore.

As they marched overland through the fog, dragging their howitzers, the *Julia's* paddle-wheel could be heard as she steamed back and forth in the distance. In Pickett's camp, as at Bellevue Farm and on board the *Tribune*, eyes tried to penetrate the fog and learn the meaning of the sound. Then the mists thinned slightly and revealed the ridge above Camp Pickett dotted with blue coats and brass buttons. A cheer went up from the camp and was echoed from the hill. The new troops were received with much clasping of hands and thumping of backs until interrupted by the officers who ordered the mountain howitzers added to the ridiculous circle of guns with which the Americans were to defend their "redoubt." But there was real cause for rejoicing: the odds were different. Now, the British only outnumbered them by two to one.

Toward noon the fog lifted enough for the *Julia* to come up to the wharf in Griffin Bay where the ammunition and a large amount of other stores were landed, without interference from the *Tribune*. While Casey was still engaged on board, an officer brought him an urgent message from Pickett, asking him to come ashore at once. For Pickett had spotted the *Satellite* coming up as though to take a position to shell the island. He seemed convinced the British were about to begin the attack.

Casey learned in haste that Pickett's current plan of defense was to fire on the landing party with his howitzers, then spike them, and retire his troops to the up-island woods under cover of rifle fire. Casey, taking command, hastily adopted the same scheme. Then looking up Paul Hubbs, he appointed him his guide to the island and ordered him at the first sound of a gun to mount a horse and lead the way inland to the "retreating grounds."

Hubbs was in utter dismay over the changed complexion of things after Casey's arrival. Everyone soon noted the contrast between the latter's preoccupation with preventing bloodshed, and Pickett's fire-eating bravado.

With his defenses looked to, Casey sent word to Captain Hornby, on the *Tribune*, inviting him to a conference. Hornby replied that he was "much engaged" just then, but would try to come. Later in the day he did come, accompanied by Captain Prevost of the *Satellite*, and Commissioner Campbell, who had followed the *Julia* over to see what was going to happen next. Casey gave his excuses for not landing his troops at the wharf and asked to be put in touch with the officer highest in command. Hornby told him that would be Rear Admiral Baynes, who had just arrived from his Pacific cruise on the flagship H.M.S. *Ganges*. The *Ganges*, said Hornby, was then in Esquimalt harbor.

As a matter of fact Admiral Baynes was not then on the *Ganges*, but on board the *Tribune*, where he was the cause of Hornby's being so much engaged. Casey did not learn this until later, and so preparations were made to go to Esquimalt to see the crusty old admiral the next day. Casey had a proposition to make, and the sooner, the better.

On the next day, having donned full dress uniforms, Colonel Casey and Captain Pickett boarded the steamer *Shubrick* and crossed over to Esquimalt harbor near Victoria. After anchoring near the *Ganges*, Casey sent an officer to the flagship with a note inviting the Admiral to board the *Shubrick* for a talk. It was that old game again: Baynes sent his regrets and invited Casey to drop over to the *Ganges*, instead.

Casey thereupon sent his own regrets to the admiral, this time sending as his messenger none other than Captain Pickett! (How that must have rankled the fiery Virginian. And one wonders how sorry Casey would really have been, had the British decided not to let Pickett go again!)

But Pickett was courteously received in Baynes' cabin, where he found Governor Douglas also present. A few pleasantries were exchanged, but Baynes still refused to budge from his own ship. Casey concluded he had "carried etiquette far enough in going twenty-five miles to see a gentleman who was disinclined to come one hundred yards to see me," and had the *Shubrick* head for home.

The proposition Casey wanted to make to Admiral Baynes was a sensible one. In order to calm the excitement on both sides, and give the home governments time to be heard from, Casey would have asked the Admiral for his word of honor not to molest Captain Pickett's troops, or prevent him from continuing to occupy the island; and in return Casey would recommend to General Harney the withdrawal of the newly arrived reinforcements. Casey would thus, in effect, have arranged a truce until an authority higher than Harney was heard from.

Admiral Baynes, a slight, lame, grey-haired Scotchman, though far cagier than Casey, was equally intent on preventing a blood bath. He had seen his decks ankle-deep in blood, he had just been saying to Governor Douglas, but he would rather shed tears than blood over a mere pig. (When *Ganges* first arrived in port, and Baynes learned what had been happening on San Juan, he was heard to mutter: "Tut, tut! No, no; the damned fools!") The admiral countermanded Douglas' orders and sustained Captain Hornby; now the redheaded captain could respire freely

71

again, for the first time since sticking out his neck a distance roughly equivalent to the width of Haro Strait.

But Casey couldn't know this as he returned to San Juan. Having felt himself rebuffed, and under the influence of Pickett, Casey would himself become increasingly "Harneyized" in the ensuing weeks. He called for additional supplies and reinforcements and was soon hard at work building permanent earthworks and fortifications from which to prosecute the very war he had been so anxious to avoid.

For a time the center of action shifted to Victoria, where the colonial legislature was in heated debate. Speaker J. S. Helmcken, who was also Victoria's doctor, commented on the American worship of the dollar and intimated Commissioner Campbell (still suspected by many of being at the bottom of the affair) could have been persuaded to see things differently for a price. Harney was excoriated for invading British territory, but "What more could be expected of a man who has spent a lifetime in warring with Indians?" The speech ended with a ringing peroration: "We must defend ourselves," said Helmcken, "for the position we occupy today would make the iron monument of Wellington weep, and the stony statue of Nelson bend his brow."

Helmcken was right to think of defenses. Victoria was swollen with armed Americans, most of them returned Fraser River miners, said to be ready to raise the Stars and Stripes over Vancouver Island at the first sign of trouble. Victoria banks, it was rumored, had transferred their money to British warships for safekeeping. Of the town's two newspapers, though the sympathies of the *Colonist* were regularly British, the *Gazette* was owned by Americans and favored the U.S. side of the dispute.* Harney's prediction that Britain would ultimately lose

* But the *Colonist*'s editor, a Nova Scotian going under the name Amor De Cosmos (as more imposing than his natal appellation, Bill Smith) was no admirer of Governor Douglas, either.

72

Vancouver Island to the United States was appearing less improbable every day.

Douglas was thinking of defenses also. His plan was the same one he had advanced for the safeguarding of Victoria a few years earlier when the Crimean War broke out: arm 50,000 trustworthy Indians as auxiliaries. On that proposal, however, the Council turned him down flat.

Admiral Baynes, too, was concerned over the effect of war with the Americans. "In the event of a conflict," he wrote home to the Admiralty on August 19, "Vancouver's Island would be completely isolated; dependent on the United States for the conveyance of our mails, no despatch could be forwarded to England except a ship-of-war was especially sent with it to Panama, a passage of between thirty and forty days. Supplies of all sorts would be stopped from the opposite shore, which would equally affect British Columbia. Four-fifths of the population of Vancouver's Island are foreigners, principally Americans; and in British Columbia the British population does not exceed 3 per cent."

Indeed, Pickett's ace in the hole had been his knowledge that several hundred American volunteers on Vancouver Island had been secretly recruited and were prepared to come to his assistance on short notice, a courier canoe being kept ready to summon them at the first shot. Pickett figured to slaughter Hudson's Bay Company livestock on the island in order to feed this motley land army for enough days to vanquish the British attack.

One of the curious civilians from Victoria whom the U.S. forces allowed to range freely around the embattled island was Angus McDonald, a Hudson's Bay Company clerk of Scottish origin. McDonald came upon a lone sentry guarding the Americans' cannon. Learning the soldier was a Gaelic-speaking Irishman, McDonald asked him how he could fight against the flag of his own country. The sentry took a hitch to his gun-shoulder and allowed that he "would like to see old England

73

catch a good drubbing anyhow," and as he paused to light an unsoldierly pipe McDonald moved on, aware — as he put it later — "that there is some account between Erin and England that never was squared."

Meanwhile it seemed that troops and supplies were zeroing in on San Juan from all over the Sound. The *Massachusetts* debarked Major Haller's company, finally, and that ship's big guns — larger than any the Americans had yet landed — were removed for use on shore. Casey ordered the old fort at Port Townsend denuded of everything that could be used on San Juan. The new one-hundred-ton schooner *General Harney* — first vessel of any great size built on Puget Sound — was hastily (and somewhat irregularly) contracted for to haul a battery and twelve tons of shell and shot to the island while her owner, Captain Henry Roeder, had the impression that "every available vessel on the Sound" was bringing in men.

Roeder later recalled the *Harney* was towed over in the night but was so heavily loaded it didn't make the island until daylight. The vessel had to pass close to the *Satellite* whose ports were open and guns apparently shotted. The *Satellite's* crew contributed to the tension by holding gunnery practice and landing exercises all the time the *Harney's* cargo was being unloaded, according to Roeder's memoirs.

Now it became Paul Hubbs' turn to add fuel to the threatening fire. Fitzroy de Courcy, the British magistrate, had decided his stay on San Juan would be lengthy enough to warrant setting up housekeeping and so made a trip to Victoria for his personal effects. Arriving with them on the mail steamer, he was met by Hubbs who, still acting as customs inspector, demanded de Courcy pay import duty on his baggage. De Courcy refused. Hubbs threatened to call on the military to prevent the goods being landed whereupon de Courcy stormed that if necessary, his effects would be brought ashore under the guns of the *Satellite*.

74

The urgent sound of boatswain's whistles and other threatening activities on the *Satellite* coincided with Hubbs' presenting himself at Camp Pickett to demand the troops help him enforce the customs laws. Only Captain Pickett was sympathetic; Colonel Casey, firmly in command, responded by posting a guard to see that de Courcy's goods *were* landed. Hubbs went off fuming that he would "report the action of the United States Troops for not sustaining us in enforcing the United States Customs."

By mid-August there were five infantry and four artillery companies — about 450 men in all — on San Juan and a small detachment of Engineers yet to come. Casey had these troops (as well as some fifty hired civilian laborers) at work building gun platforms and trenches on a ridge near the Hudson's Bay Company farm, at the spot yet today known as American Camp — about a mile west of San Juan Town.

Arrayed against these forces the British had on hand, or not far away, a total of 1,940 men distributed aboard H.B.M. ships *Ganges, Tribune, Pylades, Satellite,* and *Plumper;* while the combined armament of these vessels amounted to 167 cannon — many of them two to three times larger than the biggest guns Casey's troops had. Casey had been ordered by General Harney to choose a position out of the reach of these guns but as he pointed out, this would have entailed moving too far inland to enable defending the beaches. Taking a leaf from Pickett's book, Casey elected to risk the big naval guns in order to command the shores most likely to be landed on, as well as Griffin Bay and most of the southern end of the island.

But the British warships, while keeping up their bluff, were now under positive orders from Admiral Baynes *"not on any account whatever* [to] take the initiative in commencing hostilities."

Casey suspected something of the sort but he was not yet sufficiently Harneyized to press the advantage. In moving to the new camp he gave orders that the rights of the Hudson's Bay

Company farm were not to be infringed. Meantime, he had been put on the carpet by Harney for his conciliatory trip to Esquimalt; while the general had written Washington recommending Captain Pickett for a brevet in view of the latter's "cool judgment, ability, and gallantry."

Pickett didn't get the promotion. Instead, Harney heard from the War Department that President James Buchanan "was not prepared to learn that you had ordered military possession to be taken of the island of San Juan or Bellevue. Although he believes the Straits of Haro to be the true boundary between Great Britain and the United States, under the treaty of June 15, 1846, and that, consequently, the island belongs to us, yet he had not anticipated that so decided a step would have been resorted to without instructions. . . ."

Harney was directed to reply "by the next steamer" giving further details, particularly "whether, before you proceeded to act, you had communicated with Commissioner Campbell. . . ."

This blast closed with an admonition to "appraise the British authorities that possession has thus been taken solely with the view of protecting the rights of our citizens on the island, and preventing the incursions of the northern Indians into our territory, and not with any view of prejudging the question in dispute or retaining the island should the question be finally decided against the United States."

The crusty old Indian fighter had perhaps never considered the possibility that his government would shower on him anything but praise and glory for his course of conquest. Now even his old political friends in Washington, who had pulled him out of so many scrapes before, had had enough. He was going to have to take his medicine, and a bitter draught it would be.

Harney made a brave reply, but he was already on the skids. He had been sent to Washington Territory to put down Indian troubles, not to embroil his country in a war with a friendly power over a few paltry islands.

Without waiting for Harney's reply, acting War Secretary W. R. Drinkard summoned the general's commanding officer and long-time nemesis, Lt. General Winfield Scott, and asked him to go to Puget Sound and straighten things out. Scott was then 72 years old and in doubtful health, which was manifestly reflected in his humor though not in his judgment; but President Buchanan's anxiety to prevent war with England compelled him to ask the old gentleman to make the trip, and Scott agreed to go.

5

T HE PRESIDENT HAS BEEN much gratified," Acting Secretary Drinkard wrote Lt. General Scott on September 16, "at the alacrity with which you have responded to his wish that you would proceed to Washington Territory to assume the immediate command, if necessary, of the United States forces on the Pacific coast." Drinkard continued with a discussion of the vaguely-worded treaty of 1846 and summarized recent events on San Juan.

Mindful of the five weeks' time needed for news to reach Washington from the frontier, Drinkard went on: "It is impossible, at this distance from the scene, and in ignorance of what may have already transpired on the spot, to give you positive instructions as to your course of action. Much, very much, must be left to your own discretion, and the President is happy to believe that discretion could not be intrusted to more competent hands. His main object is to preserve the peace and prevent collision between the British and American authorities on the island until the question of title can be adjusted by the two governments. . . ."

78

The President, said Drinkard, had no objection to the plan proposed through Captain Hornby — that is, a joint military occupation of the island pending a diplomatic resolution of the boundary question; but that "American citizens must be placed on a footing equally favorable with that of British subjects."

The letter, which constituted Scott's formal orders, next passed to the thorny question of what to do if the General-in-chief were to find a "collision" — perhaps with bloodshed — had already taken place. "In that event, it would still be your duty, if this can, in your opinion, be honorably done, under the surrounding circumstances, to establish a joint temporary occupation of the island, giving to neither party any advantage over another."

And if war were already raging on Puget Sound, with Americans at arms "to assert and maintain their rights" against superior British forces? In that event, the President was confident "from the whole tenor of your past life, that you will not suffer the national honor to be tarnished. If we must be forced into a war by the violence of the British authorities, which is not anticipated, we shall abide the issue as best we may without apprehension as to the result."

Scott sailed from New York aboard the *Star of the West** on September 20, 1859, and arrived at the entrance to the Columbia River the evening of October 20. Now situated on board Captain William Dall's coastal mail steamer *Northerner*, Scott had this vessel come to anchor a half mile below Harney's headquarters at Fort Vancouver. At 2 o'clock in the morning Scott's aide, Lt. Colonel W. G. Lay, came ashore, awakened Harney, and told him of the General-in-chief's arrival.

Harney, though thunder-struck at this turn of events, rose to the occasion and offered to go immediately to Scott's vessel. Lay told him the general was asleep and did not wish to be disturbed

* Sixteen months later this same side-wheel steamer was to draw the first fire of the Civil War while attempting to land reinforcements at Fort Sumter.

until 8 in the morning, when Harney was to report, bringing with him all orders and correspondence concerning the San Juan business.

When Harney and his staff boarded the *Northerner* — now the official headquarters of the United States Army — he found Scott installed in a long cabin crowded with people. The portly old general appeared in a good mood; the sea voyage had been beneficial to his health, and he was particularly happy to learn the Americans and British had so far not come to blows over San Juan Island.

Harney was gratified when Scott's greeting to him seemed cordial. Getting right to business in spite of the bustle, Scott asked a staff officer to read aloud certain letters Harney had brought along. After a few had been read to him, the *Northerner*'s skipper interrupted to ask how long the general would be detained. Learning that Scott wished to cross over to Portland, Harney offered to stay on board during the crossing rather than delay the general's pleasure. After accepting this offer Scott, who had probably heard all he cared to anyway, abruptly broke off the conference with Harney, saying "Then it is unnecessary to continue reading at this time."

At Portland the General-in-chief was received with suitable but lengthy ceremonies while Harney fidgeted, wishing to get on with the business at hand. When it came time for Harney's departure, and Scott had still not resumed their conference, Harney sent a message requesting a private meeting. The two generals met in Scott's stateroom where Harney volunteered his opinion that the important thing was not to disturb the state of affairs then prevailing on San Juan, "until further advices from the government could be received." At this Scott broke in curtly that his course was already decided upon, namely, to offer the British a joint military occupation.

Flushing, Harney spoke out heatedly: "General Scott, I have maintained the honor of my country up to this moment and if

80

you consent to a joint occupancy I shall consider it a disgrace to the country!"

Scott's affability changed in an instant. Rising heavily from his seat to glare down at Harney's lank frame, and striking his cane on the floor for emphasis, he read the frontier general up one side and down the other. "We have both got our superiors and we've got to obey them," he concluded. The aging general's eyes were flashing and Harney said afterward he actually expected to be arrested on the spot. Rather lamely, he replied that after all he too was only trying to do what he conceived to be his duty. Then, seeing that the interview had come to an end, Harney bid his commander a good morning and departed for Fort Vancouver, a very shaken general.

Harney and Scott never saw each other again during the latter's Puget Sound trip, which lasted about two weeks. The day after their confrontation the *Northerner* left Portland for a four-day cruise up the Washington coast and into Puget Sound, meeting the Army's steamer *Massachusetts* off Port Townsend on the 26th. Scott and his entourage transferred to this vessel which became his headquarters, and to which the revenue cutters *Jeff Davis* and *Joe Lane* were also assigned as dispatch carriers. The *Massachusetts* left Townsend almost immediately for a reconnaissance of Haro and Rosario straits, and in fact kept on the move so constantly that newspaper reporters from San Francisco, assigned as "war correspondents," never were able to catch up with her.

Scott lost no time in sending his first dispatch to Governor Douglas by Lt. Colonel Lay, who sailed to Victoria on the *Jeff Davis*. This brief, forthright letter proposed "Without prejudice to the claim of either nation to the sovereignty of the entire island of San Juan ... that each shall occupy a separate portion of the same by a detachment of infantry, riflemen, or marines, not exceeding one hundred men, with their appropriate arms only. . . ."

Douglas received this missive the night of the 26th and immediately replied through Colonel Lay that he was "at a glance satisfied that no obstacle exists to a completely amicable and satisfactory adjustment..." but that he would need time to study Scott's proposal in detail. The next morning Colonel Lay, finding the *Northerner* at Victoria, sent Douglas' remarks by her to the *Massachusetts*, then nearby off Race Rocks.

As the *Northerner* and *Massachusetts* tried to maneuver alongside one another the former swung around too sharply and collided with the larger vessel. The *Massachusetts* sustained the loss of her jib boom and other minor damage while the *Northerner*'s upper works were raked and her flagstaff, with the ensign flying, broke off and fell into the bay. The flag floated away, damply and ignominiously, in British waters. A sharp order was spoken on board the *Massachusetts* and a small boat, commanded by two officers, went in pursuit. Soon the ensign was recovered and restored to the steamer, which then continued on its mail run to San Francisco, Old Glory looking rather less glorious than usual.

The *Massachusetts* headed east on a course that took her within sight of the garrison on San Juan Island. There the officers, expecting to be favored with an inspection visit by the general-in-chief, had their troops spiffing up. Instead, they watched in bewilderment as the old tub steamed by without so much as a hail; and seeing her battered rigging, Britons and Yankees alike wondered if the war had started, after all.

But *Massachusetts* was on her way to Bellingham Bay, where a day and a half were spent in recoaling and making repairs; and General Scott was reflecting on how easy his task had really been: without hearing a word more than necessary from Harney, and no words at all from Colonel Casey, Commissioner Campbell, Paul Hubbs (certainly not from Lyman Cutler!) nor most of the supporting actors in this drama, Scott was going straight to the heart of the matter with his sensible proposal to Governor

Douglas. Scott was convinced Harney's expansionist zeal, born of a desire to make a name for himself — ultimately, even, to letter his name on the White House door — was the whole crux of the matter. But Scott (who, as it happens, was himself the defeated Whig candidate for President back in 1852) had not reckoned with a certain obstinacy on Douglas' part as well. Already Scott had written the Secretary of War, John Buchanan Floyd, that the proposal of joint military occupation had been made and would "no doubt" be accepted. On this point the proud, old gentleman with the highest military rank since George Washington was due for a comeuppance; but he would be several days yet finding that out.

On Saturday, October 29, the *Massachusetts* weighed anchor in spite of the fog that was settling in fast, and headed for Port Townsend. Scott was becoming impatient. His desire to wind up this annoying little matter on the far periphery and get started East again stemmed largely from his preoccupation with the growing threat of civil war — a threat neither President Buchanan nor Secretary Floyd (but then, Floyd was a southerner) seemed able to do anything much about. Scott was eager to cast himself in the role of National Savior, having a good deal of unasked-for advice he was about to tender to government figures from the President down. For differing reasons, the crew of the *Massachusetts* — their morale rising and falling like a barometer with every change in the general-in-chief's digestion — was just as fervently longing for an end to this particular cruise.

With the fog thickening around them, *Massachusetts'* captain Fauntleroy had extra lookouts watching for little Smith Island, whose light is the standard check-point for crossing the east end of the Strait. So far the light had not been sighted and Fauntleroy was anxious to confirm his course — nothing must prevent him from getting the old general to Port Townsend on schedule. Nervously he peered once again from the wheelhouse window when there was a violent lurch and a sickening *crunch* that told him his course had been set very well indeed: the *Massachusetts* was hard aground on a sand spit, not seventy yards from the lighthouse itself.

Scott learned with unconcealed exasperation that the next tide high enough to float the *Massachusetts* would not occur until sunrise the next morning; until then, headquarters of the United States Army would be a ten-acre sandpile in the Strait of Juan de Fuca.

Fuming, the general made the best of things. The *Jeff Davis* and *Joe Lane* were kept constantly busy carrying dispatches to all points on the Sound, and when these two cutters were unable to handle all the messages, a lieutenant from the *Davis* took to an open boat in which he covered several hundred miles in the course of the next few days. But no one was bringing Scott the dispatch he wanted most — the all-important letter from Governor Douglas, accepting his proposal for joint occupation of San Juan Island.

Early Sunday the *Massachusetts* floated free and continued on for Port Townsend. Off Point Wilson she was hailed by the lieutenant in the *Davis'* whale boat: still there was no reply from Douglas. At Port Townsend the *Joe Lane* came up — again no news from Victoria. Scott's humor was deteriorating quickly. But then the fog began to thin, melting the raw morning into one of those beautiful Indian summer afternoons so common to Puget Sound. At this his mood mellowed a bit, and after only an hour at Townsend, he gave his party the day off to go hunting. For this purpose the *Massachusetts* crossed over to anchor in Padilla Bay, near what is now the ferry-terminal town of Anacortes.

On Monday the cutter *Jeff Davis* sailed from Victoria to Port Townsend, learned the general's whereabouts, found him at Padilla Bay and delivered the long-awaited missive from Governor Douglas. Scott read it quickly, skimming the polite opening sentences of diplomacy, until he caught the first hint that Douglas' reaction was negative:

I trust you will believe me [the governor wrote] when I say that if I am not able entirely to accede to your views it proceeds solely from the necessity . . . that I should take no step which might in the least embarrass the government of Her Britannic Majesty. . . . I . . . am not in possession of the views of Her Majesty's government on this matter, and, therefore, am not at liberty to anticipate the course they may think fit to pursue.

Scott recognized in this argument a stall: the whole purpose of the proposition he had made was to maintain peace *until* the home governments could be heard from and the boundary question was resolved by diplomacy.

James Douglas went on to insist that the way to restore peace was "by replacing matters at San Juan as they were before the landing of the United States troops. . . . An arrangement on that footing would bring the whole affair to a conclusion satisfactory to both parties."

There was another dig in Douglas' letter that bothered Scott:

I admit that the protection of the citizens of both nations who are now resident on the island is a matter which cannot be overlooked or lightly treated, but the principal protection that may be required is from dissensions amongst themselves, and not against hostile Indians. . . .

And again:

It is no doubt, sir, fresh in your recollection that the *sole* reason assigned to me by General Harney for the occupation of San Juan was to protect the citizens of the United States from "insults and indignities" offered them by the British authorities at Vancouver's Island.

Nevertheless the governor left the door open for further negotiations by making a counter-proposal for the withdrawal of all military and naval forces, and for a joint *civil* occupation, "composed of the present resident stipendiary magistrates. . . ."

Scott ordered the *Massachusetts* to make for Dungeness while he composed his reply. Diplomatically ascribing the tardiness of

85

Douglas' letter to "winds and fogs" he politely squashed the governor's chief point with this paragraph:

Your excellency seems to regard the preliminary evacuation of that island by the American troops as a *sine qua non* to any adjustment of the immediate question before us. I am sure that at the date of the instructions which brought me hither, and in the anxious interviews between Mr. Secretary [of State Lewis] Cass and Her Britannic Majesty's minister, Lord Lyons, residing near the government of the United States, no such suggestion was made by his lordship, or it would not only have been communicated to me, but have, in all probability, stopped this mission of peace.

Next the general rejected the idea of a civil occupation with the observation that a magistrate "on neutral territory . . . could not be subjected to the orders of any officer of the United States army, nor even to the direct control of the President . . . and therefore not to be considered a fit person to be intrusted with matters affecting the peace of two great nations." Moreover, he pointed out that the dangers of attack by hostile Indians were very real and required the presence of a military force for the settlers' defense.

Finally, Scott urged the governor to reconsider his original proposal for a joint military occupation, and enclosed a document entitled "Projet of a temporary settlement, &c." which he had penned, "the better to show its probable workings if adopted. . . ."

Since the "Projet" did eventually become the basis of the joint occupation of the San Juan Islands it is worth reading in full:

Projet of a Temporary Settlement, &c.

WHEREAS the island of San Juan, in dispute between the governments of the United States and Great Britain, is now occupied by a detachment of United States troops, protection against Indian incursions having been petitioned for by American citizens, resident thereon, and against such occupation a formal protest has been entered on behalf of Her Britannic Majesty's government by His Excellency James Douglas, esquire, C. B., Governor of the Colony of Vancouver's Island and its Dependencies, and Vice-admiral of the same —

It is now proposed by Lieutenant General Scott, Commanding in chief the Army of the United States in behalf of his government, and in deference to the great interests of the two nations, that a joint occupancy be substituted for the present one, which proposition being accepted by His Excellency, it is hereby stipulated and agreed between the said Scott and the said Douglas that the substitution without prejudice to the claim of either government to the sovereignty of the entire island, and until that question shall be amicably settled, shall consist of two detachments of infantry, riflemen, or marines of the two nations, neither detachment of more than one hundred men, with their appropriate arms only, and to be posted in separate camps or quarters for the equal protection of their respective countrymen on the island in persons and property, as also to repel descents of marauding Indians.

And whereas pending such joint occupation a strict police over the island will be necessary to the maintenance of friendly relations between the troops of the two nations, as well as good order among the settlers, it is further stipulated and agreed between the parties, signers of these presents, that the commanding officer of each detachment composing the joint occupation shall be furnished with an authenticated copy thereof by the respective signers, to be regarded as a warrant and command to the American commander from the said Scott, and to the British commander from the said Douglas, to seize and confine, or to banish from the island, any person or persons whatsoever found or known to be engaged in fomenting any quarrel or misunderstanding between the officers or men of one of the detachments and the officers or men of the other, and, further, to treat in like manner all other offenders against the peace and good order of

87

the island; it being, however, expressly understood and enjoined that such measures of correction shall only be applied to American citizens, or persons claiming to be such, by the American commander, or to British subjects, or persons claiming to be such, by the British commander.

Douglas answered this letter almost immediately but again Scott read with dismay that "the course you propose to me of a joint military occupation is one which I cannot assent to, or carry into effect, without the sanction and express instructions of my government."

On the question of protection to settlers, much insight into British policy on the frontier, as well as the attitude of James Douglas — perhaps the result of long association with the Hudson's Bay Company — can be gleaned from this passage:

". . . the expediency of affording protection to individuals who may settle on territory the sovereignty of which has not been determined may justly be questioned. Protection under such circumstances can, indeed, hardly be considered as a duty incumbent on governments; and, on my part, I am not left in doubt on the subject, as my instructions direct me to announce with reference to this colony that protection cannot be afforded to persons who, by wandering beyond the precincts of the settlements and the jurisdiction of the tribunals, voluntarily expose themselves to the violence or treachery of the native tribes."

In the next paragraph Douglas protested that British authorities had "committed no violation of existing treaty stipulations, nor been guilty of any act of discourtesy" towards the United States, but had "on all occasions during the late exciting events exhibited a degree of forebearance which will, I trust, be accepted as a guarantee that *by no future act will we seek to impair the pacific relations existing between Great Britain and the United States.**

* Italics added.

Douglas followed this with a promise to remove his naval forces if Scott would "divest the large military force now on San Juan of its menacing attitude by removing it from the island." He also assured the general that *"we will not disturb the* 'status' *of San Juan by taking possession of the island, or by assuming any jurisdiction there...."**

Although this letter was meant as a *rejection* of Scott's proposal, the shrewd old general — seizing on the conciliatory phrases indicated — deliberately interpreted it instead as a *commitment* to observe key aspects of Scott's plan. Like the camel whose nose was invited into the tent, Scott moved quickly to put the American side of the arrangement into effect and Douglas, almost before receiving Scott's next letter, was confronted with the whole camel. Scott drew up an order for the removal from San Juan of all companies but one — Captain Pickett's — and ordered the heavy guns returned to the *Massachusetts* and to the forts at Bellingham and Townsend. (This last was another slap at Harney, who had recently ordered the latter posts closed.)

Governor Douglas learned of this development with mixed feelings. On the one hand the reduced American force was an obvious advantage to the British; on the other hand he had given his word, in effect, not to take advantage of that weakness. And while he had not agreed to a joint military occupation, the Americans were already occupying — obviously intending to continue doing so — and there was no advantage to be gained by Douglas' electing *not* to put a force of his own on the island. It was a truly beautiful finesse on Scott's part.

There was just one thing. Douglas hurriedly sent Scott a private, confidential note: would he kindly station *any company except Captain Pickett's* on San Juan? It was a delicate matter, but the general would understand.

The general did understand; and on Monday, November 7, the *Massachusetts* arrived in Griffin Bay with a modified order

* Italics added.

89

for one company, under Captain Lewis Hunt, to occupy the island. Lt. Colonel Casey was given orders placing him firmly in command of the local situation, whereupon Scott took his leave, hoping to make connections with a steamer about to sail from San Francisco.

Casey's orders included instructions to look into a complaint forwarded by Governor Douglas as a sort of parting shot in the war which, the Hudson's Bay Company mogul was now forced to concede, would be fought with words instead of guns. It seems one William Moore, a British-born tradesman engaged peaceably in selling vegetables, etc., to the troops on San Juan, had been arrested by American civil officers, jailed, made to work like a common laborer on the Yankee earthworks, tried in an improvised "court house" and fined an exorbitant sum, all on trumped-up charges.

Casey's investigation turned up a quite different set of facts. William Moore, a native of Sligo, Ireland, was one of the hundreds of dejected down-and-outers crowding the tent-towns of Bellingham Bay when the Fraser River gold rush proved a bust. As the winter approached, promising more misery, Moore — illiterate, jobless, broke — took sick. Claiming American citizenship he applied to the authorities for aid. When finally restored to health his case had impoverished the Whatcom County treasury by some $300.

Moore afterward put in a garden and for a while supported his tenuous existence selling vegetables. When the San Juan trouble arose, he obtained permission to peddle his produce on the beleaguered isle, traveling to and from the San Juans in an Indian canoe. As an added inducement, and to demonstrate his gratitude to the Americans for their kindness, he offered to act as a spy, and was a main source of information on British movements in the area.

Although his deal with the Americans included a promise not to import potables along with the edibles he was selling to the troops and the Indians on San Juan, Moore soon learned there was more profit in spirits than in turnips. Before long Magistrate Crosbie was being bombarded with complaints from both British and American authorities about Moore's activities until, on evidence supplied by Moore's own partner, Crosbie had him hauled in and tried. When Moore admitted his guilt and promised to "go straight" from then on, he was released on payment of a $50 fine.

Crosbie reported the Irishman showed his "utter insincerity by engaging the very next day more extensively in the traffic than before," and so a second arrest warrant was drawn up, "to avoid the service of which he fled the island."

Moore did what many, many another would do before the San Juan business was finally settled. Paddling his canoe to Victoria, he swore his loyalty had been to Queen and Empire all along, and applied to Governor Douglas for redress. This was the complaint which Douglas, perhaps hoping for an incident to keep the San Juan issue hot, passed on to Scott.

"A set-off," snorted Crosbie, as he reported to Washington and Governor Gholson on the matter, and opined that Douglas "is determined to make trouble if he can possibly effect it."

General Scott had foreseen the likelihood of miscreants like Moore switching loyalties to avoid answering for their rascalities. One of his last acts was to lay down a rule that if any person claiming to be a British subject disturbed the peace, he should be turned over to the nearest British authority for "instant removal" from the island; and if the same man turned up a second time, the American commander could then "expel him therefrom without further ceremony." When later the British adopted a similar formula the basis was laid for a unique kind of jurisprudence with which camp commanders endeavored — with varying degrees of success — to maintain some semblance of law and order on the island for the next thirteen years.

6

AN OLD SOLDIER FADES

CAPTAIN LEWIS CASS HUNT, Company C, Fourth Infantry, commanding, assumed with mixed feelings the strange role thrust upon him. Well educated, a bit vain, and an inveterate ladies' man, Hunt held an abiding contempt for the notion of government by and for the people. He himself felt more at home in the drawing rooms of Victoria, in the company of British civil servants and naval officers, than with his own subalterns, whom he considered course and uninteresting. But, as General Scott had sensed, Hunt lacked neither patriotism nor tact; and these qualities, Scott felt, were the ones most sorely needed for the task at hand.

That task, Hunt was reflecting wryly, would not be an easy one. His responsibility was extensive: to preserve order, avoid conflicts with the British, protect the settlers from Indian attacks. As to how all this was to be accomplished, his orders said little, beyond expressing the general's reliance on Hunt's "intelligence, discretion, and (in what is of equal importance in this case) your *courtesies.*" (Hunt smugly considered the use of these terms by Scott as indicating a want of the same qualities in Captain Pickett.)

Somehow Hunt anticipated little trouble from the British — most of whom were, after all, true gentlemen. Even General Scott had remarked in his presence that only the forebearance of the English officers, particularly Admiral Baynes and Captain Hornby, had made a peaceful solution possible.*

No, Hunt expected relations with his own nationals — "patriotic brawlers" he termed them — would be the more trying. And his orders not only failed to give him the clear "dictational" powers over all things American on the island which he felt he needed to do his job, but they implied that jurisdiction over civilians was to be left largely to territorial and county civil officers! Boorish, unlettered roughnecks were these, Hunt reflected sourly; but what else could you expect from the foolishness of popular government, extended even here, on the frontier?

Worst of all, the captain knew precious little support could be expected from his commanding general, for the captain had won Harney's sure and everlasting enmity by rather openly opposing the San Juan adventure all along. Hunt felt certain the general would lose little time in finding a way to get even.

Indeed Harney, at his Fort Vancouver headquarters, was just then smarting from a further blow to his pride. In anger mixed with bewilderment he read the latest blast from General Scott, enclosing — of all things — a conditional order for Harney's reassignment to St. Louis, Missouri. "I have no doubt," Scott had written bluntly, "that one of the preliminary demands which will be made by the British government upon ours, in connection with your occupation of the island of San Juan, will be your removal from your present command."

Harney could scarcely believe his eyes.

---

* But in the nature of things political, it was Douglas who "got much praise in England for keeping the peace with the Yankees," Hornby wrote his wife in December. "That is rather good, when one knows that he would hear of nothing but shooting them all at first, and that, after all, peace was only preserved by my *not* complying with his wishes, as I felt he was all in the wrong from the first."

"In such an event," the letter continued, "it might be a great relief to the President to find you, by your own act, no longer in that command."

But, Scott went on, "If you decline the order, and I give you leave to decline it, please throw it into the fire; or, otherwise, before setting out for the east, call your next in rank to you, and charge him with command of the Department of Oregon."

Harney replied coldly that he was "not disposed to comply with such an order. I do not believe the President of the United States will be embarrassed by any action of the British Government in reference to San Juan Island; nor can I suppose the President would be pleased to see me relinquish this command in any manner that does not plainly indicate his intentions towards the public service."

Still counting on political connections to support him in his feud with the general-in-chief, Harney took his case to the Washington Territorial Legislature which passed, unanimously, on January 7, 1860, a resolution glowingly commending Harney for his strong stand on San Juan. "We respectfully and earnestly solicit the President of the United States," resolved the frontier legislators, "to continue the present able, experienced, and prudent officer (Brigadier General Harney) in command. . . ."

The general was prompt to forward a copy of this document to Army headquarters in Washington, D.C., modestly marking it "for the information" of the War Department. But that department was not overly thrilled to read there that Harney was being eulogized for, among other things, "revoking those unlawful military orders under which an attempt was made to exclude our citizens from portions of the territory." Some of the top brass in Washington City still had the quaint notion that military officers — even brigadier generals — were supposed to *follow* orders, and not go about revoking the ones they didn't like.

On San Juan, Captain Hunt found an account of the legislature's resolution in a territorial newspaper and exploded. "The

94

legitimate result of popular government," he snorted in a letter. "It was to please the dear people that Harney made his *coup*, and he did please the people, silly, blind fools that they are."

Meanwhile, Hunt was doing his best to stay on top of some sticky developments. Almost immediately upon assuming his duties on San Juan he had been confronted with the establishment of two "whisky shanties" near the army's encampment. Going into a huddle with magistrate Crosbie he gained an agreement establishing a military reserve around the camp, within which Hunt could have complete control; outside these confines, civilian authority would prevail.

Owners of one of the shanties promptly moved their enterprise into town, while the other operator "went illegal," hiding his wares under the flooring whenever a raid on his premises seemed imminent. Hunt was not long, however, in banishing him from the restricted area, which embraced something like four square miles in all.

Nonetheless, improvised bar-rooms in town continued to provide the wherewithal for soldiers and civilians alike to escape the boredom of frontier life, with the result that much of the population seemed to be drunk more often than sober. The embattled military commander appealed to Whatcom County's judge Edmund Fitzhugh who expressed his opinion that Hunt already had "full power to act against evil-doers in general"; adding that if he found difficulty in doing so, he could arrest the miscreants and send them over to the judge at Whatcom.

But other authorities doubted Hunt had the power to do either, and what with General Harney breathing down his neck — just waiting, as the captain supposed, for a single misstep — he determined to try getting rid of the whisky-sellers by a local civil action. Henry Crosbie having resigned as magistrate, Hunt applied to his successor, D. F. Newsom, and swore out complaints against three of the offenders, J. S. Bowker, Frank Chandler, and James Frazer, for selling liquor without a license.

95

Newsom convened a court, and juries were selected from the island's citizenry, most of whom, however, happened to think the state of affairs then prevailing on the island was just dandy: free land, no taxes, nobody with certain power to make or enforce laws, plenty of liquor, and a thriving business life devoted largely to inveigling U.S. dollars from the pockets of the soldiery each payday. Why change a set-up like that?

Incontrovertible evidence was presented at the first two trials that: one, the defendants were selling liquor; two, they had not obtained licenses to do so, as required by the law of Whatcom County. Nevertheless, juries gaily refused to find either defendant guilty of selling liquor without a license.

Realizing the futility of this course of action, Hunt glumly dropped the third case. While much of the population was crowding into the establishments of the exonerated whisky-merchants for a long and jubilant round of celebrating, Newsom quit his job in disgust and left the island for more civilized climes. Under the circumstances, no one could be found to replace him.

Hunt now found himself the last bulwark against total anarchy as far as the island's civilians were concerned. The opposition, on the other hand, considered this upstart army captain the final obstacle to their particular version of Nirvana, and seized on a plan to rid themselves of him for good and all. Aware of Hunt's already questionable standing with his commanding general, they drafted a memorial to Harney calling to his attention "the gross and ungentlemanly conduct of Captain Hunt" who, they charged, was guilty of "infringing" on the rights of honest tradesmen, and was trying to "drive the inhabitants from the island." In a burst of stinging if imprecise rhetoric they warned that "unless immediate steps are taken to prevent any further outrage on his part, not only the service to which he belongs, but the dignity of the country who boasts her liberty of the subject, will be compromised." The document was signed by ten "citizens of

Captain George Edward Pickett

General William Selby Harney

BOTH: *Washington State Historical Society, Tacoma.*

Early photo of American encampment on San Juan Island. U.S. artillerymen donned regulation full dress uniforms, assumed studied pose for the camera. *National Park Service.*

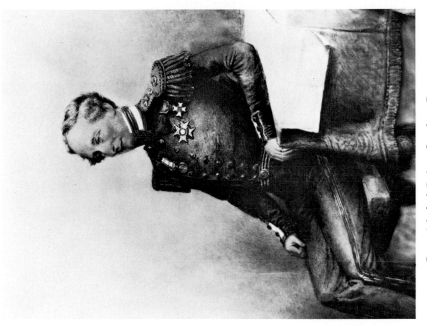

Rear Admiral Robert Lambert Baynes.
Provincial Archives, Victoria.

Sir Geoffrey Phipps Hornby, G.C.B.
Provincial Archives, Victoria.

General-in-chief
Winfield Scott, U.S.A.
*National Archives,
Washington, D.C.*

San Juan Town on the shores
of Griffin Bay. This sketch
by James Alden of
the U.S. survey vessel *Active*
shows the British warship *Satellite*,
left, and the *Active* at anchor.

U.S. SIGNAL CORPS PHOTO NO. 111-BA-1665.

Victoria in 1858. *Provincial Archives, Victoria.*

English Camp soon after Royal Marines landed in 1860.
Tents later gave way to permanent buildings.
Provincial Archives, Victoria.

American Camp on San Juan Island during the long years of joint occupation.
Provincial Archives, Victoria.

Engraving, based on a photograph, shows the permanent British installation at Garrison Bay on San Juan Island. *Provincial Archives, Victoria.*

Residence of English Camp's commanding officer during latter years
of the joint occupation. *Provincial Archives, Victoria.*

Captain Delacombe, his son, Doctors Redfern and Potter, and Augustus Hoffmeister
pose at English Camp. Hoffmeister raised cattle on nearby Henry Island
and had contract to supply the camp's mess with beef. *Provincial Archives, Victoria.*

this island," three of whom were the erstwhile defendants in Newsom's court, and the rest some of their best customers.

Harney responded with a starchy order to Hunt to cease interfering with the trade of citizens, and Hunt was directed to "make a full and complete report to these Headquarters of all your actions affecting citizens up to this time, and hereafter you will take no steps regarding them without reporting the same immediately to this office."

Hunt's reply was later described by him as "as salty an epistle as I dared write," though it seems a model of restraint considering the circumstances. To his report the captain appended a counterpetition signed by former magistrate Newsom and thirty-two "actual settlers upon the island, and tillers of the soil" who expressed full confidence in Hunt. Their statement asserted "that the peace and quiet of the island demand that a stop should be put to the unlicensed and uncontrolled liquor dealing carried on upon the island; that there is no prospect, for various reasons, that any magistrate will long continue to exercise his functions amongst us; that by the result of two recent jury trials it appears that no check exists on the part of the civil power." Harney was respectfully urged to give Captain Hunt fuller instructions, "to the end that the military power may be brought to bear promptly for the suppression of this great nuisance in our midst."

"I am now awaiting with some little curiosity the sequel," Hunt wrote a lady friend on April 20. "With Harney all things are possible, and I should not be very much surprised if he gave his wrath full swing and removed me."

Well, reflected the captain philosophically, and what if he were removed. Then it would be Ho! for Army headquarters at Steilacoom; there were some nifty numbers at Steilacoom, and Hunt hadn't had a first-class, civilized flirtation for months.

In contrast with the ceaseless turmoil in town, life at Camp Pickett — as the post was being called — was serenely pleasant. Troops were kept busy with drill and target practice, and working in the company gardens. In placing Hunt on the island, General Scott had ordered him to occupy the cluster of jerry-rigged buildings which Captain Pickett had erected near the Hudson's Bay farm. Hunt had these fixed up, and when his men had been snugly housed, he ordered his own cottage built to his particular tastes. It was of hewn logs, closely fitted together, and lined inside against the occasional spates of mean weather. On the front he had a covered veranda built — he called it a "piazza" — its roof supported by large columns cut from native trees, peeled, and the knobs left several inches long for ornamentation.

Hunt was fussy about his piazza; for the view it afforded was magnificent almost beyond description. To the south he looked out on the broad, moody Strait of Juan de Fuca, and beyond that to the snow-topped giants of the Olympic Mountains. To the west was Haro Strait (whose channel marked the boundary claimed by Uncle Sam) and behind it Vancouver Island, with Victoria in plain sight on clear days. While to the north and east lay the peaceful grandeur of the San Juan group, the imposing grey-blue humps of Orcas and Lopez Islands forming the distant skyline.

Hunt took great satisfaction and pleasure from the veranda and its view, which had a tranquilizing effect when he fell to brooding over his many difficulties. He was spending a lot of time there, these days, he reflected, as he watched a dot of a steamer approaching the wharf at Griffin Bay. That would be the mail, Hunt knew; it had been two weeks since it last called at San Juan — no doubt it would bear Harney's reply to his last letter. Maybe that letter was a bit *too* salty, thought the captain. Or, not salty enough? . . .

(Special Orders — No. 41.)
HEADQUARTERS DEPARTMENT OF OREGON
Fort Vancouver, W. T., April 10, 1860

The following disposition of troops on Puget's Sound will take effect without delay:

1. Company D, ninth infantry, Captain George Pickett, will replace company C, fourth infantry, at Camp Pickett, San Juan Island.

2. Company C, fourth infantry, on being relieved, will proceed to Fort Steilacoom, to which post it is assigned for duty. . . .

By order of General Harney:

A. PLEASONTON

*Captain Second Dragoons, Acting
Assistant Adjutant General*

So it was indeed to be Ho! for Steilacoom and that new flirtation.* But first, and quickly, before the mail steamer left the harbor, Hunt scribbled a guarded letter to a certain highly-placed major, who would see the information passed to General-in-chief Winfield Scott. Copies of pertinent communications were enclosed, "giving a history, as it were, of matters upon the island, and as showing the animus of Department Headquarters towards me."

He saw with satisfaction his letter aboard the steamer, and was soon standing upon the beloved piazza once again, gazing out toward the bay where the mail was working its way slowly into the Strait for the trip upsound. *That dull animal,* Lewis Hunt was thinking; *that reckless, stupid old goose of a general.* Well, it was a hard thing to fail, to lose a round. But he had resolved, long ago, if he were replaced, to know the reason why. Perhaps there were more rounds to come. . . .

When Captain George Pickett arrived at the end of April it was with considerable satisfaction that Hunt pointed out the problems facing an American commander on San Juan Island. And Pickett was not long in discovering his predecessor's blackly painted picture was no exaggeration. The island was fast becoming a refuge for brigands of all kinds — every scoundrel on Puget

---

* Hunt was married the following December to Abby P. Casey, daughter of his commanding officer.

Sound, it seemed, was converging on San Juan. Pickett discovered with dismay that it was his own reassignment there which largely encouraged the new influx of undesirables; the commanding general had rebuked Hunt, that fastidious spoilsport, and replaced him with the more earthy Captain Pickett! These signals were being interpreted to mean that, under its new commander, San Juan Island would be "wide open."

Pickett however had no such thought in mind. Appalled at the lawlessness increasing unchecked on all sides, he re-read his orders:

You will ... acknowledge and respect the civil jurisdiction of Washington Territory in the discharge of your duties on San Juan, and ... you are directed to communicate with the civil officer on the island in the investigation of all cases requiring his attention.

Very charming — only no civil officer had set foot on the island since Magistrate Newsom had thrown up his hands and walked off the job. How was Pickett to "acknowledge and respect" a civil jurisdiction that did not exist?

Pickett fired off an urgent appeal to Judge Fitzhugh, begging him to appoint a suitable officer. Fitzhugh decided to look matters over first. Arriving early in May, he was accompanied by E. C. Gillette, the surveyor, now a Whatcom County commissioner. After observing the situation on San Juan and listening to Pickett's pleas, Fitzhugh asked Gillette to take on the job of justice of the peace and U.S. Commissioner for the island. Gillette agreed and, promising that the latter would return as soon as he could be sworn in and get transportation back to the island, both men departed in haste for Whatcom.

Two weeks later Pickett had seen nor heard nothing further from either Fitzhugh or Gillette. A letter to the judge went unanswered. Running into Henry Roeder, another of Whatcom's leading citizens, on board a calling steamer, Pickett pleaded with him to see if something couldn't be done at once. But nothing was.

By May 20, 1860, something close to complete anarchy prevailed on the southern end of San Juan Island. Except within the four-mile military preserve, law and order were non-existent. Robbery had become commonplace. The streets of San Juan Town were unsafe for women at any time. Pickett now estimated fully two thirds of the Indians were drunk by day as well as by night. Whisky-sellers had become so numerous he had lost count of them. Meanwhile, decent citizens, living in constant fear, were entreating the captain for protection he was powerless to give them.

That evening, a Sunday, the streets of San Juan Town were thronged as usual with boisterous crowds of Indians and riffraff. From the interiors of the dozens of bars and whisky shanties came the sound of raucous laughter, fights, curses, and bawdy songs. Nearby in the drygoods emporium of one Isaac Higgins — described by Captain Hunt as the only legitimate storekeeper in town* — a group of saner citizens sat, fortressed, listening to the cacophony.

At about nine o'clock a new sound was heard — the unmistakable *krak* of a nearby pistol. The occupants of the store glanced uneasily at one another. But the riotous roar from the drinking spas never paused; seemed actually louder than before. Someone started for the door to investigate — his wiser friends pulled him back. No use to be foolhardy. Out there, now, an honest citizen wouldn't stand a chance.

Next morning at daylight the body of a Haidah Indian was found, shot through the head, near the Higgins store. His body had been robbed. All that day wailing relatives and angry friends clustered around it. Pickett, who knew the proud northern Haidahs only too well, feared their inevitable revenge-taking would fall on some totally innocent person. Orders or no orders, now he felt compelled to act.

* The distinction was short-lived. Higgins later converted his store into a saloon, too.

Pickett bought some time by giving the widow of the murdered Indian some provisions and by making assurances the killer would soon be brought to justice and punished. The catch was that nobody would or could identify the culprit until after the suspect had managed to slip off the island in a small boat.

Reluctant even to take charge of the body — obviously that was a function of civil government — Pickett opened all the stops as he again wrote the Whatcom County commissioners, reporting the murder and begging for an officer to be sent over immediately.

"My hands are tied," he wrote; "I am to assist the civil authority; where are they? Things cannot remain in this position. In order that there shall be no further delay, I now send over my whale-boat, with a *request* that you may despatch by it either a magistrate or a commission for some individual here. My commiseration for the good citizens residing here induces me to this course, and my duty will compel me to make a full report of all the circumstances if immediate action is not taken."

That evening, and for some days afterward, Pickett sent a guard of soldiers into the town to try to keep some semblance of order — "to protect the inhabitants from the Indians and each other," as he put it in a report to headquarters.

This episode at last brought E. C. Gillette hasting to the scene with apologies for his tardiness, which Pickett overlooked in his relief that the magistrate had shown up at all. Without losing time, the captain submitted a list of the worst of the hooch-merchants. Complaints were drawn up for selling liquor without a county license, and for selling to Indians.

Hauled before the new magistrate, all the defendants volubly protested the latter's authority. Most of them were openly defiant, gleefully insisting no law of any kind could touch them on the island, and fully expecting Pickett to back them up. Convening court, Gillette read to them the part in Pickett's orders about acknowledging the jurisdiction of Whatcom County, and cooperating with its civil officials. When five of the defendants still disputed Gillette's authority he called on Pickett for assistance and the five speedily found themselves incarcerated in the camp guardhouse. There would be no jury trial in San Juan Town, either; the prisoners would be held for trial before Judge Fitzhugh at the next session of District Court in Whatcom. The whisky entrepreneurs were astonished to discover not only that Gillette meant business, but that Captain Pickett did, too.

Justice Gillette turned next to investigating the Haidah Indian's murder. Learning the suspected killer had returned to the American side and was seen in Dungeness, he swore in a constable and sent him over to apprehend the suspect. A crony who just might have been implicated, and who was still in town, was arrested on suspicion.

By June 2 the Victoria *Colonist* could report a changed situation on San Juan Island. As justice of the peace, Gillette was "making havoc" with whisky dealers by prosecuting them for selling without a license; while as U.S. commissioner, he was declaring the whole island "Indian country" and any liquor brought to San Juan would henceforth be seized and destroyed.

Yet two weeks later Pickett realized he had won a battle and not the war. Liquor was simply being smuggled onto the island with ease, to be hidden in the woods and sold clandestinely — particularly to Indians. Ruefully, Pickett had to report to General Harney that whisky dealers were "still in full blast" and moreover, that quantities of northern Indian women were now being imported to the island for purposes he delicately described as "nefarious." Pickett thought it would help to have an Indian agent assigned to San Juan.

Instead, Harney resurrected part of his order of the previous summer, when he stationed Pickett's men on the island under the pretext of a protection against Indian incursions: "You will not permit any force of these Indians to visit San Juan island or the waters of Puget's Sound in that vicinity over which the United

States have any jurisdiction. Should these Indians appear peaceable you will warn them in a quiet but firm manner to return to their country, and not visit in future the territory of the United States; and in the event of any opposition being offered to your demands, you will use the most decisive measures to enforce them. . . ."

To back this up, Harney ordered Captain W. H. Fauntleroy, commanding the *Massachusetts,* to cruise the waters of the archipelago and keep northern Indians away. Any that refused to leave were to be arrested and brought to Fort Steilacoom.

Pickett was aghast as he considered the consequences of obeying such an order. Thousands of northern Indians came to San Juan in the spring of each year to fish and to work for the Hudson's Bay Company. Already there were four thousand of them reported near Victoria, and many more on their way. To oppose them with military force could only lead to the copious shedding of blood. And with a single company of men — it was seriously under strength at that — Pickett could not hope to protect the farmers scattered in isolated spots over the island. Confound that Harney, Pickett thought. He was determined to stir up trouble, somehow.

This time Pickett refused to be stampeded. He wrote Harney, pointed out the realities of the situation, and bluntly declined to "commence the war" without more specific instructions.

These Pickett would never receive. For before Harney could reply, the general was to acquire some disheartening instructions of his own.

General-in-chief Winfield Scott had been discussing Harney with the Secretary of War. He doubted the general would accede for long to the peaceful arrangement Scott had made of affairs in the Pacific Northwest. Indeed, he told Mr. Floyd, Harney was obviously jealous of what he considered interference on the part of higher authority; he probably could not be trusted to follow orders, but would soon find a new way to heat things up. Perhaps he should be removed from command before that happened? But the War Department, recalling Harney's political connections, at first preferred to wait and see.

There hadn't been long to wait. Harney's arch-enemies on the frontier, the Hudson's Bay Company, still occupied property at Fort Vancouver — it had been their fort, in fact, until the boundary treaty of 1846 placed it in Yankee territory and led to the establishment, instead, of the one at Victoria (its site having been selected over many others by James Douglas himself). The continued presence of Hudson's Bay buildings and cultivated fields, cheek-by-jowl with Harney's military headquarters, rankled the old Indian fighter beyond endurance. Finally he advised Chief Trader James Grahame that he no longer recognized the Company's right to "any lands within the military reserve," adding that if Hudson's Bay had been allowed to stay until that time, it had only been "conceded by the courtesy" of General Harney.

The Company protested — with reason — that the Treaty of 1846 guaranteed them possessory rights to the property; but to no avail. Harney gave them a week to vacate, after convening a board of three of his own officers to assess the value of the trading company's improvements. The eight buildings and four to five hundred yards of fences were put at not over $250 total, which was to be paid the company only "in the event of any compensation being allowed them hereafter by the government."

Chief Factor A. G. Dallas, with whom Harney had been locking horns over the San Juan pig business, threw in the towel and wrote Harney he was pursuing his only recourse — "to withdraw entirely from the [Washington] territory." To this the general replied, for once, with an offer of "every facility" to help them fulfill this intention. But news of this latest outburst of aggressiveness toward our brother Anglo-Saxons in the north did nothing to enhance Harney's deteriorating standing in Washington City.

105

Moreover, Harney was outstripping even his own notorious reputation for harshness toward subordinates. Soon after taking command at Fort Vancouver, there had been a disagreement between the general and his ordnance officer over some trivial matter of procedure, which the officer proposed to appeal to the chief of ordnance, whereupon Harney had him arrested, charged with disrespect to a superior officer, and relieved from duty.

Then there was the case of Lieutenant Henry V. De Hart, who had the temerity to question Harney's right to furlough soldiers so they could be put to work building the general's private residence. De Hart was no ordinary guard-house lawyer: he knew military law backwards and forwards (he later wrote the book on court martials) and was sure of his ground. When Harney preferred charges against De Hart, his nemesis — General Scott — pointed out that the charges were worthless and would surely not be upheld by Washington. Learning that the lieutenant was being held prisoner in Harney's stockade all the while, Scott peremptorily ordered the general to release him. Once again, Scott took opportunity to write the Secretary of War, that "the highest obligations of my station compel me to suggest a doubt whether it be safe in respect to our foreign relations, or just to the gallant officers and men in the Oregon department, to leave them longer, at so great a distance, subject to the ignorance, passion, and caprice of the present headquarters of that department."

Another lieutenant, Henry C. Hodges, was meanwhile being placed under arrest for the dastardly crime of omitting from a report the rank and designation of Harney's staff officer. Harney was again called on the carpet for taking such extreme measures over a minor irregularity, and Hodges was ordered restored to duty.*

* Harney was, moreover, in trouble with the Ordnance Department for trying to force the Pacific Department's ordnance officer to erect an arsenal on a tract of land owned by Harney, for which Harney was asking a tidy $3,480.

The general's stock fell yet lower when, in April, he closed down Fort Townsend for the second time, General Scott having specifically ordered it reactivated a few months earlier. When news of this reached Washington, Secretary of War Floyd crossly ordered Harney to report "on what ground it has been abandoned."

Simultaneously with this, Winfield Scott received Captain Hunt's hastily sent letter from San Juan Island, and read with mounting anger the captain's account of events culminating in his replacement by George Pickett. Laying all of this before Secretary Floyd, Scott particularly pointed out portions of General Harney's orders to Pickett which denied "within the knowledge of the general commanding" that joint occupation had ever legally been authorized, insisting that the act of the territorial legislature making the islands part of Whatcom County was "the law of the land," and warning that "any attempt of the British commander to ignore this right of the Territory will be followed by deplorable results. . . ."

"If this does not lead to a collision of arms," Scott told the Secretary gravely, "it will again be due to the forebearance of the British authorities."

By now Floyd, his disposition souring as the distant rumblings of approaching civil war began more and more to command his attention, found himself fresh out of patience:

Special Orders — No. 115.

WAR DEPARTMENT

Adjutant General's Office, Washington, June 8, 1860

Brigadier General William S. Harney, United States Army, will, on the receipt hereof, turn over the command of the Department of Oregon to the officer next in rank in that Department, and repair without delay to Washington city, and report in person to the Secretary of War.

By order of the Secretary of War:

S. COOPER
Adjutant General

7

TWO FLAGS FLYING

ALL OF GENERAL HARNEY'S tortured attempts to justify his actions in the San Juan affair were curtly disapproved by Secretary Floyd, who perhaps would have taken sterner action but for the congealing furore in the South. President Buchanan, however, supposed a fighting general like Harney might come in a bit handy before long. So he had the old Indian fighter appointed commander of the Department of the West, at St. Louis, where he could be kept on ice until needed. But Harney's continued penchant for playing the military bull in political china closets got him relieved from the post twice in as many years, and culminated in his capture by Southern forces eleven days after the fall of Fort Sumter.

One of the very first Union officers to be taken prisoner in the war, Harney was released a short time afterward and allowed to proceed to Washington, after some remarkably friendly visits with Robert E. Lee, General Joseph Johnston, Virginia's governor John Letcher and other high-up Southerners. Under these circumstances he was given no more commands and in 1863 a hard-pressed government decided the safest thing was to retire him altogether.*

Harney's old department of Oregon was given to Colonel — soon General — George Wright, who took command just as those distant rumblings of war drums were reaching the Pacific coast. Kept busy with a rising tempo of troop movements and war preparations, Wright paid a minimum of attention to San Juan Island, allowing events there to settle into their own groove. Captain Pickett was doing a surprisingly creditable job of restoring order and, once out from under Harney's impelling thumb, seemed more than willing to keep peace with the British. Wright decided to leave Pickett in command for the time being.

Meanwhile a hundred-man complement of red-coated Marines had finally landed on San Juan. There had been a great deal of intervening friction between certain "hawks" and "doves" on the British side. Back in October, 1859, when General Scott's proposal of joint occupation arrived in Victoria, doughty old Admiral Baynes took it upon himself to send a copy via pony express and Western Union telegraph — the fastest communications available then — to the British ambassador in Washington City. Douglas wasn't happy when he received orders back to accept the proposition.

Douglas' pique took an odd form. Verbally telling Baynes to land an occupying force on San Juan, he declined to show the admiral the orders directing the landing. Baynes stated he was not about to make such a move just on Douglas' say-so. But the governor maintained that, as representative of the Queen, he could not "delegate" his instructions to anyone, and steadfastly refused to show Baynes the order. The deadlock was not broken until Baynes wrote the Admiralty in England for a copy, which was not received until February.

There was another month's delay while a site for the encamp-

* Toward the end of the war, Harney was awarded a brevet in recognition of earlier successes.

ment was selected. Captain Prevost, the *Satellite's* surveyor-skipper, scouted several possible locations, recommending a certain "convenient slope of prairie land, with a running stream of fresh water within 400 yards of it; convenient of access by boats; also a safe harbour for ships, of any size, at all seasons of the year."

The site — later to become Friday Harbor, the county seat — was rejected by higher-ups, perhaps because it was on the eastern slope of the island and twice as far from Victoria by water as any site on the western coast.*

A pleasant spot on the northwestern shoulder of the island, near present-day Roche Harbor, was settled upon instead; and troops were landed there on March 27, 1860, under the command of Captain George Bazalgette.

Bazalgette, a firm disciplinarian though affable enough socially, had been granted authority to keep order among British subjects. His power was thus, in contrast to the restrictions placed on his American counterpart, absolute. If offenses were committed by any of Her Majesty's subjects, Bazalgette was empowered to deal with the case however he judged best, or if necessary, simply to expel miscreants from the island "by the first opportunity."

In the interests of peace, Bazalgette was also instructed, should there be any doubt as to an offender's nationality, not to act before consulting with the American commander, "and not even then unless your opinions coincide."

Bazalgette's troops were at first simply quartered in a neat white tent row along the shores of Garrison Bay. Their equipment, more suitable for a short bivouac than a protracted occupancy, consisted of cooking equipment and a few basic tools. For no one dreamed then the two "opposing" camps — one under the Stars and Stripes, the other flying the Union Jack — would

---

* Prevost's estimate of the "safe harbour for ships of any size" may have been overenthusiastic. Years afterward a patriotic visit to Friday Harbor by the historic U.S.S. *Constitution* ("Old Ironsides") was cancelled when her officers deemed the harbor's confines too tricky for the venerable vessel.

continue to occupy their respective ends of the island for year upon year while the boundary question went without solution.

But America's statesmen were now preoccupied with the more pressing business of staving off, if possible, a civil cataclysm of potentially horrible proportions. The little cloud no larger than a man's hand, dimly foreseen by Buchanan in 1859, became a dreadful nimbus, its awesome portent only too clearly understood by Lincoln in 1860. Politicians of both North and South played out their feverish roles, observing with mounting horror their collision course, but unable or unwilling to alter that course. Britain, too, was anxiously watching events to see what dangers they might bring to her interests in North America. Concern over a few small islands in far-off Puget's Sound withered away quickly in London as in Washington.

And so the two encampments on San Juan Island took on more and more the appearance of fixed installations. At English Camp the row of tents gave way to a cluster of whipsawn, white clapboard barracks, commissary, and shops. A two-story log blockhouse was erected on the beach — not so much to safeguard against attack by the Americans as from Indians. A large area was cleared for a parade ground, and a double row of Douglas fir seedlings was planted, in honor of the governor. Gardens were put in and fenced, fruit trees set out. A well was dug near an ancient broad-leafed maple — a tree which is today still growing, and bears a plaque claiming it to be the oldest of its species in the world.

As the camp area spread further and further up the hillside extensive limestone terracing was added. Ultimately there were tennis courts and croquet grounds and seven-room homes for the subordinate officers. Bazalgette's own residence had ten rooms and two large halls, including a billiard chamber and ballroom. The transplanted Britishers were determined, it would seem, to make this dot of tentatively-held empire into a comfortable likeness of far-off England.

Around the camp Bazalgette established a military preserve similar to the Americans'. Relations between the two commanders were good, and among the troops, fraternization was the order of the day. The wagon-road built to connect the two encampments was well-traveled.

With the firing of Fort Sumter in April 1861, the agony of Rebellion began. While the lives of civilians in distant Washington Territory were scarcely touched, the Army was plunged into a ferment of fevered activity. Colonel Wright was hastily ordered to supply by steamer to San Francisco, for shipment to the scene of war, most of the troops in his command. To comply, he was obliged to withdraw forces from garrisons all over the Territory, closing most of them down altogether. One of the camps ordered closed was the one on San Juan Island.

Wright had misgivings about this wholesale removal of troops from Puget Sound: it was an open invitation to still-bellicose Northern Indians to wipe out, one by one, the settlements of whites clustering its shores. Rethinking the matter, he decided San Juan Island — lying in the midst of the Sound's approaches — was the key spot for defense against canoe-borne war parties. "Indeed," he wrote his superiors, "I believe that a strong garrison on San Juan Island, with the aid of a small steamer, would afford ample protection for the whole sound, and that all other posts might be dispensed with."

Wright's letter crossed with a one-line dispatch from his commanding general in San Francisco to "re-establish Camp Pickett" and was followed by instructions to maintain the post on San Juan Island "as having a national importance." Washington City agreed, and the maintenance of Camp Pickett throughout the long years of the North-South conflict was assured.

Pickett himself, torn between loyalties to the Union he had sworn to serve and to the Virginia he loved, concluded to cast his lot with his native state. Having tendered his resignation as an officer in the Army of the United States, Pickett was granted leave of absence on a pretext — which fooled nobody — of returning to Virginia to collect a legacy. After turning over his government property at Fort Steilacoom, he departed by way of Panama and joined the Southern forces. And his brilliant exploits as a Confederate general, particularly the valiant (though fruitless) charge at Gettysburg, were followed with pride by Americans on San Juan, in spite of their solidly Union sympathies; for this man who stood up so valorously before overwhelming British forces at Griffin Bay would long remain the island's foremost local hero.

Pickett was replaced temporarily by a brother officer and close friend, Captain T. C. English, in the San Juan command. English too was a Southerner, and toward the end of 1861 he was in turn relieved by Lieutenant Augustus G. Robinson, an artilleryman.

The theory has been advanced that perhaps Southerners like Harney, Pickett, Paul Hubbs and others, had deliberately provoked the British over the San Juans in hopes of a collision with England that would either prevent the Civil War from taking place at all or, at the least, would give the North the disadvantage of fighting on two fronts. No solid evidence to support such a view has ever been uncovered and it seems less than credible that frontier soldiers and settlers in the farthest reach of the land could have foreseen clearly in that momentous July of 1859 what the most prescient statesmen in Washington City scarcely dared to surmise.

It was February 1862 before a permanent commander was assigned to Camp Pickett and by then San Juan Town's mischief makers were again in full swing. Captain Lyman A. Bissell had barely set his foot on the island and assumed the command before being besieged with complaints of all kinds from the honest settlers over misdeeds on the part of the town crowd. Whisky flowed freely once again, and drunkenness was the order of the day — and of the night. Justice Gillette had left his public office to become partner in a thriving lime producing concern at Roche Harbor; and the new justice of the peace, one E. T. Hamblet, struck Bissell as being far too friendly with the whisky sellers to inspire his confidence. Hamblet had his office — and held court — in a barroom belonging to his closest crony, none other than J. S. Bowker, one of the defendants in those abortive jury trials back in Lewis Hunt's day. And Bowker himself was still doing business without a county license.

When Bissell referred the citizens' complaints to Hamblet, nothing came of them, as juries were somehow always composed of men who sided with the offenders. Bissell, still under orders to "respect" the civil authority, seemed powerless to do anything about it.

In August the murder of an Indian near British Camp brought matters to a head, impelling Bissell to take more vigorous measures, just as a similar killing had induced Pickett to do. It seemed an American named William Andrews, living near the British encampment, had brought on the tragedy by dispensing copious quantities of fire-water to the parties involved. Captain Bazalgette complained formally to Bissell against Andrews, pointing out that a similar complaint had been made against him the previous year when Pickett was in command.

Pickett had been unable to get a conviction in Andrews' case, and Bissell doubted he would be any more successful. What particularly ired him about Andrews was that he was a Southerner — an impudent "Johnny Reb" brazenly flaunting the law of the land and the power of the Union Army.

The more Bissell thought about Andrews, the angrier he got. At last he took the unprecedented (and unauthorized) course of simply expelling the man from the island by military force.

Then, having set his hand to the plow, he proceeded to give the rest of a long list of trouble-makers 24 hours to leave the island, or be tossed into the guard house.

Stunned, they all left.

Bissell next established a military police which searched every boat touching at the island, and refused to allow those carrying unauthorized whisky to land.

There was a decline in the number of drunken Indians and a period of comparative law and order, although at least one saloon — the one operated by magistrate Hamblet's friend — continued in business. Apparently Bissell was not opposed to citizens' taking a peaceable nip now and then, but no boisterous carousing was to be tolerated. So when a high-spirited covey of "sports" from Victoria sailed over intent on having a spree at Bowker's hooch emporium, they were met by soldiers who peremptorily ordered them to get back into their boat and leave the island. They did, after which the Victoria *Colonist* muttered darkly about the "martial law" imposed by the embattled American captain.

Indeed there was now no question about who was running San Juan Island. When some minor trouble erupted between the settlers, Bissell even dictated a system of compulsory arbitration which by-passed the civil authority altogether. At least one land boundary dispute between an American citizen and a British subject was settled in this manner, though the Britisher certainly was under no compulsion to submit to it. The fact that he did indicates the system must have been a fair one.

For the first time in years, an American commander felt on top of things on San Juan Island. Still, Bissell felt a gnawing suspicion in his gut: someday he would be called to account, results or no. Looking to justify his actions, he resurrected the correspondence between General Scott and Governor Douglas as proving that Washington Territory had *no* rightful jurisdiction

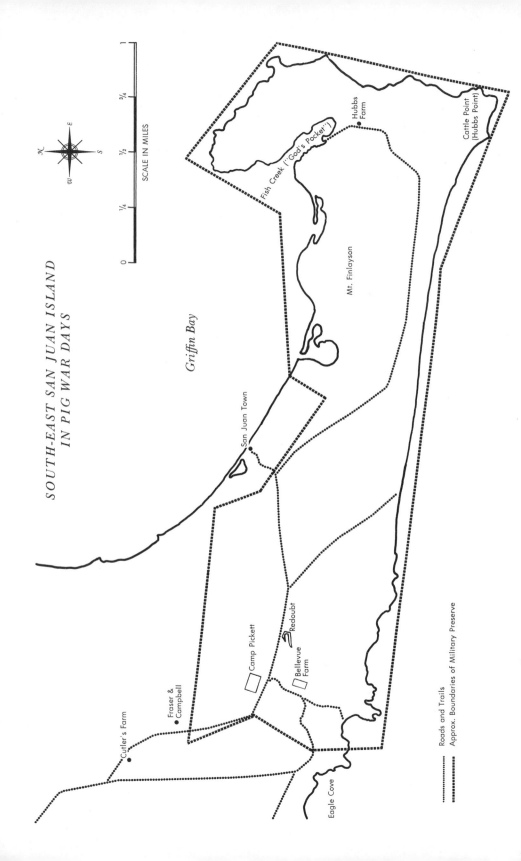

SOUTH-EAST SAN JUAN ISLAND
IN PIG WAR DAYS

SCALE IN MILES

0   ¼   ½   ¾   1

Griffin Bay

Cutler's Farm

Fraser & Campbell

Camp Pickett

Redoubt

Bellevue Farm

Eagle Cove

San Juan Town

Fish Creek ("God's Pocket")

Hubbs Farm

Mt. Finlayson

Cattle Point (Hubbs Point)

Roads and Trails
Approx. Boundaries of Military Preserve

over the island — subsequent Army orders to the contrary notwithstanding.*

Justice Hamblet, of course, didn't see it that way, and came to Bissell in a huff over the latter's having virtually proclaimed himself the island's dictator. Bissell calmly pointed out that the only alternative seemed to be island-wide anarchy, and asked Hamblet if he and the other citizens could suggest a more workable way of maintaining law and order.

Bissell posed the question casually, in a rhetorical sense. But Hamblet seized on it as an invitation and was soon posting the following

NOTICE

According to the wish of Captain Bissell, as expressed to me, I hereby request the citizens of this island to meet at Frazer's house, in the woods, on the road to the garrison, on Sunday, February 1, for the purpose of making such laws as we shall deem necessary for the settlement of differences between settlers concerning land claims and for the enforcement of good order upon the island.

E. T. HAMBLET

Some thirty persons showed up at the log house near Cutler's "pig garden" where Robert H. Frazer and a man named Campbell had installed a rustic saloon; but if they expected to have an opportunity for resolving any questions democratically, they quickly discovered otherwise. The meeting was scarcely brought to order before Hamblet, himself, had somehow been elected chairman. Pushing through the thick knot of settlers crowding the diminutive cabin, Hamblet had not even reached his seat at the front of the gathering before he began appointing a "resolutions committee," to be headed by Isaac Higgins,

* In refuting Douglas' suggestion of a civil occupation of the island, Scott's November 2, 1859 letter observed that a judge or justice of the peace was "not to be considered a fit person to be intrusted with matters affecting the peace of two great nations."

postmaster, and proprietor of one of San Juan Town's noisiest barrooms.

Higgins promptly stood up, pulled from his pocket a piece of paper, and handed it to the secretary — whom the settlers recognized as none other than M. W. Offutt, one of the men Bissell had banished from the island for selling liquor to Indians.

When Offutt began reading this document aloud the respectable settlers, who knew a sell-out when they saw one, turned in disgust and walked out. In consequence, Higgins' resolutions were adopted unanimously by those remaining, and the meeting adjourned. The whole proceeding took ten to fifteen minutes.*

Hamblet lost no time in forwarding a copy of the "Preamble and resolutions" thus adopted to General Wright, now commanding the entire Department of the Pacific from San Francisco. The general read with dismay that San Juanians "cannot concur with Captain Bissell in thinking that he is our Governor, or that he has the power to authorize us to make laws by which we will be governed, it being evident to us that, according to the arrangement made by General Scott and His Excellency Governor Douglas, the military were placed here to exercise a police supervision over the citizens and subjects of their respective Governments, and to aid the civil authorities of these Governments in enforcing the laws upon their respective subjects and citizens, or in protecting them in their lives, property, and all the rights to which they are entitled."

The ploy of Hamblet, Higgins and company was of course intended to bring back the good old days of civil law — i.e., no law at all — and it very nearly succeeded. But Wright could smell the rat. Observing the resolutions were "somewhat enigmatical," he wrote Bissell for clarification of the meeting's "real object."

* This rigged procedure would have earned the special censure of a young engineering officer in charge of building San Juan's earthworks. He was Lieutenant Henry M. Robert, later the famed originator of the standard *Rules of Order* familiar to parliamentarians.

118

Meanwhile, Wright ordered Brigadier General Benjamin Alvord, now commanding at Fort Vancouver, to go to San Juan if necessary and "arrange any misunderstanding that may exist between the captain and the settlers." To Alvord he gave instructions that while he had "no objection to the American settlers having civil officers within the limits occupied by them, yet he will not consent to their exercise of any jurisdiction except on the end of the island in our possession."*

Alvord, hoping to avoid making the trip, wrote Bissell for a full report. Accompanying Bissell's lengthy reply was a statement endorsed by twenty-six law-abiding residents who protested they were not represented by Hamblet's railroading party. "We fully approve the actions of the commanding officer of this post," they advised the general, "as calculated to maintain order, to keep disorderly characters away, and to maintain the present good understanding between the British and American commands and their respective governments."

Bissell was also supported by a summation of the whole San Juan situation as penned by Edward D. Warbass, a civilian of excellent reputation who had been post sutler (storekeeper) on the island ever since Pickett's time. Warbass, who had been on the Pacific coast since California gold-rush days, was later the founding father of Friday Harbor.

"American settlers," Ed Warbass assured Alvord, "would be contented to have the laws of Washington Territory in full force, and with rigid vigor executed, but are prepared to believe that the general will agree with them that under the law as executed by Mr. Hamblet we have something other than the laws of our country."

Warbass himself had meanwhile become a victim of one of Hamblet's shenanigans, involving the hopeless confusion over

* This error would for a time compound Lyman Bissell's difficulties by apparently limiting his authority to a certain "portion" (undefined) of the island instead of extending to all Americans living on it.

property rights on the contested island. Where previously there had been plenty of open land for all comers, disputes over the choicer sites were beginning to erupt; and with no clear-cut notions as to whether title could be granted by one kind of law or another, or by a combination or by none at all, the scene was set for a wrangle unique in the annals of jurisprudence.

San Juan Town itself, for example, was part of the original Hudson's Bay Co. farmsite, and still claimed as such by the company's present agent, Robert Firth, with the support of the British camp commander. The same property had been staked by young Stephen Boyce, an American who hoped to make a farm there if and when Britain lost out in the boundary question. Now, in early February of 1863, postmaster Higgins came forward with a claim of his own to the townsite, and was appealing to his friend, justice of the peace Hamblet, to confirm the title. In anticipation that this would be done, Higgins began plowing up the road used by Hudson's Bay Company, soldiers, and settlers alike to get from town to the dock, and — using materials dismantled from some of the Hudson's Bay outbuildings — began fencing in his "homestead."

Warbass, who had bought and paid for a house and farm in this area in 1860, was suddenly confronted with Higgins' demand to "relinquish possession" of the property Warbass thought he owned, except for the lot on which his house actually stood; and on that, Higgins was demanding $25 for rent. When the doughty pioneer refused both demands, Higgins swore out a complaint before magistrate Hamblet, and Warbass was summoned to appear in court. Meanwhile, intervention by the British commander put an end to Higgins' efforts to fence in the disputed land.

Before the date set for Warbass' trial, Hamblet ordered another islander, an Englishman named Roberts, to appear and "show cause by what authority" he held a land claim on the northern tip of the island — which happened to contain valuable lime deposits. The complaint was made on behalf of a young lawyer and wool smuggler, L. W. Tripp, who was not a resident of San Juan, but was prepared to come to the island and operate the lime kiln as soon as his good friend E. T. Hamblet had completed the necessary arrangements.

Roberts* answered Hamblet with a polite little note declining to appear, and pointing out that as a British subject, he was scarcely answerable to the justice's authority.

Hamblet ordered an immediate trial, which was held without Roberts' presence in Bowker's barroom, at night, with participants as well as onlookers smoking, drinking, and gambling during the proceedings. Not surprisingly, the court ruled in favor of Hamblet's friend, Tripp.

Hamblet and a covey of his cronies were about to eject Roberts by force when the matter was reported to Captain Bissell. Bissell understandably hit the roof, and not having — fortunately — yet received General Wright's orders confirming the jurisdiction of civil officers, he ended the whole matter by peremptorily suspending Hamblet as a functionary of Washington Territory.

All this Warbass reported to General Alvord in so convincing a manner Alvord urged the department commander, General Wright, to give Bissell authority to "banish from the island any person fomenting any quarrel or misunderstanding between the British and American residents, or troops, . . . it being enjoined that the power shall not be lightly exercised, but reserved for occasions imperatively requiring it." Alvord pointed out that according to the Scott-Douglas agreement, British subjects and Americans were to have equal rights and unless the commanding officer were granted the powers requested, "I do not see but that American citizens have greater impunity in crimes, besides having equal rights."

Wright concurred, and Bissell subsequently received a special

* This Roberts — not to be confused with the American engineer-parliamentarian — died by drowning the same year.

order bestowing on him his long-desired authority, which did much to restore peace and order to the island.

It also, of course, strengthened even more Bissell's position as the highest overseer of all things American on the island. Later that summer James Kavanagh, sheriff of Whatcom County, traveled to the island to collect license and poll taxes. He returned eight days later, grumbling in his diary that he had not succeeded in his mission, "because of interference of Captain Bissell. Military law is supreme on the Island."

Just how supreme, he described in a letter to General Wright, alleging — among other things — that Bissell was making arbitrary and fanciful decisions in land-dispute cases, using his power of banishment frivolously, and interfering on behalf of his friends in matters of debts.

Wright bucked the letter to Alvord, who wrote the sheriff that while difficult questions were bound to arise in such peculiar circumstances as existed on San Juan, "it seems to be the duty of patriotism at this trying crisis in our history to practice forebearance and await patiently the progress of events."

By this time both Alvord and his department commander were sick and tired of the continual annoyances arising on the far-off island with its puny hundred-man post. Wright threw up his hands and "confided" the whole mess to Alvord, who chose to follow the path of least resistance, which he later described as "administering opiates and staving off puzzling questions."

The following year Wright's successor, General Irvin McDowell, and Washington Governor William Pickering, visited San Juan Island on an inspection tour. Pickering concluded not to appoint any more justices of the peace, and ruled that no civil authority of any kind might be exercised on the island "save by or through military officers in command.*

* McDowell on this trip straightened out the remaining tangle over division of the island, pointing out that authority was to be exercised "not as to territory, for that is the matter at issue, but as to individuals. . . ."

Thus the American Camp commander, once hampered by possessing too little power, now found himself confirmed as the supreme authority over every American on the island. It was a circumstance ripe with temptation for any man with latent despotic tendencies; but Lyman Bissell was not that kind of man. For all his aggressiveness in dealing with situations that demanded aggressive measures, Bissell was basically a fair-minded, life-loving fellow without a spoilsport bone in his body. Throughout his tenure on the island, there was a great deal of partying. Each year both the Fourth of July and the Queen's birthday brought convoys of boats from Victoria with scores of merry-makers intent on joining San Juanians of both nationalities in their revelry. There were always good times to be had when Captain Bissell was in command.

All that changed abruptly in 1865 when Bissell was replaced by Captain Thomas Gray, a man as austere and unbending as Bissell was fun-loving. When a large group of "pic-nickers" came over from the Canadian side to help celebrate the Fourth, Gray had the boats met by soldiers and brusquely ordered away, to the disgust of the Americans, who had gone to considerable trouble and expense preparing to entertain their Britannic friends.

Gray proved a martinet as well: wholesale desertions and even suicides began to occur among his troops. So many were slipping over to Victoria — without intending to return — that Gray put announcements in the papers there, offering to restore "without trial or punishment" those who voluntarily came back. Then, to keep them from going over the hill again, Gray passed an order requiring all boats on the island to be kept under lock and key. Patrols were established which made the rounds of the island, and when a boat was found on the beach unlocked, it was simply bashed in without ceremony and thus rendered unseaworthy.

Trouble erupted when one of Gray's patrols staved in a vessel belonging to a British subject who had business interests on the

123

island. The Britisher, Daniel McLachlan, checked his rage until confronted by the same patrol a week later. This time he lost his temper and ordered them off his company's property, whereupon he was arrested and tossed into the camp lock-up for — as he put it later — "threatening the majesty of American military law."

After weeks of imprisonment, while purportedly awaiting a trial, McLachlan was released when business associates prevailed on the British commander to intervene.

Meanwhile, Isaac Higgins (the man Captain Hunt once described as San Juan Town's "only legitimate store-keeper") was having a run of troubles. Shortly after taking command, Gray induced Higgins — whose stint as the island's postmaster had ended — to take over hauling the government mail between San Juan and Port Townsend, at an attractive salary. But the deal was made verbally, and three months later Gray changed his mind and cancelled the arrangement.

Disgruntled and jobless, Higgins decided to take up farming again, and soon was engaged in fencing, for the second time, those fields at San Juan Town which he still claimed were his.*

About the time his crops were in and growing, Gray's second in command, Lieutenant W. P. Graves, came down and told Higgins to remove the fences. Higgins, who later stated Graves seemed less than sober at the time, ignored the order.

Two weeks later, on returning from a trip to the mainland, the would-be farmer was met at the dock by soldiers who again ordered him to take down the fences "and fill up the postholes." When he refused, the soldiers did it for him.

Outraged, Higgins stormed up to the garrison where he found Lieutenant Graves in command of the post, Captain Gray being off the island. A heated discussion of the affair ensued, cul-

---

* The claim was based on a paper granted him by Captain Pickett, acknowledging Higgins was already residing on the place when Pickett's men landed on the island in 1859.

minating in Higgins' angry promise to "seek every legal method of redress," whereupon he too found himself installed forcibly behind the bars of Gray's pokey.

After languishing there a week, Higgins was hauled out and ordered to leave the islands and "never return to them again." Refusing to leave willingly, he was placed in an Indian canoe and paddled across to the mainland under guard. He was not (he later claimed) allowed to take any food, blankets, or possessions of any kind. Ejected penniless on the beach six miles from the nearest town, Higgins' only consolation was the sarcastic observation of one of the soldiers that "You are now back in the land of civil law."

Higgins hired the best lawyer he could find, and sued both Gray and Graves for malicious trespass. A grand jury in Olympia indicted the two officers and a sheriff presented himself on the island with warrants for their arrest. The pair refused to be arrested, whereupon the judge, Charles B. Darwin, angrily ordered the sheriff to return to the island with a posse and bring the men in.

The posse arrived to face Gray's troops prepared for battle and, convinced the officer really meant to open fire, the sheriff again withdrew empty-handed.

Judge Darwin promptly announced he intended to see the civil law enforced if it took all the force of the Territory, and issued an order to any sheriff in the district to arrest both Gray and Graves on sight. Graves was indeed arrested subsequently, and was obliged to post bond guaranteeing his appearance in court the following term.

Neither officer appeared when the case came to trial, but Higgins was awarded damages totalling $6,000 for his losses. It was a mere moral victory, of course, as both defendants refused to pay up.

Protests over this sort of high-handedness on the part of San Juan's military dictators were springing up like green shoots after a Puget Sound rain. The Washington *Standard* complained it was "sick and tired" of hearing reports of arbitrary property confiscations and banishments, without a hearing of any kind, at Gray's whim. "No civilized people on earth," declaimed the *Standard*, "are subjected to the same degrading petty despotism as is practiced upon the reserves of San Juan Island," where "Americans are denied all law and subjected by the force of the bayonet to obey the caprices of a petty military officer," and "subjected to outrages nowhere else tolerated among civilized people." And on the island itself, the first commercial message to be sent over a newly constructed submarine telegraph line was a $45 wire to San Francisco, protesting the "arbitrariness, injustice," and "tyrannical caprice" of Thomas Gray. The telegram was composed and paid for by Charles McCoy, the blue-eyed giant who raised that Fourth of July flag at Paul Hubbs' cabin back in '59.*

Eventually the Washington Territorial Legislature got into the act by drafting a strongly-worded memorial to Congress, deploring martial rule on San Juan Island. Thus encouraged, and still hoping to collect his court-awarded damages, Higgins sent to Washington, D.C., a petition containing charges against Gray which were so outspoken even the sympathetic Victoria *Colonist* declined to print them.

It was a bad move on Higgins' part; for after looking into the matter, Secretary of State William Seward not only denied the petition, but confirmed officially that "for reasons of high public expediency," authority on San Juan Island was and would continue to be "exclusively military" until a final boundary settlement.

Isaac Higgins' case was thus effectively closed, and with Seward's categorical pronouncement, one might suppose all questions as to jurisdiction on the disputed island had at last been

* For reasons now unknown, McCoy had in the interim changed his name to McKay.

settled. Nothing could be further from the truth; for the tangled events surrounding the Higgins case were as nothing compared with the legal confusion to arise out of a bizarre episode the following spring.

8

THE CASE OF THE CONSTIPATED KILLER

SIX YEARS HAD NOW PASSED since Captain Bazalgette, together with his company of red-coats, first set foot on the northwestern shores of San Juan Island. As soldiers will, his troops had scarcely settled into their new Garrison Bay "home" before they had begun informally scouting out their environs. It was only a short time before the word got around that the numerous outcroppings of a soft, whitish rock they found in the neighborhood was limestone — an unusually pure grade of it, and so accessible, and in such staggering quantities, that a few knowledgeable people quickly recognized an opportunity for making some easy pin-money.

Bazalgette's men were soon filling in the time by wielding pick and shovel in the nearby quarries, hewing out great chunks of the valuable stone, which they burned in crude pot kilns. The lime thus produced was packed, it is said, in miscellaneous containers — ranging from empty meat barrels to whisky kegs — and shipped to various world ports aboard merchant ships and even British naval vessels. In this simple manner was born what would be the island's only major industry — aside from farming — for the next hundred years.

Profits at first were modest. But the potential was there, and the foresighted scrambled to gain title to land containing the most likely-appearing deposits. The scramble was not always a gentlemanly one — witness Justice Hamblet's efforts to take away the claim of the Englishman, Roberts, and give it to his American friend — and considering the unresolved dispute over the island's sovereignty as well as the muddled question of civil versus military law, it was hard to tell who owned what in the best of cases.

Lyman Cutler, the erstwhile pig-slayer, was one of the first to try striking it rich in the lime game. Another American who took the plunge early was the energetic E. C. Gillette, one-time surveyor and justice of the peace whose resignation from the latter post left Captain Pickett high and dry in his 1860 battle with San Juan Town's whisky merchants. Cutler and Gillette became partners in the enterprise they named "The San Juan Lime Company."

Gillette sold his interest the following winter to one Augustin Hibbard, a heavy-set, large-boned Canadian from Montreal who claimed to be an American citizen. Hibbard did not seem to be producing much lime at first, giving as his excuse a lack of barrels, or of coopers to make them.

But in the meantime, Hibbard had another means of trying to make ends meet. He was one of the signers of the protest rigged by Hamblet, Offutt and company to try to get rid of Captain Bissell; and Bissell was pretty sure the real reason for the paucity of Hibbard's lime production was that the weighty Canuck was preoccupied with a wholesale bootlegging operation. Confronted with the accusation, and proof that his fire-water was winding up in the hands (and gullets) of soldiers and Indians, Hibbard assumed a pained air and insisted he only sold the stuff to his own employes. What they did with it afterward was, of course, no responsibility of his.

Augustin Hibbard surrounded himself with a bizarre group of generally unsavory individuals, one of whom was a man by the

129

name of Thomas Wheeler whose arrival in this country was as unorthodox as it was unplanned. Wheeler had been living a beach-comber's life in Hawaii. With three natives, he somehow got adrift in a small boat one day and was blown far out to sea. After days with no food, fearing all would die of starvation, Wheeler and two of his companions fell upon the third, killed, and ate him.

Subsequently the survivors were picked up by the British vessel *Topaze*, which was bound for Victoria. Arriving there penniless, Wheeler learned the San Juan Lime Company was looking for barrelers. Having been a cooper by trade, and being now reduced to the awful fate of working for a living, Wheeler shortly found himself in the employ of the Hibbard-Cutler operation.

The newcomer and the company cook took an immediate and violent dislike to one another and one day after the cooper had been imbibing overfreely of his employer's sideline stock-in-trade, he entered the kitchen and began annoying the cook, William Gibson. In the ensuing altercation Gibson picked up a cleaver and gave Wheeler a gash in the biceps. Although the wound did not seem serious, it continued to bleed, and by the time the English Camp's medical officer could be summoned, Wheeler was weak from loss of blood. Taken to the infirmary, he seemed to be regaining strength for a time; but the next day he began to fail, and was dead by evening.

Whatcom's sheriff James Kavanagh, then in the midst of his correspondential struggle to regain control of San Juan from the military, made his second trip to the island in three weeks — the first having been for the unsuccessful attempt to collect poll taxes. Kavanagh interrogated Gibson and had him committed to stand trial at Port Townsend the following month. Cutler and several other witnesses attended the proceeding, no record of the outcome of which has been found, though Wheeler's deathbed-statement accepting responsibility for the incident presumably absolved his unintending slayer.

At the same session of the Territorial court another San Juan Island man was tried for assaulting Charles McKay with a knife and inflicting a deep throat wound which nearly cost the pioneer's life. These events in the fall of 1863 show that while civil officers were unable to collect taxes or try minor offenders, the Territory's power to prosecute the more serious crimes of murder and assault remained intact. In a short time, even this power was to come into question.

Under the iron-fisted supervision of Captains Bissell and Gray, Augustin Hibbard turned his attentions more and more to making a paying proposition of his lime concern. In the process, Lyman Cutler somehow dropped from the status of a partner to that of mere employe. By 1869, according to the books of the American commander, Hibbard was sole owner. But as a matter of fact, Hibbard had acquired a couple of silent partners in Victoria; this information went unreported to the military, though, since the Canadians owned exactly a half interest, which they suspected might lead to all sorts of perplexing complications, if it were acknowledged. And though he was actively running the business, Hibbard himself by now held less than a half interest, having sold a quarter of his share to a short, wiry-framed man with an unpredictable disposition and the as yet undistinguished name of Charles Watts.

Watts, on the basis of his one-eighth ownership in the firm, secured an agreement with the Canadian owners entitling him to board at the kiln and receive the very respectable salary, for those days, of $43 a month. The 38-year-old Watts was not husky enough to work in the quarries, and had no apparent skill that could be put to use in any other part of the operation, but he was expected to putter around for a while in order to find some way of working into the scheme of things and, insofar as possible, earn his salary.

Watts' idea of working into the scheme of things included

setting up housekeeping with an Indian woman, as many of his fellow bachelors had done, and otherwise entering whole-heartedly into the island's social life; but as far as productive labor at the lime kiln was concerned, the little fellow seemed unable to find any useful work he was capable of doing.

Not that he wasn't trying. For fully six months Watts made, in Hibbard's view, an unholy nuisance of himself in one department after another. Finally, unable to fit in anywhere else, a very frustrated Charles Watts wound up in Robert Williams' cooper shop. There he tried his hand at making barrels and, while the results of his first crude efforts would hardly be considered a credit to the trade, Watts himself proudly announced to Hibbard that he had discovered he "could make a passable barrel" and would continue working as a cooper.

Hibbard's opinion of the little man's achievement in the coopering line did not coincide, and the two had a heated argument, with Watts insisting on his "rights" as agreed to by the other owners, Hibbard maintaining his position as foreman entitled him to bar Watts from the vital barreling plant, and both refusing adamantly to budge a single inch from their respective positions.

His mind irretrievably made up now, Watts proceeded the next morning to begin constructing a workbench for himself in the cooper shop. But after knocking off at noon and eating dinner with the rest of the men, Watts returned to the shop to find the partly finished workbench in pieces on the floor. When he learned Hibbard had torn it down, he went looking for the larger man with blood in his eye.

In the angry squabble which followed, the most printable epithet uttered was Watts' calling Hibbard a "damned scoundrel." That the two men did not come to blows was probably only because the heavy-set Hibbard, at well over twice Watts' scant weight, could afford charity, while his plucky adversary at least had the good sense not to aim the first punch.

Two or three evenings later, his still-smoldering passion having apparently produced a state of irregularity, Watts excused himself from the group of men finishing their supper in the company's dining room and went upstairs to fetch some epsom salts. Having poured himself a supply, he looked for some paper and string to wrap it in. Finding none, he wandered next door into the company's business office, where he came upon Hibbard, who was cutting tobacco for his pipe.

Apparently Watts had been removing his effects from the building, and was now living several miles away with his Indian helpmeet, Kitty, for Hibbard took the occasion to accuse Watts of also removing some shirts and other items which belonged to Hibbard. Watts angrily denied this, insisting that, on the contrary, there were still a water pitcher and several other things of Kitty's on the premises, which he intended to take.

Hibbard retorted that there was only one item in the place belonging to the woman, and that was a chamber-pot lid, which Watts was free to take if he wanted to.

Watts declined that item of crockery and again denied stealing Hibbard's shirts, whereupon the husky foreman stood up suddenly, called Watts a "thieving son of a bitch" and moved threateningly toward the smaller man. As Hibbard appeared to reach for a chair, Watts jammed his hand into a pocket and hauled out a small four-shot pistol, thrust it towards Hibbard's livid countenance, and pulled the trigger.

Taking the shot full in the face, Hibbard stopped momentarily, threw up his hands to his wound and then made for the still-open door, in front of which Watts was standing, the little pistol in his hand, surrounded by a cloud of thin smoke.

From the corner of one eye Watts caught sight of a rifle hanging from a peg on the wall next to him. Thinking, perhaps, his adversary was trying to reach this firearm, Watts pulled the trigger a second time, and a third. Still on his feet but barely alive, Hibbard stumbled to the door, shouldered weakly past his assailant and lurched out into the hallway.

Downstairs, the small group of men still gathered about the dining tables supposed Charles Watts had gone up to catch an after-supper nap. No sound of the altercation taking place over their heads penetrated their noisy conversation until the first report from Watts' four-shooter. Young Jim Fleming, hearing it, shushed his companions: "Boys, there is a shot upstairs!" he called, already making for the foot of the stairs several yards away.

Just as he reached the bottom of the stairway the second and third shots rang out in succession. The next instant Fleming looked up and saw, emerging through a wraith of pistol smoke, the figures of Watts and Hibbard jammed together in the office doorway.

Hibbard staggered past the immobile Watts and, holding both hands tightly to two raw face wounds, threw himself down the stairs into the arms of Fleming, moaning, "Oh, my God! I am a dead man!"

Struggling under the weight of the huge man sagging against him, Fleming hollered for help. Above him, Charles Watts stood looking down at the head of the stairway, still clutching in one hand his smoking pistol and in the other a large bottle of epsom salts.

Fleming, seeing the pistol still — as he thought — pointed toward them, was afraid Watts was going to shoot again. "Don't," he called beseechingly just as several companions reached his side and began taking Hibbard from him. Others dashed upstairs to disarm Watts, who stood dazed watching the knot of men carry his bleeding victim into a nearby bedroom.

Lyman Cutler and Ed Ziegler were summoned to sit with Hibbard while young Fleming went for the doctor. Besides the face wounds, they found an ugly hole in Hibbard's right breast which had begun slowly spreading a deep scarlet stain across his shirt. Unable to breathe in a reclining position, the dying man sat gasping on the edge of the bed next to Ziegler. Watts, too, sat dumbly by in the same room.

After ten minutes Ed Ziegler began to feel Hibbard's body lean heavily against him as the big man's strength wasted. Then he simply toppled over sideways into Ziegler's arms, unconscious, barely breathing. Two hours later on this June night of 1869 the doctor arrived, and pronounced Augustin Hibbard dead.

Word of the killing reached the American Camp during the absence of the officer then commanding it, Captain J. T. Haskell. But Haskell's own superior, Lt. Colonel Charles Bird, happened to be on the island. Bird went immediately to the lime kiln with a guard of soldiers and arrested Watts, marching him unprotestingly off to a cell in the camp's much-used guard house.

Bird investigated the killing himself and after three days concluded Watts should stand trial for the crime of premeditated murder. A complete report of the affair, including formal charge and specifications signed by Bird, was forwarded to the War Department in Washington. Mindful of Secretary Seward's categorical pronouncement of the preceding autumn that the island's "tenure" was to be "exclusively military," Bird noted the crime had been perpetrated outside the jurisdiction of the usual courts and proposed a military commission be appointed to try the prisoner.

Washington's brass were not so sure. There was something basically un-American-sounding about military commissions trying civilians for crimes — especially capital crimes — against other civilians; people were sensitive about such things in this post-Civil War reconstruction stage. No one could be found to sign the order. Instead, there ensued a prolonged period of hedging and buck-passing, during which the fattening Watts file traveled from office to sweltering office through a hot Washington summer.

It was a long, rainless summer on San Juan Island, too, where Charles Watts was experiencing his first months of imprisonment

— months which, though he could not know it then, would stretch into long years before his fate would be finally settled.

Meanwhile, Colonel Bird was facing the problem of what to do about the now apparently proprietorless San Juan Lime Company. For starters he had seized the entire plant, ordered all work stopped, impounded the company books, and after inventorying the property turned everything over to a non-commissioned officer for safe-keeping.

Very shortly the absentee Canadians, named Bailey and Huntington, presented themselves to Bird as co-owners of the establishment and demanded to be allowed to take charge of their company and get on with the work. Bird refused. First, he told them, they would have to get permission from the new British commander, Captain William Addis Delacombe, to become residents of the island.

Unfortunately for the Canadians, Delacombe refused them this permission — perhaps as a penalty for having improperly concealed their interests in the company. Bird therefore reported to his Army superiors that it might be best to "have the whole thing sold to the highest bidder and pay the creditors as much as possible." Bailey and Huntington would be permitted "to become creditors" in order to claim whatever amount they had put into the firm.

But a simpler alternative to this drastic action, Bird proposed, would be to have the late proprietor's next-of-kin — he had brothers living in Montreal — appoint an agent to take over operation of the enterprise, or come out and run it themselves, leaving Messrs. Bailey and Huntington out of the picture altogether.

This last course was decided on and an heir of Hibbard's, Thomas Maskey, ultimately took over operation of the reactivated lime kiln. Unfortunately for him, the company's hard-luck streak had not yet run out; Maskey himself died a mere two years afterward.

Meanwhile, Bird's charges against Hibbard's killer had gone all the way up to the Secretary of War, who secured from the Judge Advocate-General an opinion that "there exists no legal authority for the trial of the case by military commission." The Watts affair was thereupon bucked to the U.S. Attorney-General, who lost no time in passing it along to the U.S. Attorney for Washington Territory, Leander Holmes.

Holmes must have winced at reading the brief, almost casual letter with which Acting Attorney-General Wallbridge Field dumped the whole mess in his lap. Field neatly glossed over the tangled questions of jurisdiction, noting merely that "The United States claim that the Island of San Juan is within the limits of the United States, and the courts of the Territory will, I suppose, follow, in determining the boundaries of the Territory as against a foreign nation, the opinion of the political departments of the Government."

Almost as an afterthought he remarked that, of course, the courts themselves would no doubt decide any questions of jurisdiction that might come up. Assuming that Her Majesty the Queen of Great Britain and Ireland raised no objection, Holmes was to proceed with prosecution of the case on behalf of the United States.

On September 1 Holmes, together with a posse headed by a deputy marshal, embarked on the steamer *Success* for San Juan Island to claim their prisoner. But in spite of the auspiciousness suggested by their vessel's name, the party made their trip for nothing but the scenery. Captain Haskell, very much in command of this little island on which civil authority of all kinds was simply unrecognized, quite firmly refused to deliver Watts up. Nothing Holmes could say had any effect. The official documents he showed Haskell — even the one signed by the Acting Attorney-General of the United States — were brushed aside. Haskell told Holmes he would turn the prisoner over to him when — but only when — he had explicit instructions from his own *military* superiors to do so.

Holmes, who was the Territory's number-one barrister and had a deserved reputation for golden-throated persuasiveness, tried for two days to change Haskell's mind before returning empty-handed and ill-tempered to the mainland. A week later, after the proper orders were executed and presented to Haskell, Watts was at last brought over by steamer to stand trial in the District Court of Washington Territory, at Port Townsend.

While Queen Victoria did not object to Watts' trial, some Canadian newspapers did so with vehemence when British subjects began to be served with subpoenas to appear as witnesses. "The civil court has no power to try Watts," expostulated the Victoria *Colonist*, "and even if it had, it possesses no power to enforce a subpoena served upon a British subject resident on San Juan."

"Pure unmitigated humbug," retorted the Port Townsend *Message*, assuring the *Colonist* that the "treaty" of joint occupation fully authorized such trials. Nobody was being coerced, the *Message* told its colleagues across the line, and assured them the British subjects that had been summoned were only too happy to appear voluntarily in the American court.

"We thought it about time for the *Colonist* to get up another mare's nest," sniggered the *Message*, "but this one has positively no eggs in it."

Even so Judge Orange Jacobs, suspecting the Victoria paper's "mare's nest" might not be all that eggless after all, was at pains to inform witnesses they were at liberty to decline to testify, if they wished; but all testified anyway.

Watts retained as his lawyer the noted pioneer attorney Frank Clark, who had distinguished himself more than once as a cannily resourceful courtroom in-fighter. This led Leander Holmes — aware of the peculiar international complications of this celebrated trial (and perhaps the opportunity for making some political points) — to attend personally to prosecute the case for the United States.

Holmes' witnesses told their straightforward story of the quarrels between Watts and Hibbard, the shots overheard from the upper floor, Watts' appearance with the smoking pistol in his hand, and particularly his reported confession to an employe named Thomas Sutcliffe that he had killed Hibbard. Clark relied on character witnesses (cooper Robert Williams testified Watts had a reputation as a "peaceable and quiet citizen") and Watts' own account, by which Hibbard was on the point of attacking him with a chair when Watts shot in self-defense.

Clark's moving summation, designed to create in the jury's mind the reasonable doubt needed for acquittal, was so skillfully delivered it seemed for a while his client might actually get off. But all hope was buried abruptly beneath the avalanche of Holmes' violent oratory, studded with blood-thirsty invectives. After deliberating a respectable period, the jury filed in to pronounce Watts guilty of first-degree murder.*

Attorney Clark remained undismayed for, characteristically, he still had his best cards up his sleeve. Appealing Watts' conviction to the Territorial Supreme Court, Clark cited various errors in the trial, the chief one being his contention that the United States had no right to bring the case at all. Federal jurisdiction, Clark pointed out, according to a 1790 law, was limited to areas in which the U.S. government had *sole and exclusive jurisdiction* and, since San Juan Island was jointly occupied and in dispute with Great Britain, obviously the jurisdiction there was not "sole and exclusive."

Three Supreme Court justices pondered this ticklish puzzle.

---

* The next case after Watts' on the Port Townsend docket was also a murder trial, in which Clark again represented the defendant, with the evidence very much against his client. Determined not to lose two in a row, Clark went to work on Holmes with flattery and, having gotten him in a receptive mood, prevailed on him to make the defense summation for him. He did, and Clark won the case.

Each reached a different conclusion and three separate opinions were written. For Charles Watts, the important thing was that two of the three agreed his trial should not have been on the part of the United States, thereby reversing the conviction.

Watts was promptly charged again, this time on the part of Washington Territory, which claimed jurisdiction on the grounds the crime was committed within the confines of Whatcom County. Retried in the same Port Townsend courthouse in February 1872, Watts was again found guilty of Hibbard's murder, and sentenced to hang.

For the second time, attorney Clark appealed to the Territorial Supreme Court — this time claiming that Washington Territory didn't have jurisdiction, either! For, argued Clark (and not without ample justification) time and time again in recent years the civil jurisdiction of the Territorial courts had been shown to be inoperative on San Juan Island.

Thus, the military having declined to prosecute, the highest Territorial court having ruled out prosecution by the United States, and the Territory itself demonstrably lacking jurisdiction, attorney Clark had seemingly found the loop-hole through which his client might escape the wrath of society and go unpunished for his crime.

And the maneuver might well have worked, and Watts gone free, had not the worthy justices of the Supreme Court acted with equal resolution to plug — technicality or no technicality — the loop-hole which would have made murder legal in the San Juans. This time the judges' finding was unanimous: unwilling, they said, for Watts to obtain "more justice than he deserves," they refused to admit "that not even the laws of the Territory" could reach him, and they let his conviction stand.

Clark appealed their finding to the Supreme Court of the United States, and for the next three years, while that august body — which knew a hot potato when it saw one — considered whether to consider the appeal, Watts languished in the Port Townsend pokey.

During the years he waited, the "peaceable and quiet" nature testified to by witness Williams gradually dissolved into a perpetual surliness which made him the despair of his jailors and kept him at loggerheads with his fellow prisoners, whose comings and goings — particularly goings — irritated him greatly. The climax to this phase of his career came in July 1875 when he became angered at a fellow guest named Smith and, somehow procuring a small hand axe, just about chopped Smith's head in two. After this, Port Townsend officials arranged to have him transferred to the tender keeping of Kitsap County, where he was lodged in the Port Madison jailhouse.

Port Madison, a mill town, was located on the northern tip of Bainbridge Island, across the bay from Seattle. Its *skookum house*, reputedly the most secure lockup in the Territory, routinely boarded the other counties' most dangerous prisoners. This fortress was actually a sort of basement underneath the courthouse, the only access being a trap-door in the courthouse floor. Prisoners once tried to escape by burning a hole through the floor, only to find iron spikes interspersed among the timbers.

Keeper of this frontier oubliette was portly, red-cheeked Sheriff Theodore O. Williams. "The." Williams was also the town wit, a fact presumably not related to the one thing that was wrong with the Port Madison jail: it had been built in the wrong place. Through some error Kitsap County held title, not to the lot on which its building stood, but to the one adjoining it. Until this tangle was set in order, the county's commissioners were understandably reluctant to put any further money into the place. Meanwhile, since "The." Williams could not see consigning ten or twenty human beings to the perpetual dank gloom of this crowded latter-day dungeon, the prisoners were let out from time to time for exercise and to work the truck garden which fed them. As a Seattle paper observed pointedly, "A sixteen or eighteen foot

141

fence is more needed around this building than anything else."

Such was the residence of Charles Watts, now 45, his complexion sallowing, black hair graying at the edges, the tenth day of January 1876 when the judges of his land's last court of appeal handed down their decision. Chief Justice Morrison Waite opined that Watts' case was not subject to review by his tribunal, since it "no where appears that the Constitution or any statute or treaty of the United States is in any manner drawn in question."

What Waite was really saying, as far as Watts was concerned, was that the Territorial necktie party in his honor could commence anytime now, and that the next Judge before whom he would plead would be the Highest One of them all.

Word of the Supreme Court's dismissal of the Watts appeal reached Washington Territory some weeks later, whereupon the case was promptly redocketed at Port Townsend. But Watts' date with the hangman was never met. It was not even set. A few days after the pronouncement by the high court was made known, Watts and two other prisoners were being marched back to their island pokey after eating supper in the outlying cook house. When the guard turned his back, Watts dodged behind a building and headed for the brush. Moments later he was missed, but it was too late. Searchers beat the bushes in all directions but with darkness falling, San Juan's most notable badman was not to be found.

"The." Williams spread a description and offered a generous reward, but Charles Watts was never seen again. He certainly made good his escape from Bainbridge Island, and assuming he negotiated with safety the moat that is Puget Sound, and arrived whole on some mainland beach, he probably found little difficulty in assuming a new name and a new life in another quarter of the frontier. In those days before fingerprints, mug shots and social security numbers, when it was always injudicious to inquire too closely into one's neighbor's past, even a Charles Watts could carry it off.

142

9

END OF AN OCCUPATION

ALL DURING THE LONG YEARS when the American North and South were preoccupied in spilling each other's gore the San Juan question remained far in the background, a minor diplomatic trifle to be disposed of after things were calm again. When at last the shooting stopped, first aid for the country's political and psychic wounds became the overriding care of its statesmen. Only in the late 1860's did the nation's attention gradually refocus on the San Juans — which now assumed the importance of an overlooked chess pawn suddenly rediscovered on a vital square.

For relations with Britain had about hit bottom. Much hard feelings stemmed from that country's having allowed the South to use British-built and outfitted vessels in an aggressive program to harass Northern shipping, an operation so successful something like half the country's total merchant fleet was sunk or captured, raising insurance rates to the sky and all but wrecking the North's economy. (That, of course, had been the idea.) Hysterical demands that Britain pay indemnities for these losses were climaxed when a senator close to President Grant totted up the amount supposedly due and announced, in all seriousness, that the only way Britain could pay it was to cede to America the whole of Canada.

When England's response to this notion proved less than enthusiastic, Grant himself observed Canada could be taken by force, if necessary, in thirty days.

For a time, fever to annex its northern neighbor one way or another gripped Americans everywhere. Seward, purchaser of Alaska from the Russians, envisioned now a "magic circle of the American Union" embracing the entire North American continent. Even within Canada, an annexation movement was finding voluble sympathizers.

But these were in the minority; most Canadians had no desire to become stars on the American flag, and were willing to fight to prevent it. And if it came to a fight — now or later — both sides had become acutely aware of the immense strategic importance of far-off San Juan Island, dozing astride the entrance to Canadian and American inland waters.

"The possession of San Juan commands the ship channels to British Columbia," orated an alarmed speaker in the B.C. legislature. "Any ships passing from the Pacific or Victoria ... must pass this island in range of its guns." And in England, Viscount W. F. Milton, scribing an impassioned book on the San Juan question, warned: "Should the island of San Juan fall into the hands of the United States the mainland of British Columbia would be cut off from intercourse with each other (*sic*) by the batteries of the United States erected on San Juan."

As for the Americans, the spectre of British guns at the entrance to Puget Sound was equally scarifying. War Secretary Rowlings told the Senate Great Britain could bottle up all the principal harbors of the Pacific Northwest if the island fell to the British, whereupon Secretary of State Hamilton Fish bluntly informed Britain that the United States "must have San Juan" no matter what.

Speaking semi-officially for the Army, Major General Silas Casey (the old San Juan hand who, as a Lieutenant Colonel, had brought Pickett reinforcements by mail steamer under cover of fog) pointed out in a New York newspaper another important consideration. America was linking East and West with mighty steel rails — granting the railway companies up to forty miles of land on each side of their right-of-ways as an inducement to build these arteries. As the western terminus of the Northern Pacific line was likely to be on Bellingham Bay, British guns commanding the rail line from San Juan Island emplacements would have all sorts of dire consequences.

But not everyone took the matter so seriously. The Toronto *Globe*'s tongue-in-cheek suggestion: solve the impasse by sending "a gang of labourers to spade the seven by nine hill into the sea and let the channel go right through it."

Meanwhile the two countries probed for other possible solutions. U.S. offers to buy San Juan, or trade part of Alaska for it, were turned down. British suggestions of settlement by arbitration were rejected, since the Americans were steadfastly unwilling to chance the decision's going against them.

Next the United States proposed unofficially to forget its hopes of annexing Canada, and scale down its other claims on Britain, in return for "cession" of the disputed island. The British fired back the categorical reply by return cable: "Her Majesty's Government cannot cede the Island of San Juan." Period.

Finally, in January 1871, the two countries — each hopelessly unyielding over San Juan but willing to horse-trade other differences — agreed to call a joint high commission for the negotiation of all Anglo-American problems. Meeting in Washington, each country represented by a blue-ribbon delegation of high-powered statesmen, the talks went amicably enough — until the San Juan question came up.

Tempers flared when State Secretary Hamilton Fish led off by accusing the British of deliberately misreading the 1846 treaty in order to wrest San Juan from its rightful owners. Under no circumstances then, Fish enunciated, would the United States agree to any solution which would give San Juan to the British. Shocked, the staid English diplomats reported home that the Americans had become "ugly" on this point, so much so that they were considering walking out of the meetings. Instead, it was agreed the boundary question be put aside until the last, rather than jeopardize the settling of other issues on the agenda.

One note of hope was struck with an American proposal that whoever got the island should guarantee not to fortify it. Canada's prime minister was pleased. Such a promise would cost nothing in peacetime, he exulted privately, and England — "so long as she is mistress of the seas" — could easily seize an unfortified San Juan Island on the first sign of war, and "hold it against all comers."*

Once the same thought occurred to the Americans, that idea was quickly quashed.

By late April, American opposition to submitting the boundary to a foreign head of state for arbitration began to soften, perhaps because there was simply no other rational solution possible, and other concessions won from Britain at the conference hung in the balance — just as the British diplomats had foreseen.

Trouble was, the British had so far insisted on giving an arbiter three choices: Haro Strait, as claimed by the United States; Rosario Strait, asserted by Great Britain; or, as a compromise, San Juan Channel, running tortuously down the center of the archipelago. America felt the arbiter would be almost certain to settle on the compromise "middle channel" solution, giving the more numerous smaller islands in the group to the U.S. and delivering the real prize — San Juan — to Britain. The United States, therefore, would agree to arbitration only providing

* Canadian confederation, taking effect July 1, 1867, did not yet extend to British Columbia which remained a British possession until July 20, 1871.

146

the possible decisions were limited to two: Haro Strait, or Rosario.

On this all-or-nothing basis the Treaty of Washington was at last signed in May, naming the Emperor of Germany as arbiter and binding all parties to accept without appeal his decision. James Prevost, former head of the Boundary Commission and now an admiral, was to present the case for Great Britain to the Kaiser. America's side would be argued by its minister to Germany, George Bancroft.

Bancroft's shrewd presentation was based on correspondence between statesmen at the time of the 1846 treaty, showing, he said, that American and English negotiators alike had Haro Strait in mind when speaking of "the channel" between Vancouver Island and the mainland. Prevost presented numerous charts and log books showing Rosario Strait was the one regularly used by British vessels at the time, particularly those of the Hudson's Bay Company, and was the most navigable channel because of slower currents and better anchorages.

Bancroft also pointed out that in 1846 Haro Strait had a name, which Rosario did not; that Haro was plainly the widest, deepest, shortest, and most conspicuous channel of the two; and that maps published in 1846 or earlier — including those in Germany's own Royal Library! — invariably showed Haro but not Rosario.

Kaiser Wilhelm the First did not, of course, decide personally the merits of the two cases. He chose as judges (after a suggestion subtly advanced by Bancroft) a panel of German experts, including the vice president of the Supreme Court of Berlin; a jurist renowned for his writings on commercial law; and Germany's foremost geographer. These three went into seclusion for some months, each to study the presentations of the opposing governments as the world waited to learn from them which of two flags would continue to wave in the salt-tanged breezes of San Juan Island.

Meanwhile a suspicion was growing among the British that they had been "had." Was not this George Bancroft, they were asking, a personal friend and political admirer of the German chancellor, Bismarck? Had not Bancroft once boasted of how "Bismark loves to give the United States prominence in the eyes of Europe as a balance to Great Britain"? And was it mere coincidence that the American minister at The Hague, J. L. Motley, an old school chum of Bismarck's, had just offered to come by for a neighborly visit with the Chancellor — for the first time in years? British statesmen were grumbling in private their fears that Bancroft was even then "hugger-muggering" the distinguished German experts whose decision was so long in coming.

And in British Columbia the decision was awaited with a pessimism tinged with the conviction that, if the award went to America, British citizens on the island would be unceremoniously booted off the homes and farms they had lived and worked on for years, to be supplanted there by underserving Yankee sundowners. Worse yet, that the Americans would lose no time in turning the place into a fortress, its gun muzzles menacing the shores of British Columbia from Esquimalt to the mouth of the Fraser.

On the disputed island itself there were now some hundred families living. The population of the entire archipelago stood around 800. Most of the heads of families were British, technically; yet their allegiance seemed not so much to one nation or the other, as to the San Juans themselves. The place had a way of capturing the hearts and loyalties of its inhabitants. (It still does. Scratch an islander and you will find a poet, lyrically in love with every crumb of soil under his feet, every pebble on the beaches surrounding, and every wave of salt chuck washing its shores.)

Times were good, life was sweet. Farms prospered. In spite of the military presence of two opposing nations, the most belligerent sound to be heard was generally the sharp snap of shepherds' whips as their great flocks were herded leisurely. There was church every Sunday — and no longer was it presided over by an itinerant missionary from Victoria either, but by San Juan's own resident Bible-banging, hell-fire preaching, sandy-sideburned beloved T. J. Weekes. And school every day, the youngsters hiking miles to classes in the little one-roomer on Portland Fair Hill, where the older boys made shy calf eyes at Miss Naylor, their pretty young teacher. A fellow with a girl friend could come calling with two horses — riding one, leading one — to take her to a quiet church social or spirited schoolhouse dance.

In such an atmosphere, the cerebrations of three learned pedants on the opposite side of the globe seemed singularly unimportant. Only let this good life proceed undisturbed, the typical islander felt, and the color of the flag overhead seemed not to matter much.

Only in the seats of power away from the Islands did it appear to matter very much indeed. By September, hints of an imminent decision were leaking hard from Germany. "The gentlemen of the press and other Germans," the British minister joylessly cabled London, "to whom Mr. Bancroft has communicated his case and countercase in gorgeous gilt bindings expect the Imperial decision will be in favour of America. . . ."

The Victoria *Colonist*, too, was predicting the Kaiser would sustain the position of the United States and run the boundary through the Canal de Haro.

In the Territorial capitol of Olympia, the local baseball team was getting ready to play Victoria. Mysteriously, a fake telegram appeared, purportedly from Washington: "Emporor William has decided to let the result of the coming baseball game between Olympia and Victoria dictate his decision to the international

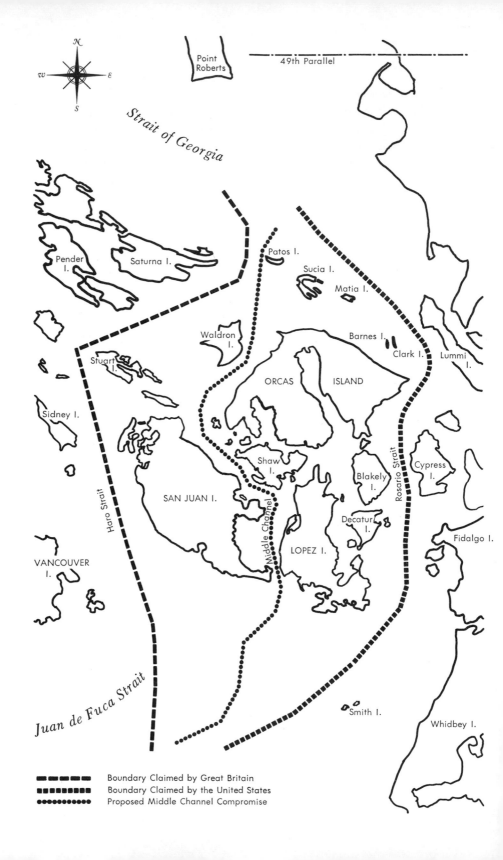

boundary question." Both teams were caught up in the fun of the joke and while both played their hardest, the Americans won the game. Strangely enough, it was just afterward that the Kaiser's decision was announced.

The German emperor's panel of experts just may have wished they could settle the question on such a basis as a ball game. Pressed to come to a unanimous decision, they found they could not. The consensus among them seemed to be that neither Rosario nor Haro Strait answered the treaty description. One went so far as to suppose the treaty referred to *no* particular channel; what was meant was *the totality of waters* separating Vancouver Island from the mainland, and the boundary should run down the middle of those waters, splitting in two the islands that happened to be in the way.

But, such a choice being — like the compromise middle channel solution — unallowed by their instructions, the experts at last rather grudgingly voted two-to-one in favor of Haro Strait and the Americans:

"We, William, by the grace of God, German Emperor, ... find ... the claim of the Government of the United States ... is most in accordance with the true interpretation of the Treaty."

Word of the momentous decision reached Puget Sound at the end of October. As might be expected, wild rejoicing erupted on the Yankee side which was matched only by the dark grumblings heard across the newly-confirmed border. There, Canadians fumed over the award but reserved most of their disappointment for the British diplomats who, as they felt, had allowed the wily Yanks to outwit them once again.*

On San Juan, settlers instantly began laying plans for a gigantic celebration, to be held as soon as the islands were

* James Douglas, now in retirement in Victoria, was not to be consoled. "Well, there is no help for it now, we have lost the stakes and must take it easy.... The Island of San Juan is gone at last! I cannot trust myself to speak about it and will be silent," he wrote his daughter, Martha, in England.

formally handed over to them. Among other things an ox was to be roasted whole — "No reflection, of course, upon John Bull," the Victoria *Colonist* observed drily.

That celebration was not long in coming, once official word of the award came through channels to the Navy at Esquimalt. H.M.S. *Scout* dropped her hook in Garrison Bay on November 18 with orders for the evacuation, intending to return on the twenty-second to embark the men, stores, ammunition and armament.

Baffling winds and freezing temperatures marked the *Scout*'s return on the appointed day. Dancing, icy spindrift sucked in clouds from the water's surface by the blowing cold, hung over the gale-lashed Sound and painted white the smoke-stacks of ships. The marines snugged their chilled faces into caps and collars as they trudged between the camp and the beach, carting the Queen's property to long-boats in which it was transferred to the waiting warship. A crowd of well-wishers — of both nationalities — stood by watching.

At 11 in the morning the troops were assembled and inspected. Captain Cator of the *Scout* gave an order, and the men marched smartly to the beach to take their places in the boats. Sensing that the occasion called for a speech, Cator made it a short one in deference to the violent weather. "Marines!" he bawled above the wind's bellow. "You—are—a—credit—to—your—country!" When his words had been applauded by three lusty cheers from the assembled islanders, the marines returned the compliment, their *hurrahs* echoing and reechoing from the fir-topped slopes of Young Hill behind them to Hanbury Point across the bay. Then the oarsmen dipped their blades in the boisterous waters and pulled away for the *Scout*.

H.M.S. *Petterel* joined the *Scout* in Garrison Bay but with the storm's mounting viciousness — veteran pilots were calling it the worst ever encountered on the Sound — neither vessel sailed until the twenty-fifth. Around noon of that day the little handful of officers and men still on shore came to attention before the Camp's flagstaff, from which the crimson and blue of a huge Union Jack floated majestically as it had done there for thirteen years. Standing rigid they watched as the ensign was now slowly, slowly hauled down and taken from its halyard.

With considerable pomp the flagstaff itself was cut down and sawed into pieces, the largest one to be brought around to the dockyard at Esquimalt for a souvenir, smaller pieces to be distributed among the men.

At two in the afternoon the emptied buildings and "betterments" — worth, according to the *Colonist*, at least $25,000 — were handed over to a detachment of American soldiers commanded by a Lieutenant Epstein who took charge on behalf of the United States. Then the British camp commander, Captain Delacombe, his lieutenant, and their families embarked on the waiting ships, and these set their course for Esquimalt. The joint occupation had ended.

Yet in spite of the cheers, and the good relations between American and British islanders personally, a good deal of mistrust remained. Americans were peeved over the flag-pole business: chopping it down had thwarted their plan to run the Stars and Stripes up promptly in the Union Jack's place — and they suspected this was the real purpose of the ceremony.

For their part, Canadians steeled themselves against the Americans' next move which, they fully expected, would be some trick to snach away their hard-won homes. Thus when Washington's new governor, Elisha Ferry, visited San Juan the following month, British eyes and ears scrutinized his every move and tried to read between all the lines uttered by this ebullient, glad-handing American.

Actually Ferry, who had only been in office a short time, was on a mere junket. Innocently, all smiles, he was bounding from farm to farm on the island, making little speeches — and passing out off-the-cuff remarks on the workings of the U.S. homestead

153

laws. Of course, the law required American citizenship. His office, by the way, would have something to say formally in two weeks' time.

Ferry couldn't dream the Canadians were dissecting his words, so casually spoken, nor that he himself — a friend and appointee, after all, of President Grant, that would-be annexer of Canada — was suspect. He was astonished to learn, later, that his remarks had been interpreted as a tacit order for Britannic citizens to take out their first American papers within two weeks, or lose their homes.

Ferry had meant no such thing, but before he could learn of the misunderstanding and set things straight again, there began a great rush of business at the District Court in Port Townsend. By the time the governor's supposed "deadline" had passed, seventy-seven British heads of families — all but one of those resident on the island — had filed their intention to become American citizens. And if some of them felt any regrets at giving up their allegiance to the Queen, it was overshadowed by a feeling of security in having preserved their homes against any threat of Yankee shenanigans.

Imagine, then, the uproar which followed not long afterward when it was learned that San Juan Island — and most of the rest of the archipelago too — was being claimed *in toto* by the Northern Pacific Railroad Company! Scarcely anyone had remembered that the company had long ago been granted by Congressional charter all unsurveyed government lands lying within forty miles of their projected right-of-way. Scarcely anyone, that is, except the sharp-eyed N. P. R. R. lawyers, who now pointed out that the San Juans had never been surveyed, no homestead patents had been granted, and most of the archipelago lay within forty miles of the projected terminus on Bellingham Bay. Thus the island clearly, said the company, belonged to the railroad.

As Northern Pacific officials were thought to be on the point of actually dispossessing property-owners on the island — Americans and Britishers alike — the Victoria *Colonist* smothered its indignation with a prediction the railroad would "find it a difficult task to wrench the islands from the grasp of the hardy pioneers who hold them — and would hold them if necessary by armed force."

It was Governor Ferry who delighted the hearts of all islanders — but especially the ex-British — by going to bat against the Northern Pacific. Claims that had been staked before the line's plat was filed would be respected, he promised. Settlers who came later would at the worst be given an opportunity to buy their own homes back from the Company at fair prices. And, Ferry was asking his friend President Grant to see if even more couldn't be done.

Grant obliged with a proclamation withdrawing the San Juans "from sale or disposal of any nature" until the claims of British citizens had been taken care of, under the guarantee of various treaties still in effect. And he appointed General Hazard Stevens, son of the Territory's first governor, to go to the islands and adjust the British claims. Meanwhile, the government's plans to survey the San Juans were postponed.

It was some years before the survey was finally made, and by that time the Northern Pacific had all but gone bust, its scandal-marked financiers wriggling mightily to escape prison or poor-house or both. New interests took it up and decreed the line would terminate not in Bellingham but in Tacoma. So while the legal ownership of land in the San Juans remained a many-tangled thing for years to come, it was at least clear that none of it belonged to the Northern Pacific Railroad.

Meanwhile Canada's other fear — that San Juan would be fortified against her — appeared rather less groundless. The *Colonist*, having gotten wind of an Army plan to stake some military preserves on the island, commented dourly: "It would appear from the above that brother Jonathan has no intention

155

of permitting grass to grow up on his new acquisition. The earnest haste with which these preparations are to be made, sets out in still bolder relief the blundering policy which deprived the British crown of the island."

Indeed, $10,000 had been appropriated for a military look-see at the San Juans. A team of Army Engineers headed by General Nathaniel Michler arrived early in 1874 and set about locating, in the *Colonist*'s words, "the most favorable sites for the erection of fortifications in the different islands."

Michler spent the summer of 1874 scouting the islands and by September had located seven government reservations, surveyed their boundaries and sounded their harbors. Two sites were selected on San Juan, two on Shaw, two on Lopez. The seventh reserve was little Canoe Island, between Lopez and Shaw.

Canadians fully expected to see a formidable array of shore batteries erected on these reservations as the next step. Their agonizing over this prospect became all the more excruciating when none other than William Tecumseh Sherman — hero of the legendary march through Georgia and now commanding general of the Army of the United States — visited San Juan personally.

Horrified, the *Colonist* reported on the general's visit to the site of the old English Camp, just across Haro Strait from Victoria. Giving considerable rein to its imagination, the paper concluded Sherman must have decided to place fortifications here, too!

"From this site the Canal de Haro passage may be swept by a shore battery and communications with the mainland completely blocked at any time," moaned the paper, adding that "a single battery on Lopez Island would command Rosario Straits, and a speedy end would be put to Canadian commerce in the Pacific, should hostilities between Great Britain and the United States ever occur.

"It is rumored," gasped the *Colonist* in conclusion, "that the American government await the report of General Sherman before commencing work on these fortifications, and that an

156

appropriation for the purpose will be asked from Congress at its next session."

But — the dreaded fortifying of the San Juans never took place. Sherman's visit to English Camp was no more ominous than that of any other rubber-necking tourist to a site of historical interest. And the scheme the Army's brass had in mind was something quite different from the *Colonist*'s apocalyptic predictions. Their plan: to enable Griffin Bay to become, in the event of hostilities in the unnamed future, a "harbor of refuge" for American ships. All the military reserves were chosen because they overlook the approaches to that bay, and they were intended for defensive purposes — the safeguarding of U.S. vessels against the might of British sea power.

The fact is that settlement of the San Juan Islands boundary issue marked the end of the last remaining territorial dispute between England and America, and the beginning of a long-lasting period of friendship, one token of which is the long, totally undefended border between Canada and the United States. As for the military preserves in the San Juans, no artillery has ever been mounted in anger on any of them. No buildings have ever been erected on them for military purposes, no troops quartered there; in short the Army has never used them for any purpose at all.*

The most lasting effect of the Michler-Sherman visits was on an altogether different front, for Mrs. Michler was passing her time in that 1874 summer collecting money toward the construction of a new Presbyterian church on the island. The "church festival" she engineered (featuring those fixtures of frontier socials: bazaar, post office, "Rebecca's well," supper and dance)

---

* An exception is the rather extensive 1961 War Games in which the Army successfully repulsed a Griffin Bay landing of "Aggressor Forces"; but this was long after the spot had ceased to be an Army reserve. The games took place largely on private lands and cost the Army thousands in repairs to roads, fences and other property.

157

cleared $150, in addition to the $400 she and the Reverend T. J. Weekes managed to raise from the Presbytery in Seattle.

The military lands staked by General Michler, after being mostly leased out to private use for long years at a time, were one by one given up by the Army altogether, no sign now remaining of their one-time military earmarking. While the pretty little country church islanders built with money raised at Mrs. Michler's festival still stands, elderly but revered and lovingly preserved. And serene in the graves of the churchyard surrounding it sleep many of the chief actors in the stories this book has yet to tell.

10

The fires of spring bathed with
golden stillness the San Juan Island greens and blues of that
first American May. Snug in a hillside home not far from
American Camp a young girl bent, smiling, over her needlework,
her nostrils drawing in with pleasure the musky-sweet bouquet of
fresh-turned sod outside. The distant clank of harness and stamp
of hoofs rose and fell, rose and fell as share ripped through loam
and left furrow paralleling furrow in the field before her.

She as much felt as heard the thumping discharge of a firearm
somewhere outside, rose, and went to the door to learn the
meaning of the sound. But the distant scene which appeared to
her was unreal, as much so as the near one: the man facing her,
the contorted, dark-featured face and slight frame giving a
momentary impression of a wolf's head mounted incongruously
upon the body of a youngish boy.

The reality was the long-barreled weapon of death in the
assassin's hand as he rushed straight for the house where the
girl retreated, numb, behind the door, locked it and pulled away
the key. The wolf-face appeared at the window and she saw him
take aim. Her arms went out to ward off the shot, not in front
of her face but in front of her belly, where her child grew yet

159

unborn. "Oh, please," she breathed, "my baby!" Wolf-face pulled the trigger and she felt the ball enter her side and it surprised her how warm the blood felt as it ran from the wound, and she ran into the kitchen so he wouldn't do it again, but then Wolf-face was at the kitchen window too, and she came back to the living room and took down the shotgun from its peg. She found the trigger just as the enemy reappeared behind the broken pane and took aim again. She fell when he fired, the muzzle of her own weapon arcing toward her and discharging as the stock met the floor.

Wolf-face forced the door and stood over the pellet-riddled body of the girl an instant and then kicked her probingly in the face. But he needn't have done that. She was quite dead.

It was hard for a San Juan Island settler in late 1872 to see that the boundary decision really changed anything. To be sure, the British troops left the island promptly enough — and after being mustered out in England, some of them just as promptly returned to become settlers themselves. The American soldiers stayed on longer (for reasons to be noted) and then many of them, too, swapped the Army blue for homespun, and the soldier's life for the pioneer's, on this island they had come to love.

Hudson's Bay sheep no longer roamed the hillsides, having been recalled to Britannic pastures, and were replaced by goats imported by an enterprising rancher. With the sheep had gone most of the Hawaiian herdsmen and their families, many of them settling down near Victoria or on Canada's Saltspring Island; though some remained on San Juan. A few of these became solid citizens — but mostly they squatted in a shack town around shallow, mud-bottomed Kanaka Bay on the island's southwestern shore.*

* Now known as False Bay. North of it lies a smaller cove called Kanaka Bay on today's maps.

The Reverend Thomas J. Weekes,
pioneer minister of the San Juans.
Friday Harbor Presbyterian Church.

The Islands' first schoolhouse, on Portland Fair Hill,
San Juan Island. *Courtesy Mrs. Leith Wade, Friday Harbor.*

Royal Marines in formation at Garrison Bay, shortly before the evacuation. *Provincial Archives, Victoria.*

British blockhouse, most enduring of the structures at English Camp, in a recent picture. *National Park Service.*

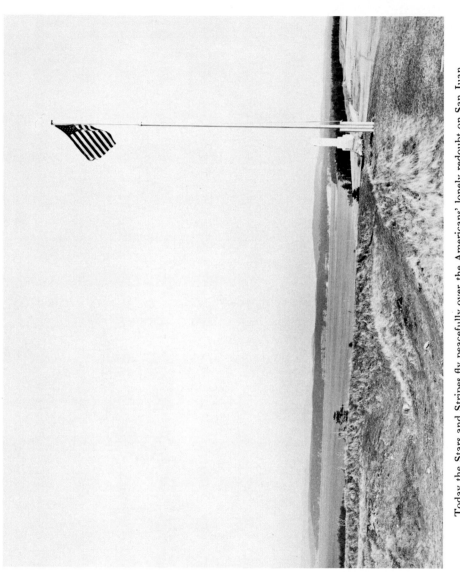

Today the Stars and Stripes fly peacefully over the Americans' lonely redoubt on San Juan. *National Park Service.*

Elisha P. Ferry, governor of Washington Territory at time of the boundary settlement. *Washington State Historical Society, Tacoma.*

BILL HOLM

Kanaka Joe, youthful San Juan Island killer. Artist's re-creation based on descriptions of newspaper reporters.

Friday Harbor in the 1880's. At left are William Douglas' hotel and the Sweeney Mercantile Company. At right the building with the rounded front is John Douglas' Saloon Best.

San Juan Island Historical Society.

Patriarchs of San Juan Island: Edward Warbass, Charles McKay, and Stephen Boyce.
San Juan Island Historical Society.

Joe Sweeney, pioneer Friday Harbor merchant, and family.
Courtesy Mrs. Leith Wade, Friday Harbor.

Governor Ferry had seen to it that military rule of the San Juans was yielded up to the civil government of Whatcom County, which was thus able finally to collect taxes on the island. (They found, to their chagrin, that these revenues were more than offset by the cost of county services — road building, for example — which islanders immediately began importuning them for; but that was Whatcom County's problem.)

Perhaps the chief difference, so far as the daily lives of islanders were concerned, was over the customs situation. Formerly a note from one of the camp commanders was all the authorization one needed to bring articles on or off the island, or trade San Juan produce for goods obtainable at mainland towns on either side of the border. Any settler could catch the tide in his canoe or sailboat, make the trip to Victoria and trade garden truck for staples, tools and the like. Those who lacked a boat — or the inclination to risk the modest dangers of such a trip — could have their trading done for them by someone like Harry Dwyer, master of the sloop *Alarm*, which made regular trips between Victoria and the Islands.

Young Dwyer, a ham-handed, perpetually-grinning, oversized Nova Scotian, lived in Victoria where he moonlighted as a fireman with the "Tiger" Engine Company. Just about everybody in town knew the popular Captain Harry, who bowed to no man in his zest for life. And in the fall of 1872, life was mighty good to Dwyer: his boat was paid for, business was booming; he had money in the bank; and he had just met the most beautiful and rapturously charming girl the world had ever produced. When the object of his dreams felt her heart palpitate correspondingly for this strapping man of the sea, their joy became boundless as the blue salt chuck Dwyer supposed he would be sailing, on and on forever.

They were married in September, to the joyous pealing of the Tiger Company's engine-house bells.

But Dwyer's world tumbled a few short weeks later. With the

San Juans awarded to America, a line was drawn down the middle of Haro Strait — a line Harry could not see from the deck of the *Alarm* but which might as well have been built of brick or stone. For no longer could one sail with freight on a bee-line the thirteen sheltered miles from Victoria to San Juan; now one must clear the United States custom house at Port Townsend, detouring dozens of miles across the treacherous Strait of Juan de Fuca, and pay a sizeable duty on many of the articles being imported.

To San Juan farmers, the change meant looking for new markets; for Harry Dwyer, it meant looking for a new job.

About this time Dwyer's lovely bride, Selina Jane, blushed and whispered a bit of news in his ear, and Harry decided — what with one thing and another — the time had come to give up the sea-faring way. Providentially, he had bought a piece of run-down farmland a few years before, over on San Juan Island. Harry decided to sell his sloop, fix up the place and settle down.

The Dwyers were welcomed with genuine warmth by their new neighbors, especially the Jim Hannah family, long-time friends and former customers of Dwyer's. The Hannahs put Selina up for the first few days while Harry neatened up the cabin on his place. Evenings were spent around the big fireplace in the Hannahs' comfortable home, yarning over the day's news.

They talked, for instance, on the strange disappearance of a neighbor, William Fuller. Fuller, an elderly, recently-retired Englishman, was a house-joiner by trade, builder of some important homes over Victoria way. With his full beard — except for a roundish, clean-shaven spot at the chin — he was the picture of British dignity, and although he didn't parade his wealth around, he was obviously rather well-to-do.

Fuller had turned up missing one day about the time the British troops were evacuated. A friend calling at his home found the doors all standing open, and Fuller's dog Jinnie in a great frenzy. After several days spent fruitlessly scouring the nearby woods, islanders were led by the frantic Jinnie to a fern flat under an aged madrona tree. There, hidden beneath a pile of heavy field stones, Fuller's battered and lifeless body was discovered.

The American Camp physician announced Fuller's death was due to a single bullet, fired at close range into the back of the victim's head. Afterward, the body had been brutally mangled by the great stones which were heaped over it. But no one could produce a clue to the murderer's identity.

The settlers' suspicions fell on the Indians. Fuller had had an altercation, a few years before, with some Northern red-skins — in the process of which he had killed several. Now, most islanders felt, their friends had returned to exact vengeance.

Ed Warbass, the island's solidest citizen, was just then tapped by Whatcom County to be the new justice of the peace. Frankly worried, Warbass' first act was to write to the Army, asking them to maintain their post on the island for a time, in case Fuller's death augured more Indian troubles to come.

Meanwhile Harry Dwyer had secured a pair of horses and was industriously plowing the fields, reclaimed from swampland, in front of his house. March had been unusually wet and windy, April little better, and now in mid-May Harry was hustling to get caught up with the spring's work. Selina Jane spent her days happily on the front porch, watching Harry make furrows in the field before her while she knitted little things for the baby they were expecting.

One Monday morning Dwyer took time out from his plowing to pay a visit on a neighboring farmer, Benjamin Terrell, who had a calf for sale. Dwyer bought the calf and left, driving the animal awkwardly down the four-mile trail to his farm. Ben Terrell and wife were amused — as a country gentleman, Dwyer was still a pretty good boatman. Still, they admired his industry. They were sure he would do well, with time.

Four mornings later the Terrells awoke to find the calf had

163

come back to them during the night. Now they were not so amused. Dwyer was not only awkward, he was careless; one of them would have to take half the morning from their own work to see about the animal's return, and all because Harry had forgotten to close a gate.

After breakfast Mrs. Terrell started down the trail to tell Dwyer to come get his errant calf. As she approached the Dwyer place she caught sight of Harry in the field, the horses standing patiently still in a half-plowed furrow. Dwyer, the reins looped about his heavy body, was on the ground next to the plow handles, where Mrs. Terrell supposed he was tinkering with the plow, or catching a bit of rest. Or more likely, he had seen her coming and was having a little joke.

"You can't fool me, Mr. Dwyer," she called gaily as she came up to him, but he didn't look up. Then she saw the back of his head was gone.

Dried blood crusted the edges of the wound. Around it buzzed a knot of large green flies. Under the exhausted horses, great gaping holes had been pawed out of the loam in the animals' attempt to escape; but their bitted mouths were unable to pull free from the heavy man lying dead across the reins.

Mrs. Terrell's screams echoed against the distant hills, but no other sound came to her in reply. Casting a horrified glance toward the ominously silent house at the edge of the field, and sensing it contained nothing she wished to see, she fled down the path.

By noon, alarm was spreading all across the island. Ben Terrell had run to the Hannah farm and found only Mrs. Hannah and her daughter, Lila, at home. These two women agreed to return to the Dwyers' place and look for Selina, while Terrell went to fetch Ed Warbass.

Minerva and Lila Hannah averted their eyes as they rushed past the grisly scene in the field and approached the Dwyers' house. Finding the door hanging broken on its hinges they entered and saw, inside, bits of newly-sewn clothes and a pair of scissors scattered about the floor. A trunk stood open, its contents strewn helter-skelter along with bits of glass from a shattered front window.

At the entrance to the bedroom the Hannahs found the dead body of Selina Jane Dwyer. In her hands, and drenched with her blood, were the front-door key and a scarlet baby dress. A broadbrimmed "sundown" bonnet sat askew on her head, which was discolored with bruises. Next to her, propped neatly against the wall, was Dwyer's shotgun, its stock black with smears of dry blood.

By telegraph, news of the tragedy was flashed to Victoria. There the couple's countless friends were shocked, anguished, unable to believe. Soon, all fire-house flags were drooping at half-mast. The Tiger Company, together with Dwyer's lodge, collected $500 overnight to be given as a reward for the killer's capture. Distrustful, perhaps, that the Americans on the scene could handle a murder investigation properly, Victoria unofficially sent Robert McMillan as a special officer to San Juan to help in the detective work.

But by this time Justice Warbass was holding a very competent inquest over the deceased, and had collected some important evidence: a list of property missing from the Dwyers' house (two watches and a small amount of money); a description of boot-prints found next to Dwyer's in the newly plowed field (size 7 shoes, with seven rows of nails); and another item, which Warbass was keeping mum about for the time being. Then he released the bodies, which were taken to Victoria for burial.

The double funeral was preceded by "the most melancholy cortege ever formed in our city," according to the *Colonist*'s emotional account. The procession moved to the slow accompaniment of "the melancholy throb of the engine-house bells (the self-same bells that only a few months before pealed for joy on the occasion of the wedding of the man and woman whose requiem they now sounded)." At the church where they were married, the minister who had united them read over their bodies the burial service of the Church of England.

Back at San Juan Island, apprehensive settlers were reacting to the terrible knowledge that an unknown and ruthless killer was at large among them. Nearly everyone supposed the Dwyers' murderer had killed Fuller as well. And when Special Officer McMillan pronounced that the assassin was likely a white man (since Indians rarely wore shoes) islanders began looking warily at one another. Farmers would let their chores go, rather than leave their families home alone; nearly everyone slept with an open eye — and a firearm under the pillow. Mass meetings were held, the settlers toying with the idea of a vigilante-type volunteer police force — but who could be trusted to serve on it? (An innocent visitor, barging in suddenly and unannounced at one of these get-togethers, narrowly missed being shot to death by his jittery neighbors.)

Meanwhile, Minerva Hannah was quietly totting up a fact or two and coming to her own suspicions. To Warbass she suggested, privately, a discreet visit to the Kanaka Bay shacktown, to see if anyone might be missing — particularly a couple of young brothers named Joe and Kie Nuanna. Just a few days before the Dwyers were found dead, the boys had asked to borrow a shotgun from the Hannahs to go pigeon-shooting. Minerva had loaned it to them, along with a small pouch full of shot. Joe had returned the gun the same evening, but acted strangely; and afterward she found blood-stains on the stock.

Warbass considered the story for a moment. After all, it was only one of many tales islanders were bringing him about people who had "acted strangely" lately. He asked her one question: where was the shot pouch she had loaned the two boys? Well, that was another thing: they had not returned it, and she had not seen them to ask about that.

166

At Kanaka Bay, Warbass found that both Joe and Kie had crossed over to Victoria "to have a time." With them was a Canadian Indian known as Charlie, who had been on San Juan for a while, palling around with the Nuanna boys. Warbass looked up Special Officer McMillan, who telegraphed the information to Victoria, and the next day police were on the look-out for all three.

Joe and Kie Nuanna were the teen-aged sons of a Kanaka father and an Indian mother. Joe, the older of the two, had more of an Indian than a Hawaiian appearance. He was short, but fairly thick-set, with coarse, straight black hair neatly combed back of his ears, and had high cheek bones and a sharp, straight nose. He had grown up on San Juan — had even gone to school there — but now Joe was growing to look the part of a full-blooded Stikine warrior. Still, neither he nor his brother had been regarded as particularly troublesome.

Joe was walking serenely down Victoria's Yates Street when a constable spotted him. He seemed surprised at being arrested, but mighty uneasy, too. Asked about Dwyer's murder, he told the officer "Charlie knows all about that" — and was marched off to gaol by the constable, who suspected Joe knew quite a bit about it, too.

Charlie's reputation was not very good. He had been in trouble several times in Victoria, where the *Colonist* described him as "a villainous and dwarfish-sized Indian." Police caught up with him on Fort Street the same day Joe was arrested. They also hauled in an Indian by the name of Tom, a friend of Charlie's who was under suspicion for several unsolved killings.*

Special Officer McMillan took passage to Victoria and interviewed the prisoners. Counting the rows of nails in Joe's boots

* James Cowan was murdered, in a similar manner to Fuller, in 1862 on Waldron Island. Murders in like circumstances had occurred on Canada's Saltspring Island. In the 1880's, killings committed on Orcas Island were still being blamed on "Skookum Tom" but nothing could be proved.

and finding there were seven of them, he returned in hasty excitement for another look at the prints left by the killer. His examination convinced him that Joe was the man who had walked with the unsuspecting Dwyer before blowing the ex-seaman's brains out.

McMillan was the star witness at Joe's hearing, held before a Victoria magistrate early in June. Kie, Indian Charlie and an indigent Kanaka named Kami were also placed at the bar, where a lawyer asked on behalf of the United States that the prisoners be held pending extradition.

McMillan's evidence was given with the air of a man presenting an open and shut case. There were Joe's boots which, he swore, exactly matched the killer's prints. There was the gun Joe admitted borrowing from Minerva Hannah, and the odd way he acted when returning it. His brother Kie was along when the gun was borrowed, and Joe himself had implicated Indian Charlie. Just where Kami fit into the picture was not yet clear; but he was a countryman of Joe's and a most suspicious character no matter how you looked at it.

Promptly the court-appointed defense barrister began to tear McMillan's case into shreds. Under cross-examination the special officer admitted he "measured" the prints left by the killer with a bit of willow stick. No, he did not have the stick with him when he examined Joe's boots. That time he had used the span of his hand as a measure. Yes, it was true, the prints left at the murder scene had been all but obliterated by rubber-neckers when he got there. Yes, it was also true that seven rows of nails was a very common feature of American-made shoes.

Turning with an indignant snort, the defense attorney asked the magistrate to dismiss the prisoners. "If men are to be judged by the number of rows of pegs in their boots," he declaimed acidly, "about half those now in court should be placed in the dock." He drew applause when he concluded that "Kie was arrested because he happened to have a brother who had seven rows of nails in his boots."

His Honor held that the evidence was pretty thin indeed, and he was inclined to let all four prisoners go free. But the American representative, alarmed, demanded that Joe, at the very least, be held. The magistrate responded that he would give him one week to come up with more tangible evidence against Joe. The other three were discharged.

At this point Charles McCoy, or McKay, the spunky Fourth-of-July flag-raiser of 1859, re-enters our story. McKay was now industriously farming the place he had staked out in Pig War days, and since it was not far from the Kanaka Bay settlement, he had gotten to know Joe rather well — in fact, had done him some considerable favors recently, and supposed the young half-breed looked on him as a trustworthy friend. But McKay, a long-time pal of Harry Dwyer's (McKay, too, hailed from Nova Scotia) was pained beyond toleration to imagine his compatriot's murderer being let off by a Canadian judge for lack of evidence. McKay caught the next tide and headed for Victoria.

Oozing compassion, McKay entered Joe's cell for a fatherly visit. What a pity to see him languishing so; surely no one who knew him as McKay did could think the boy capable of such a dastardly crime! But then the authorities were out to hang someone, and he would have to be honest about it, things looked mighty black for poor, innocent Joe. Yes, Joe would no doubt hang for the crime.

Now that evil-hearted Indian Charlie, McKay went on; *there* was a villainous type — one could easily imagine someone like Charlie committing such a foul murder. What a shame Charlie would doubtless go scot-free! Actually, given the least shred of evidence, the police would far rather hang him than Joe for the crime. Why, even supposing Joe *had* been mixed up in the affair — tricked into participation, for example — by turning state's evidence there was every chance of his being pardoned for

169

his part in it. In that case, well, Charles McKay would move heaven and earth to see Joe escaped the hangman after all.

Joe rose with alacrity to this bait and was soon dictating to an accommodating gaoler his version of how the crime was committed — a version in which he, Joe, stood innocently by and watched the friend, Charlie, shoot Dwyer from behind.

"I then saw Dwyer's wife come out of the house," Joe related. "Charlie ran to the house and looked in at the window, having taken [the Hannahs'] gun out of my hands. I then saw him shoot through the window at Mrs. Dwyer."

Wounded, the young woman began pleading for the life of her unborn child, Joe went on, at the same time retreating into the back part of the house.

"Charlie then ran around to the kitchen door and came back to the window and shot at Mrs. Dwyer again. I then saw Mrs. Dwyer fall on the floor. As she was falling, she fired off a gun which I saw in her hands.

"We then broke down the kitchen back door and entered the house. Mrs. Dwyer lay on the floor dead. Charlie kicked her three times on the head and face.

"I took the gun that was lying by Mrs. Dwyer's side and placed it against the wall. In doing so, I got blood on my hand, which accounts for the blood on [the Hannahs'] gun. Charlie told me to go out and watch that no one came, while he was searching the boxes."

Charlie's search of "the boxes" netted the pair their trifling booty, including the two watches of Dwyer's. Asked where the watches were now, Joe described their hiding place in the Kanaka district of Victoria, where police soon recovered them.

Everyone supposed Indian Charlie would by now be long gone, but one of the lawyers ran across him strolling blithely down one of Victoria's main streets, obviously unaware that he was again being sought by police. The canny barrister told him Joe wanted to see him, and Charlie walked unsuspectingly into a cell, whereupon the jailor slammed the barred door. The following day both prisoners were again brought before the Police Court judge, Indian Charlie objecting angrily that he had been "framed."

Unfortunately for Joe, Charlie was able to account rather convincingly for his time on the afternoon he supposedly spent butchering the Dwyers. Nor was it any help to the Kanaka youth that no prints of Charlie's bare feet had been found in the furrow next to the murdered man, while boot-prints just like Joe's were all over the place. On the other hand, Joe's detailed recital of the way the murder had been committed, and particularly his ability to tell just where the stolen watches had been secreted, were about as incriminating as a photograph, portraying him in the act, would have been.

As if that weren't enough, an American official now produced the Hannahs' missing shot pouch, which Joe had borrowed, and which Ed Warbass later found on a root-house at the rear of the Dwyer home.

Next day a crestfallen Joe, who knew an all-up game when he saw it, called in his jailor and confessed to the murder of William Fuller months before. Again he implicated an Indian companion — this time a Songish by the name of Kill who, he said, had a string of quail traps near Fuller's place.

The elderly Englishman had been destroying Kill's traps, Joe said, and the two boys went to Fuller's house to complain about it. Fuller told them the traps had been catching his chickens, and assured them he would continue to break up the traps as fast as they were set.

Peeved, the boys lured Fuller out of his house, Joe continued, by pretending to lead him to a spot where — they said — one of his sheep was caught in a tree. A hundred yards from the house they shot him from behind and, after pounding his head with rocks to make certain he was dead (and helping themselves to the money in his pockets) they hid the body by covering it with boulders.

Joe then returned to the house, he said, and swiped a pair of Fuller's shoes, which — he added with a wry grin — he wore to the old gentleman's funeral a week or more later.

Kill, picked up by police, vehemently protested his innocence. After some weeks spent in the Victoria pokey, during which time no evidence could be found to support Joe's allegations against him, the Songish was discharged.

In the meantime Joe had changed his stories once more, now claiming he alone was responsible for the Dwyers' deaths, whereupon the Canadian police judge again released Indian Charlie — over strenuous objections from the Americans, all of whom were convinced Charlie was indeed a partner in the Dwyer killings.

Charlie declined to risk being brought to the bar a third time and lit out while he had the chance, returned to the bosom of his Indian brothers up north — and was never heard from again. Doubtless his own tribesmen, who were also satisfied of his guilt, quietly executed him for the crime of bringing disrepute on their tribal name.

Kanaka Joe was extradited to the juridical mercies of Washington Territory late in October. It was a crisp fall morning when he was loaded aboard the *Eliza Anderson*, rather pale from the long months of confinement, a bit paunchy from the good jailhouse food and little exercise, but cocky and self-pleased with the attention he was getting from the assemblage of reporters. The newsmen noted he "seemed as happy as though he were starting on a wedding tour, or was about to visit a circus." But when they asked questions, he merely grinned at them. When someone expressed pity over his probable fate, he burst into laughter.

Joe's escorts were taking no chances. As soon as they had him on board the steamer, a chain was welded around one leg and locked to a stanchion of the vessel.

Joe's trial for the Dwyers' murder took place during the

November term of District Court at Port Townsend. Half the citizens of San Juan Island, it seemed, were there. Evidence given by Minerva Hannah regarding the borrowed gun and shot pouch were conclusive, according to her daughter Lila's account, written long years afterward. The trial lasted three weeks, but no one had any doubt what its outcome was to be. Kanaka Joe was convicted, and sentenced to hang the following March.

By the time the execution date came around, Washington's Legislature had passed an act taking the formerly disputed islands from Whatcom County and creating instead a new county to be known as San Juan. Steve Boyce, a popular, no-nonsense farmer who was a veteran of the California and Fraser River gold rushes, and a San Juan settler since the Pig War, was elected sheriff. In this capacity Boyce went to Port Townsend to supervise the hanging.

Port Townsend had never had an execution before, and townspeople prepared for it as for a picnic. A site for the gallows was chosen to accommodate the great crowd expected — on the beach at Point Hudson, close to the present-day site of Chetzemoka Park. A nearby brewery prepared for a record day's business.

The appointed morning dawned raw and bleak, but saloons and stores opened early to a thriving trade. Visitors had been arriving from all points on the Sound for days; someone from San Juan noted that particularly large numbers of Indians had come for the gala occasion.

At least two hundred people were on hand in town as Boyce and his Jefferson County colleague, Sheriff J. J. Van Bokkelen (another Pig War actor) brought Joe from the jailhouse a little after nine-thirty. A reporter, set to glimpse a "ruffianly demon," noted with a shock that the prisoner seemed nothing more or less than "a mere boy" to him.

Joe's last meal — a hearty breakfast — was prepared for him by Mrs. Van Bokkelen, who felt the boy needed mothering more than hanging. Boyce said later the only sign of tears was when Joe said good-bye to her.

Joe walked stolidly up the beach to the scaffold, accompanied by the two sheriffs and a Catholic priest. His hands were unbound: he had begged Boyce not to put irons on them, and promised not to give any trouble. As he trudged unfalteringly this last mile — literally — it seemed to one San Juan islander just as though "he were going to some grand party."

Stephen Boyce was not sure whether the boy's remarkable composure was making his job easier or harder. "Will you be afraid tomorrow, Joe?" he had asked the night before. "Oh, no," Joe replied. "I hope *you* won't be afraid. I want to die quick." To which the sheriff promised, "Be a good boy, and I will treat you as well as I can."

An even greater crowd was waiting by the gallows. At ten o'clock virtually the whole town — children included — was on hand to see Joe trot up the steps to the platform and then, asked if he had anything he wished to say, the youngster doffed his soldier's cap and addressed the crowd.

"People, I am very sorry for what I have done," said the teen-aged murderer of William Fuller and Harry and Selina Dwyer. "Now I have to go. All hands — good-bye."

Sheriff Boyce reached for Joe's hands and began securing them behind his back, and at this the boy's confident expression suddenly went slack, his knees nearly buckling beneath him. Boyce nodded to Father Manns, who began speaking quietly to the youth. A black cap was dropped over his head, the noose fixed in place. Boyce nodded again and the priest stepped to one side. At five minutes past ten o'clock, Sheriff Boyce knocked away the bolt holding the trap, and Joe's body was thrust into the emptiness beneath.

Because the rope was new and stiff, and the young boy small and light, the hangman's knot failed to slip tight as it should have. Instead of a merciful, quick snapping of the spinal column

174

— the purpose of the knot — the noose simply cut off the boy's wind and began slowly choking him to death.

Horrified, the men on the scaffold looked helplessly at one another for a moment. Finally Boyce grasped the quivering rope in both hands, swung himself over the gaping trap and kicked hard on the knot, closing it. But it was twenty minutes before the doctor could pronounce the boy dead.

Hundreds carried the vision of Joe's last anguish to their own death-beds. Port Townsend never had another hanging, and when after twenty years the next San Juan County murderer was condemned to Joe's fate, Stephen Boyce — who could still hear Kanaka Joe's confident wish to "die quick" in his ears — was on hand to see the deed done in far different circumstances.

II

JOE FRIDAY'S HARBOR

For all the yankee doodle fervor with which islanders embraced the end of the boundary dispute and were now joyously wrapping themselves in the folds of Old Glory, this is not to say they were prepared to submit with equal ecstacy to the established functionings of American civil government. The truth is that the San Juan settlers had become a mighty independent breed. They had, after all, resisted the rule of Britannia and the Hudson's Bay Company; nose-thumbed the might of their own country's military; and treated with sneering contempt the kind of civil authority practiced across Rosario Strait in Whatcom County, of which political subdivision the islands at first found themselves a part.

It did not increase the warmth of the love match when Whatcom welcomed the San Juans to its bosom by slapping an 8-mill-to-the-dollar tax on islanders' personal property.

It was thus an event about equally gladsome as the Kaiser's momentous decision when, in November 1873, by act of the Territorial Legislature, the new County of San Juan came into being. It was a small county, population-wise: only some two

176

hundred settlers, plus wives, children, Indians and bums. About two thirds of the total resided on San Juan; of the rest, most were living on Orcas and Lopez Islands.

But among these few hundred islanders there were some highly capable men, including the tall, pleasant-mannered fellow with the Santa Claus beard, Edward Warbass. Warbass, a West Coast pioneer since the first batch of forty-niners headed for California's Eldorado, had gotten himself elected to the Legislature and engineered the bill creating San Juan County almost before Whatcom's politicos knew what was happening. For Warbass and his friends were determined, if they had to be under the thumb of a county, that they would jolly well have their own and run it their own way.

Three commissioners were named by the bill to appoint the county's first slate of officers. Charles McKay was one. A bitter northeast storm kept one of his colleagues — an Orcas sheep rancher — away from their first meeting, but McKay and the third man had the fledgling government in operation within minutes.

Their first act was to appoint Ed Warbass county auditor. Warbass was on hand at the time (indeed, the commission was meeting in his house). He immediately posted his bond, took the oath of office and pitched in to work.

Warbass was a man of vision — vision acquired the hard way. Had he not once turned away a chance to buy for a few dollars property that was now downtown Portland, Oregon? (All pioneers claimed to have had such chances, but Warbass really did.) And was not one of his early campsites, which he could have claimed by merely setting a few stakes, chosen by later settlers as the townsite now growing by such leaps and bounds and bearing the name Seattle? Warbass was convinced the San Juans would some day have the greatest metropolis of them all.

But Ed Warbass was also convinced that San Juan Town, its reputation tarnished by memories of the whisky-dealings and

177

scofflaw practices of Justice Hamblet's day, was not the fit place to seat the government of the fine, prosperous county he envisioned. Besides, it was not well located. He much preferred a spot a few miles to the north, that "convenient slope of prairie land" which the British Captain Prevost had once recommended for English Camp. There was plenty of fresh water, and a beautiful protected bay which, Warbass confidently predicted, vessels of all kinds would some day be entering and leaving every five minutes.

No one was living on the site now — no one but a gentle Kanaka named Joe Friday and his family. The only roads into the place were the meandering trails of Friday's sheep. And it was such a beautiful spot: Eden must have looked like this. Ed Warbass couldn't understand how it had been passed up by homesteaders.

About the first thing Warbass did was to stake the best 160 acres on the shores of Friday's bay — not for himself, but for the county. He knew that by U.S. law, government land could be taken up for county seat use. His fellow officials were pleased: what a splendid idea! The county could sell lots to the business men who would soon be flocking in to locate their fine big buildings and neat homes. San Juan County would have a rich treasury — and no need for oppressive taxation. So the commissioners dispensed with the eight-mill tax imposed by Whatcom County.

Warbass was no carpenter, but he managed to throw together a small building of rough boards near the water, just below the babbling spring where Joe Friday's sheep were watered. This 16-by-24-by-10-foot shack was designated the courthouse, and served as the office and residence of the county auditor as well.

Two years later Warbass' was still the only building in Friday Harbor. Not only had the county dads failed to attract newcomers — even the town's namesake, Joe Friday, had moved away inland with his sheep. It was all so frustrating. But Warbass and his confreres had missed a decisive point: newcomers to the county could take up a whole quarter section of land under the homestead laws for less than San Juan County was asking for one of its town lots. The county commissioners pondered lowering the price; but Warbass wouldn't hear of it. Friday Harbor was destined to become a great city, he assured them. It was only necessary to wait for men with vision — and money to back it up — to see that, and there would be no stopping the place.

Meanwhile, settlements were springing up at other locations in the islands, and there were any number of stores now. The biggest one was at San Juan Town. The proprietor was Israel Katz, a genial, hard-working fellow with a penchant for licorice — he chewed the stuff the way most men chawed tobacco. He was a great favorite — a "comer" as they used to say — and one of the most influential men around. His establishment was part of the Waterman and Katz enterprise, whose main store at Port Townsend was presided over by Israel's brother Solomon.* And Israel Katz was sticking by San Juan town.

Then there was Hi Hutchinson's store and post office over on Lopez, where the best farmland was. Hi was doing well too, and so was Lopez, which had some smart boosters. They were forever getting letters printed in newspapers and magazines around the country, praising Lopez to the skies, and running down Friday Harbor.

Even Paul K. Hubbs, the feisty customs man stationed on San Juan since Pig War days, had deserted the island and was store-keeping over on Orcas. Hubbs was an odd one: had a good education — had even lived abroad for a time — but ever since a falling-out with his family when still very young, he leaned toward the solitary life of the backwoods. Truth to tell, he much preferred living with Indians to life with his own kind.

By 1868, San Juan had gotten too crowded for Hubbs. He

---

* Inevitably, the Port Townsend store was called in the vernacular "Solomon's Temple."

sold his Cattle Point farm to a retiring soldier and moved to Orcas, settling down by a secluded, smallish cove across from Blakely Island. Through some kind of finagle he got exclusive rights to run sheep on Blakely — a sizeable island he was content to let census officials believe was a mere five square miles in area.

Hubbs had at his home the only grindstone on Orcas Island. When this intelligence came to be known, his solitude began to be increasingly violated by settlers and Indians who dropped in to get acquainted — and just happened to have with them tools that needed sharpening. Eventually Hubbs decided to capitalize on the popularity he hadn't sought, and put in a small store. It did so well, for a bit Hubbs was caught up by the great American dream of Success, which he pursued diligently until the day he took to his bed with chest pains, gasping for breath and ashen-cheeked. Doctors told him it was heart disease and recommended he move to one of the mainland towns where they could keep an eye on him.

Hubbs turned many things over in his mind as he sat convalescing, gazing out over the placid waters of his cove which everyone now called Grindstone Bay. His happiest years, he felt, were those spent among the Indians, years when he scarcely ever saw another white man. He wished he could live those years over. Well, why not? Who ever heard of an Indian with heart disease? It was white men, living in towns, striving to collect dollars, who had heart attacks. Towns were noisy, confined, dirty. How could a town be anything but unhealthy?

Live in a town? Hubbs decided he would rather die.

Quietly he disposed of his material belongings, abandoned his Grindstone Bay home. He would become a recluse — an island-hopping nomad, here today and somewhere else tomorrow, living on clams and berries, roosting in a tent or under the stars. For as many years as God might yet give him, he would live this way, despite the dire warnings of his doctors. (But of course the physicians were right. Hubbs died of a stroke — thirty-eight years afterward.)

The closing of Hubbs' store left Orcas Island with a commercial vacuum, into which there soon stepped a jolly, moon-faced Irishman name of Joseph Sweeney. The thirty-three-year-old Sweeney opened a trading post which, although doing a quite modest business — most of his customers were Siwashes — seemed to be making its proprietor a rich man in astonishingly short order. Cynics, noting the Irishman's habit of taking long moonlight cruises in the direction of Canada, suspected he was augmenting his trade with a little innocent smuggling, but no one ever caught him at it.

One of Sweeney's best customers was a middle-aged Tennessean, John H. Bowman. Bowman had settled on a quarter section at what is now the village of Olga. A well-educated man, he was running a small private school to keep in pocket money. He was also drawing modest pay as the county's first judge of probate, and impressing the right people with his political acumen and plain horse-sense.

By 1876 Ed Warbass had spent three years in the little auditor's shack on the shores of Friday's bay, and so far had sold not one county lot. The voters, thinking it was time for a change, elected John Bowman to Warbass' job and sent Warbass back to Olympia and the Legislature. Bowman looked the situation over at Friday Harbor, moved his things into the county building Warbass had just left, and then looked up his friend Joe Sweeney. Bowman convinced him that together they could likely get Friday Harbor moving at last — and at the same time turn a penny or two for themselves.

Sweeney handed his Orcas store over to his younger brother Stephen and moved to San Juan Island, locating for a time just outside Friday Harbor. Bowman, meanwhile, was talking turkey to the county commissioners. Over the almost apoplectic objections of Ed Warbass, it was agreed that Bowman himself would buy 56 acres — the choicest parts of the townsite — for just $171. Moreover, the purchase price would be paid in installments, out of Bowman's auditor fees. It was also agreed that Bowman could sell the remaining county lots at vastly reduced figures — whereupon Joe Sweeney stepped up and bought a big chunk of them.

Sweeney (who had been a logger before coming to the Islands) fell to clearing the timber from his lots and in due time he erected a handsome store building at a convenient spot which would become the corner of Spring and Second Streets — in other words, the exact center of town.

Ed Warbass was incensed beyond words at the commissioners for selling, for a few paltry dollars, property he was sure would some day be worth a great fortune. But the county fathers were in trouble: with almost no money in the bank and little more in sight, and unwilling to impose a burdensome tax rate on their own and their neighbors' farms, they were already issuing warrants to cover the county's mounting debts. The proposition Bowman had warbled, sweet as the first lark of spring, struck them as well worth the millions supposedly lurking in Warbass' hypothetical bush. Nevertheless the full-bearded father of Friday Harbor was inconsolable, and swore he would never live in the place again himself.

Yet even after the Sweeney Mercantile Company opened for business hard by the town's gurgling spring, the rush to build up the county's lawful seat still refused to happen. A few settlers were locating in the environs — mainly because there was simply less and less land to choose from now — but the real seat of politics and commerce continued to be San Juan Town, or "Katzville" as everyone had taken to calling it. Even the precinct meetings at election time were held in rooms close to the bustling saloon of Israel Katz' well-patronized store. It rankled Warbass to come here, to see the gentle Hebrew's smiling countenance and wonder at the secret of his unflagging popularity.

Warbass' one achievement of late had been to convince Uncle

Sam to establish a post office at Friday Harbor. A settler named John Taylor was cajoled into lending his name as postmaster. Yet the mail steamer continued to dump off a mountainous stack of mail sacks at San Juan Town (postmaster: Israel Katz) on each trip through the Islands, and — there being nary a letter addressed to Friday Harbor — proceed on its way without even stopping at the county seat, to Warbass' unspeakable botheration. At last he took to riding horseback to San Juan Town once a week and posting a letter addressed to himself at Friday Harbor, so the mail boat would *have* to stop.

Taylor's tenure as postmaster was short. About the time Bowman and Sweeney came to town, a settler named William H. Higgins located some two miles out from Friday Harbor. Higgins, a carpenter by trade, wanted to be on hand for the Friday Harbor building boom — if it ever took place. Meanwhile he was taking any kind of work he could get, and was easily recruited to assume the not very time-consuming job of postmaster.

Higgins worked hard at supporting his family of four daughters. (One of these, as a small child, sat down — hard — against a hot teakettle on which were the raised letters IXL. She was to bear that unique brand on her netherest parts all her life.)

William Higgins farmed some and hired out to others, and he also worked for the revitalized San Juan Lime Company, now operated by James McCurdy and N. C. Bailey. Under the industrious Bailey's management, the kiln was turning out to be a money-maker: upwards of 20,000 barrels of superior lime were being shipped annually. The company had their own schooner, the *Ontario*, and employed a fairly large crew of workmen besides providing pin money to moonlighters like Higgins, who put their spare time to account cutting the stacks and stacks of cord wood consumed by the company's voracious kilns.

Up at the north end of the island was an even more promising system of lime deposits. The whole of Roche Harbor, and all the hills behind it, seemed made of solid limerock of the purest kind.

Out in the bay little Pearl Island appeared to be one massive chunk of the stuff. Joe Ruff, who had homesteaded the place but had no plans to develop it, quietly sold out to Israel Katz. Now this genial entrepreneur was making noises about starting up quarrying operations which promised to be the most extensive in the western United States.

But the lime kilns were miles from Friday Harbor; their prosperity — real or potential — would scarcely be felt at the county seat.

In spite of his pique, Warbass was still plugging away. As a legislator he worked successfully at getting a U.S. customs officer stationed at Friday Harbor. The coming of the deputy inspector, John M. Izett, swelled the town's population by fifty percent — to a grand total of three souls.

Even the new Presbyterian church — the one for which General Michler's wife had raised the first money — was being built not at Friday Harbor but out in the country on property donated by a Norwegian settler, Matthias Lundblad. A good share of the county officers were on hand for the cornerstone laying in August 1878; John Bowman had to admit it was a beautiful spot — high up on a hill-top overlooking the island's central valley on one side and the broad waters of Fuca Strait on the other. What bothered the few Friday Harbor boosters was that a minor boom of settlement was already shaping up around the unfinished church. Lundblad (whose hobby of raising canaries perhaps accounts for the presence of the wild yellow songsters on the island yet today) was himself living on lot number one of a subdivision laid out by a fellow Scandinavian named Peterson. Others were bound to follow. And the island's Catholics were talking of building a second church just across the road from the Presbyterians'.

Of course, the churches' influence was limited to a distinct minority among the island's populace. Vastly more islanders were numbered among the congregations at the bar and card tables of the Katzville saloon, in spite of the solemn imprecations regularly thundered from the pulpit of the Reverend T. J. Weekes of a Sunday morning.

Even among his own flock, it seems, Weekes had few allies for the righteous battle against demon rum. True, there was a flurry of pledge-taking in 1879 when a series of temperance meetings ended with the organizing of a Good Templar lodge. Allan Weir, editor of the Port Townsend *Argus* and an indefatigable advocate of teetotalism, addressed the assemblages — and afterward scared off any topers who might have been wavering by recommending in his paper that, in the absence of intoxicants, "the best drink for working men is a thin oatmeal with water and sugar."

Weekes' beautiful little Gothic church, constructed almost wholly by volunteers of the congregation and without incurring any indebtedness at all, was four years in the building. Those four years saw a continued influx of new settlers to the Islands — none of which evinced any interest whatever in Friday Harbor and its county lots, the prices of which auditor John Bowman was, in desperation, pegging lower and lower and still lower.

The town had, however, gained one more family: that of Matthias Paul Rethlefsen. A native of Germany, he wanted very much to be called Martin Brown; but what with his broken, gutteral way of speech, couldn't quite make it stick. Rethlefsen had come across the plains from St. Louis to California in 'fifty-six, coming every step of the way on foot. Then by boat up the coast to the Fraser River excitement two years later, stopping at San Juan on the way. He returned to the island in 'sixty-one, settled and endeavored to farm for some years on a promontory called Bald Hill which, he joked good-naturedly, was obviously made of solid gravel; for no matter how much he culled the field stones from his clearings, more kept rising to the surface.

The joke was on him: Bald Hill *is* almost all gravel, and in ensuing decades would be mined copiously for domestic road-building as well as for export to other Sound points, U.S. and Canadian, with scarcely a sign of even denting the supply.

Rethlefsen had a neighbor, in those early days, called "Uncle" Jack Montgomery — a man then in his sixties, less than five feet in height, weighing not one hundred pounds; but a man with a quick temper and a trigger-finger to match. One day "Uncle" Jack discovered an Indian peering through his cabin window, and without waiting to ask questions, assuming his visitor was up to no good, the diminutive settler grabbed his rifle and attempted two or three times to shoot the supposed intruder. But the weapon refused to fire, and the Indian began a hasty retreat. Montgomery finally pointed his rifle at a tree, whereupon it performed perfectly; but by then the Redskin was far, far away.

But later, "Uncle" Jack learned the Indian was friendly and had come to warn him of a dangerous war-party of Northerns that was in the vicinity.

Not long after this, Montgomery left his cabin for a hunting trip and returned to find a party of five Northern Siwashes prowling his place. Again without thinking, he raised his rifle and felled one big Redskin who was trying to make off with "Uncle" Jack's winter spud supply.

The rest of the marauding party took off to the beach in haste, one of their number pausing long enough to get in one shot, which grazed the settler's chest causing a painful though superficial wound.

The Indians began launching their war canoe and "Uncle" Jack watched them leave with great satisfaction until it suddenly dawned on him that every man in the party had just become his mortal enemy, and none would rest until his balding head graced a door-post of the tribe's home lodge. So the settler again put firestick to shoulder and, skillful shot that he was, began picking off the fleeing Northerns one by one.

After the last body had slumped and all oars were slack against the drifting canoe, Montgomery was in a sweat to get away from

186

the island before the murdered men's kin swooped down to exact their revenge. He hurried to Martin Rethlefsen's cabin, told his gory tale and advised Rethlefsen to leave, too: Indians were not awfully particular and were as apt to take off one man's noggin as another's.

But the cool-headed German calmed his visitor and the two went down to the beach where the tide, now incoming, washed the canoe and its grisly cargo ashore. Together they collected the bodies and buried them in one large grave, and burned the canoe until no scrap was left.

Soon several canoe-loads of Northern Indians came prowling through the Islands, asking after their missing tribesmen. Rethlefsen and Montgomery had sworn secrecy, of course, and were keeping their vow. No one else knew anything, and the Redskins, after poking about fruitlessly for a while, gave up the search.

No word of the story was breathed for many years. Later, when Rethlefsen had decided the danger was past, and Montgomery himself had been dead for some time, he told of the incident. But nobody believed him. Not, that is, until he conducted a group of doubters to the spot where the Indians had been buried, and went to work with a spade. For there was nothing mythical about the human bones he was shortly exposing in triumph to their view.*

Eventually Rethlefsen abandoned his Bald Hill rockpile and moved in nearer to Friday Harbor, to John Bowman's delight, as did a few others — there was Charlie McCarty, who settled around the bay at Channel Prairie where the University of Washington's famed Marine Laboratories (more popularly known as the "bug station") would be located in a future century. A French-Canadian named Charles Barney (even he couldn't say

* In 1938 two elderly relatives of Rethlefsen's revisited the island and after disinterring the "evidence" a second time, visited the office of the Friday Harbor *Journal* where, to the dismay of the editor and his wife, they displayed the bones and related the details of the adventure after exacting a promise not to print it during their lifetimes.

187

how he came by that un-French moniker) had a place nearby, and even Ed Warbass had broken down and filed on 160 acres adjoining town. He called the place "Idlewild" and for his residence he hired a young fellow by the name of Jack Douglas to move one of the island's first lumber-built houses — claimed to be the one constructed in 1859 for Captain Pickett — from the site of the old American Camp.

Still, a scattering of homes around the fringes was a far cry from the commercial-industrial center the town's founders were longing to see rise from the banks of Joe Friday's bay. Then in May 1882, Jack Douglas' twenty-nine-year-old brother William came under the spell of Warbass' Friday Harbor dream and succumbed to the proposition put to him by hard-talking John Bowman. Douglas could have any lot in the place, except along the water, for the rock-bottom price of ten dollars. Waterfront would cost him twenty.

Douglas reached in his pocket, pulled out a ten-dollar bill, and became the only person besides Sweeney and Bowman to own business property in Friday Harbor.

Young Douglas built a store and dwelling on his lot and, with his modest savings of $400 for capital, acquired a stock of goods. The reactions of Joe Sweeney are not recorded; but two general stores in a town whose population is something less than six would suggest competition might get irksome. Douglas admitted, in the evening of his life, to having "cut prices a good deal."

It is certain that both Sweeney and Douglas were looking for ways to attract the greatest possible share of the island's custom, and one of the first steps taken by each, as an accommodation to out-of-towners whose travels had produced an advanced state of thirst, was to install a discreet place of refreshment in a back room.

The result was almost magical.

For soon both entrepreneurs had a back-room business going which was at least as brisk as the trade out front had been slack.

And business in the front was picking up right along with it. Why, islanders who for years had been riding the greater distance and patronizing the genial Katz at San Juan Town (where an hour or two spent in the attached barroom was an obvious social obligation) were at last discovering how much more convenient was the location of Friday Harbor. Besides, was it not a citizen's duty to support the county's legal seat? Anyone with half an eye to the future could tell you, now, the commercial center of the archipelago was bound to shift from Katzville to the booming village on Friday's bay.

In other words, a two-saloon town beats a one-saloon town every time.

And truly, within months, both Sweeney and Douglas were outgrowing their buildings and planning to expand. Douglas had to pay $200 for property nearer the water (he could have got it for $10 the year before) where he built a vastly fancier saloon, and put in a hotel across from it. The new place opened in May 1884. Impressed, an Anacortes newspaper reported Douglas was offering no mere frontier rotgut, but "a choice stock of wine, liquors and cigars. We bespeak for him a liberal patronage." The same issue commented that "five-cent beer" was making Friday Harbor "lively" and that the same village was "resonant with the sound of the saw and hammer, and building is being pushed forward in a way that is unprecedented in the annals of the place. . . ."

Joe Sweeney, too, was busy expanding his mercantile enterprises, for which he purchased considerable property along the bay, and constructed a wharf at which increasingly frequent steamers began to tie up. (Of course, Sweeney was not neglecting the all-important saloon business which made the rest of it possible.)

Jubilant county officials erected a more commodious building for the transaction of their growing business, and put John Bowman's shack up for sale. At this point Israel Katz himself threw in the towel and good-naturedly joined in the rush to build up the seat of the county, occupying the erstwhile auditor's edifice until he could build something better.

After that, "Katzville" simply died on the vine. Even the post office quietly picked itself up and moved north to Argyle — a languorous little community of gentle souls four miles up the coast, where the notable attractions were the island's only grist mill and the doctor's residence.

Within a few years, the historic old village on Griffin Bay became a ghost town, its buildings vacant, its streets empty and soundless. What property Israel Katz still owned there was left in charge of a caretaker, an elderly immigrant islander known as "Whispering Pete" Seary (so-called in honor of a fog-horn voice acquired during a lifetime spent as a bull-teamster).

One dry September day in 1890 Seary set fire to the ruins of an old stable some distance away. A brisk, hungry breeze arose, pushed the flames quickly across a hay field and ignited the decaying structures of San Juan Town. In minutes, the historic village was no more. All lay in ashes — all but the memory of a rowdy, roistering town Captain Pickett once called "bedlam day and night," a place where a man could raise a thirst and quench it, a shack-town dedicated first, last, and always to the four b's: beer, booze, "broads," and brawls.

Not that the town's heritage of boozing and brawling had disappeared from the island. It had simply moved up north a piece to the booming village at Joe Friday's harbor, where it was yet to enliven things for many another bright year.

12

ORCAS ISLAND'S PAINTER-PARSON

Barely two miles of pictur-
esque, islet-studded waters separate San Juan from Orcas, which
lies placidly to the northeast. Shaped like a bulky, inverted letter
U, Orcas is almost sliced in two by a long, narrow fjord called
East Sound. The fat western half of the island is similarly
indented by a shorter arm of the sea known, not inconsistently,
as West Sound. These features, along with other irregularities of
the coastline, have endowed the island with vastly more waterfront property for its size than any other island in the group. Thus
Orcas in modern times has become a tranquil place of summer and
retirement homes, tourist resorts, camps and parks, and the
busiest people around are real estate agents.

Orcas also has a greater area than San Juan. But though its
fate was equally at question during the Pig War drama, little
attention seems to have been paid it by either side in the dispute.
Cannon balls used to be found on its western shores, giving
credence to old settlers' tales that the island was used by San

Juan artillerymen for target practice, but that seems to be the extent of Orcas' involvement in the fracas.

In the 1850's the Hudson's Bay Co. sent an occasional French-Canadian trapper to Orcas' shores, and during the Fraser River gold excitement of '58 it was a way point for American miners heading in that direction. But there is no firm record of any real attempt to settle on Orcas earlier than 1859, when Hudson's Bay officials stationed a party of four deer-hunters on the island to keep Victoria larders supplied with venison. Two of these men, William Bradshaw and Louis Cayou, elected to settle down near the hunting ground, which came to be known as Deer Harbor.

Bradshaw was killed soon afterward in some sort of accident, and thus Louis Cayou is generally credited with being the first permanent white settler in the area.

Cayou, like many of that era, married an Indian maiden who subsequently presented him with numerous offspring. Most of the sons and daughters were predictably dark-complexioned, and took to hunting, fishing and such outdoorsy pursuits more readily than to "book-learning" and the more cultural sides of life. But one son — Henry — was visibly lighter of skin, and markedly more studious, sensitive and enterprising than his four brothers and six sisters. Henry Cayou was to live ninety years lacking a few weeks in the Pacific Northwest, mostly in the San Juans, and by combining brains and instinct with his brawn would make and lose a succession of fortunes in the fishing business. Near the end of his career it was estimated he had caught more fish than any man alive. He also served the county of San Juan in various public offices and was a prominent citizen in every regard.

But the apparent differences between Henry and his siblings gave rise continually to whispered questions as to his paternity — whisperings which no one supposed reached the ears of Henry himself. But they did, plaguing him in youth and leading him in middle age to pour out his feelings in this poem, published in the San Juan *Islander* in 1911:

The Inquiry*

Tell me, ye roving winds,
    That whistle 'round my face,
Do you not know some spot
    Where scandal has no place?
Some lonely mountain top,
    Some island on the sea,
Where weary ones may rest
    And be from slander free?
The wild winds sighed and whispered low,
    But firmly answer "no, oh no."

Tell me, ye little birds,
    That flit from shore to shore;
Do you not know some place
    Where tattling is no more?
You go from north to south,
    From east to west you rove,
Do you not find some land
    Where all is peace and love?
The sweet bird answered from the nest,
    "There's no such place where you can rest."

Tell me, bright sunbeams
    That shine in every clime,
And in your beauty bright,
    Are dancing all the time;
Do you not know some land,
    Though far beyond the sea,
Where from the slanderous tongue
    Poor mortals may be free?
The sunbeams dancing in their mirth
    Just paused to whisper, "not on earth."

* The poem is actually a paraphrase of Charles Mackay's "Tell Me, Ye Winged Winds." Mackay — the poet, not the San Juan Island pioneer — was a noted Scottish writer during the mid-Victorian era.

193

Other settlers "drifted down" to Orcas as the 'sixties wore on, and many of them were colorful types. There were, as an example, Allan and John Robinson, who with a third brother had struck it moderately rich in the gold fields of California. Following the crowd to the Fraser in 1858 they decided this time they would play it smart, and foregoing the hard work and uncertainties of the pan and sluice box, would invest their pile in a Victoria hotel instead. For they had been shrewd enough observers of the California scene to know it is generally easier to dig gold from miners than from mines. So a luxurious hostelry was built to their specifications at a lavish cost of $90,000 — and finished just in time for the gold rush to fizzle out. The Robinsons were left with the whitest elephant in town. They sold it, finally, for $3,700 — and were glad to get it.

With this diminished capital the Robinsons acquired a sloop and put in a stock of store-goods which they traded at the many little waterside settlements in the San Juans. (Paul Hubbs' pioneer trading post at Grindstone Bay was one of the several such establishments they kept supplied.) Then about 1867 the brothers settled down on adjoining farms in the Crow Valley area of western Orcas. Neither ever married.

Another minor influx of settlers resulted from closing down the coal mines across the way at Whatcom. The mines were subject to sulphur seepage and had a habit of catching fire, which could only be extinguished by flooding the pits with salt water. The succession of fires and floods ruined the mines, to say nothing of the morale of the miners, many of whom found their way to Orcas in the later 'sixties.

Among this latter group of newcomers was Charles W. Shattuck, a one-time Michigan mule-skinner and alumnus of both the California and Fraser River gold excitements. Shattuck's first dwelling on Orcas was a tent on the beach at the head of East Sound; afterward he hauled in a boatload of lumber and built a small cabin a short distance inland, where he operated a store of sorts. There being no other white settlers within miles, his first customers were almost all Indians.

When the boundary dispute was settled and it became possible to do so, Shattuck filed under the homestead laws for land encompassing half of what is now the village of Eastsound. The other half was staked by his neighbor, Ephraim Langell, another ex-Fraser River miner who passed through the Islands in 1860 and came back for good a decade later.

By 1873 — a year after the Islands were awarded to America — Orcas' population amounted to some forty souls. Three years later there were three times that many, with heavy settlement in the fertile Crow Valley area. There, farmers were growing excellent crops which, when hauled down to the beach, could be sold to traders at good prices. Michael Adams, an Eastsounder who had arrived soon after Charles Shattuck, was having particularly good luck growing fruit: The Port Townsend Weekly *Argus* reported Adams' output would reach a thousand boxes in 1877.

The atmosphere on Orcas in those pioneer days was a far cry from San Juan's. Orcas Islanders kept too busy playing out the quiet drama of life — tending their farms, raising their families, engaging in an exhausting but wholesome frontier social life — to engage in booze and violence to the extent practiced by many of their compatriots across the way. The island had a constable and a justice of the peace, but there was little for them to do, so when in 1882 a real crime was committed, no one knew quite how to handle so unprecedented an occurrence.

The offense was murder, and resulted from an altercation between one Lars Brown, a burly, gruff-natured blacksmith from the island's southern shore who could have modeled for Longfellow's famous poem, and an easy-going French-Canadian fisherman named Yves J'Affret.*

Brown was a Dane, and a mystery man. No one knew much

* Probably *Jaffret*, but existing records insist on the apostrophied version, so it has been retained here.

about his past life, and Brown preferred it that way. Unusually skilled at metalworking, he was a downright genius when it came to fixing firearms; that may have contributed to the legend that he once had something to do with the U.S. arsenal at Harper's Ferry, and that this association — or the ending of it — had in turn to do with his appearance on this far-off island, and his reticence to speak of the past. What was known was that he had a physique that wouldn't quit (kept in shape by daily skinny-dips in the Sound, irrespective of season or weather) and a temper to match, so that women gave him a wide berth, and men had best to treat him with restraint as well as respect. All this was well known to everyone on Orcas.

Unfortunately, Yves J'Affret was from Waldron.

It seems that at the end of a strenuous working day, both men repaired to an Indian encampment or "rancheria" serving as a sort of frontier-era speakeasy. J'Affret, it is said, in pulling a handful of money from a pocket dropped some five-dollar gold pieces on the ground. Brown benevolently stooped down and picked them up for the Frenchman, who after counting them accused the blacksmith of keeping one of the fives. (That either man was by this time fully in condition to count anything, is open to question.) Brown denied the allegation thickly and after a brief but highly vocal wrangle, went home to bed.

Later the same night Brown was awakened by an insistent pounding on his cabin door. Answering it he found J'Affret in an even fouler mood than before. The ensuing argument pivoted from gold pieces to an alleged relationship between J'Affret — a family man — and a certain Indian maid known as "Ginny," in whom Brown himself evinced a good deal of jealous interest. J'Affret called the charge a slander, whereupon Brown simply picked the smaller man up bodily and heaved him out of the house.

When J'Affret again started beating on the door, the blacksmith threatened to shoot him if he tried to enter. "You're a coward," cried the Frenchman, "and I will chance it." He flung open the door and started for Brown, who was now holding a pistol.

As the two men closed, Brown discharged the gun. J'Affret took the shot full in the stomach, and pitched against his adversary. Brown, not realizing J'Affret had been hit, grappled with him momentarily and then threw him out the door again. This time the Frenchman lay still on the ground, where he died in less than an hour.

Brown was hauled before the local justice of the peace, James N. Fry, who admitted his knowledge of juridical procedures was a bit skimpy, but resolved not to let this stand in the way of justice. Empaneling a jury of twelve good men and true, he swore each of them in on this rather remarkable oath: "Do you solemnly swear that the verdict you shall render in this case shall be the truth, the whole truth, and nothing but the truth, so help you God?"

Next, the defendant was placed on the stand and directed to give his account of the shooting, which he did.

At this point a question of procedure was raised, namely, whether witnesses who had seen the shooting, and were therefore acquainted with what actually took place between the two men, could testify. It was ruled they could not, as their knowledge of the facts was clearly prejudicial to the case under consideration.

Instead, "Judge" Fry turned to the jury members, each of whom was invited to testify as to the good character and "veracity" of the defendant. Then the judge retired the jury, after instructing them thusly: "Gentlemen, you are all intelligent men and know about as much about the law as I do. You will render a verdict of guilty or not guilty."

The jurers took one look at the powerful Dane, who had been glowering at them in a menacing manner throughout the proceedings, and found him not guilty.

The court's next order of business was to raise money to

pay the trial costs. It being apparent the victim of the homicide had no further use for his worldly goods, his boat and other possessions were ordered confiscated and sold. J'Affret's widow and business partner were, however, poor enough sports to raise certain objections to the order, so that ultimately the property was reconfiscated from the confiscators and returned to them.

J'Affret's friends sent to Friday Harbor and complained to the county prosecutor about the affair, suggesting something less than justice had been dealt. At first there was some question whether Brown could ever be retried, under the constitutional guarantee against double jeopardy, but the county attorney decided to overlook this complication. Terming the Orcas Island proceeding "unmitigated, and worse than a mutiny" he instructed the sheriff to ignore the earlier farce and hold Brown for a real trial.

Meanwhile, Lars Brown's neighbors were treating him more circumspectly than ever. One, having blundered onto the Dane's property, found himself staring at the business end of an axe head and retreated under a rain of invective, including a warning of being "quartered" if he ever came that way again. Another islander noised it around that Brown was keeping a loaded pistol by, and had opined publicly he'd "have to shoot some more damned fools" before the business was over.

Brown was at last arraigned in the regular way and stood trial at Port Townsend in September 1882. This time witnesses to the fracas were allowed to tell what happened, but the verdict was the same — not guilty. The jury seemed too confused about the whole thing to be able to conclude beyond reasonable doubt that the big Dane had acted other than in the defense of himself and his home.

Orcas Island at the time scarcely had anything to fit the term "village." The nearest thing to it lay at the head of East Sound, for which Charles Shattuck's store, which was now a post office as well, had been named. Shattuck's nearest neighbor, a short hike down the beach when the tide was out and a stiff climb through the woods when it wasn't, was "Judge" Fry. When not ad-libbing innovations to the American system of jurisprudence, the portly, goateed Fry operated a kind of hotel. It consisted of a log building onto which a rough lean-to had been added in case of an overflow.

Upbeach in the other direction, a one-room schoolhouse sat on a knoll overlooking the bay, just within hailing distance of Ephraim Langell's neat home. And that, except for fir trees and a few deer trails, was Orcas' leading community in the early 'eighties.

There wasn't even a dock where steamboats could land. Vessels anchored out in deep water and put passengers, freight, and mail ashore in a launch or lifeboat. Cattle were unceremoniously pushed into the drink and made to swim. (This was accomplished by facing them in the desired direction and prodding with a pole at a certain point on the posterior anatomy. When the blow was precisely aimed, some animals could almost make it to shore in a single jump.)

If passengers were fastidious they could arrange to be put ashore a couple of miles down the beach at Port Langdon, where a San Juan outfit had a lime quarry and a kind of dock. The landing was easier there, but it entailed a rigorous tramp through the woods if one's destination was Eastsound.

One evening early in 1883 a party of three gentlemen in city suits came ashore at Langdon, presented themselves at the door of a nearby settler and asked to spend the night. Two of the visitors were elderly, and introduced themselves as prominent Episcopal churchmen from Olympia and Seattle. They had in tow an engaging, red-headed, pink-whiskered chap in his forties by the name of Sidney R. S. Gray. Gray was the eager type, and looked as though he ought to be a real estate salesman, instead of a budding clergyman, which he was. The object of the clerics' visit was to organize a church of their denomination on Orcas

199

Island and Gray, though not yet ordained, was to head this as a lay missionary.

Elder Gray, as he came to be called ("Sid" to his closest friends) was born in England to a prominent family, and educated at Eton and Oxford. Upon displaying a fair talent for art, he was sent by his indulging parents to study under the famous Bostonian James Whistler (who, though his famous "mother" portrait was still to be accomplished, was then making a great stir among London daubers). Gray himself attained neither fame nor fortune with oil and brush, but happily the family wealth was such that he did not want for income. His parents asked only that he conform in basic ways to their concept of English aristocratic life.

But in 1877, at forty-two years of age, Gray fell in love with a Teutonic miss by the name of Alma Mecklenburg. Alma's father was none other than the Duke of Mecklenburg-Schwerin, a formerly independent duchy recently absorbed into the German state. The Mecklenburgs were nobility of a very high order, and the former duke was aghast to think his young daughter planned to marry a British commoner. Considering that he was also, in a sense, newly out of work, it is not so surprising that the duke celebrated their marriage by cutting off Mrs. Gray, *née* Mecklenburg, without a pfennig.

The Grays were equally unecstatic about the nuptials. To them a foreigner was a foreigner, and a German even moreso. Consequently they too took economic reprisal against their recalcitrant son, leaving the Grays destitute — save for the sizeable sum young Sidney was fortunate enough to have deposited in his own name at London banks.

Unwelcome both in England and in Germany, the newlyweds came to the United States for their honeymoon, and elected to stay on. Gray came west, got hooked up with the clergy, and so was assigned to organize a church on this remote island in Puget Sound.

None of this family history was known to residents of Orcas. To local people, Sidney and Alma Gray were just two more transplanted Europeans who had drifted around a while and finally landed in the San Juans, for reasons that were their own business.

Scarcely had Gray arrived when he had opportunity to call all his ecclesiastical influence into play. It was learned a waterfront lot at Eastsound had been purchased from Charles Shattuck by a man who intended building a saloon. Now Orcas had never had a full-fledged boozery, although one or two Indian rancherias were suffered to dispense a bit of firewater to those who just had to patronize such a place. Taking San Juan Island as the horrible example, a fair segment of Orcas Islanders were determined not to let it happen to them.

Rallying the temperance-minded forces around him, Gray led the fight while the saloon-keeper-to-be, apparently unmoved, worked at clearing his lot of timber. But with each huge tree felled, and each trunk rooted out or burned, the voices of the anti-booze faction (many of them women) became louder and shriller. By the time the prospective grog merchant had cleared out the last giant fir and begun placing the foundation for his building, the strain was showing.

Likely the would-be barkeep might have persisted in his plans — after all, he intended getting a county license, which would make the whole thing quite legal — but for an unnerving detail. One of the shrillest and most determined voices among the opposition belonged to auburn-haired Sarah Jane Fry, wife of "Judge" Fry, a sample of whose novel approaches to the administering of the law has already been chronicled. Fry himself was known to tipple on occasion, but the aspiring saloonist shuddered to contemplate the kinds of trouble the J. P. — egged on by his dry-minded spouse — might be expected to visit on him, license or no license.

So the saloon project was abandoned, its entrepreneur departed for more favorable climes, and Charles Shattuck took back his lot. Thereupon Sidney Gray and the forces of righteousness in the community approached Shattuck and got him to donate the vacated site for the new church Gray wanted to build. Thus Orcas Island's first church edifice enjoys the distinction of standing on land cleared, and on the foundation built for a saloon. When the congregation turns to hymn number 564 of a Sunday and sings "How firm a foundation . . . Is laid for your faith," the song has a special meaning for them.

(It might also be commented here that the island *never did* have licensed premises of any kind, nor did it go in much for unlicensed ones, until the cocktail lounges and one or two reasonably quiet taverns, associated with grocery stores, of very recent years.)

Gray designed his church himself, patterning it after his recollections of small country churches in his homeland. Quietly, he dipped into his London capital for funds with which to build, assisted to some extent by Episcopal missionary societies and in a limited way by members of his own congregation. When it was finished, the Bishop came up from Tacoma to dedicate the structure, which is still one of the prettiest rural churches to be found in all the Puget Sound country.

To Elder Gray, after six years' travelling about America, Orcas Island was like coming home to England. The climate he found similar — only better; and there was much to remind one of Britain among the flora and fauna of Orcas. Along Crescent Beach, he reveled at seeing wild rose bushes — the first he'd found since leaving the old country. And gradually an ambitious plan was forming in his fertile mind: to turn Orcas into a model English village, with not just the church but schools and farms and businesses, all patterned after the best of English life. And the crowning touch would be the selective recruitment of desirable English families to emigrate to Orcas, bringing with them the "tone" (and pounds sterling) to build up the place properly.

Islanders were dubious. Eastsound lacked utterly the industrial base to support the good clergyman's dream village. Lime quarries on the island had proved second-rate (Langdon's was about to close down altogether). Farms were strictly one-family affairs. How would all those newcomers support themselves?

Gray found an answer in Mike Adams' highly profitable orchards. Now not only Adams but also a young fellow named Von Gohren (a son-in-law of "Judge" Fry and his saloon-busting wife) were cashing in on the discovery that Orcas soil was phenomenally suited for raising certain kinds of fruit. Von Gohren, who had been trained as an engineer and was of a scientific turn of mind, had been experimenting systematically. Elder Gray talked to him and learned that climate and soil conditions were excellent for the production of certain types of apples, and even better for raising a variety of plums known as Italian prunes.

Armed with this intelligence and his own persuasiveness, Gray talked several Puget Sound financiers into forming a large concern with the unimaginative moniker of Orcas Island Fruit Company.* For starters the company bought out Mike Adams' entire operation, which they ran while acquiring vast amounts of additional land. Meanwhile, Gray was engineering the organization of more enterprises, such as the Orcas Island Canning Company, the Orcas Island Buying Company, and even the Orcas Island Hop Company.

While all across the island, private individuals likewise rushed to ascend the horticultural bandwagon. Apple and Italian prune trees were planted from one end of Orcas to the other. Acre upon acre were swiftly cleared of tall fir and pine, and replaced with spindly fruit stock. Evenings were liable to be spent mentally banking the huge profits-to-be.

By now the indefatigable Sidney Gray was the uncontested

* One of the backers was J. D. Lowman, a partner in Seattle's pioneer printing and stationery house, Lowman and Hanford.

number one citizen of Orcas Island. Besides preaching twice on Sundays, he was the island's foremost real estate salesman, the local notary public, and superintendent of most of the business enterprises he had enthused into existence. In what spare moments remained to him, he was even platting the drawing-board community to be called "Village de Haro" and launching a cash-raising campaign to fund two high-class private institutions for learning, to be known as the De Haro and St. Agnes schools for boys and girls, respectively.

By 1890, these projects had progressed to the point where "Village de Haro" had been mapped and its as yet nonexistent streets named, while the twin schools were soon due to pass from the paper-work to the construction stage. Meanwhile, Gray was bombarding old contacts in Britain with letters, painting with words pictures of Orcas Island more alluring than anything he had ever created on canvas. And Britishers were actually arriving on the island: their clipped old-world accents could be heard more and more now from Deer Harbor in the west, to Doe Bay on the eastern shores.

Likely none of that year's crop of newcomers, much less the older-timers on Orcas, were aware that in far-off Argentina, a profligate president was spending that nation's finances into the red-ink department. Only when the pampa republic defaulted on its bond payments; which left British banking houses to hold a 100-million-dollar bag of liabilities; in turn leading Baring Brothers and Co., one of Britain's largest financial institutions, to close its doors; thus causing panic among American bankers, many of whom were controlled by Baring; resulting finally in the closing of every bank on Puget Sound, the calling of notes, the refusal to extend credit, and barrel-head cash demanded for every dime's purchase in any store in the country, did it come home to Orcas Island settlers what hard times could mean.

Sidney Gray, for one, lost everything. The model village, the private schools, the huge complex of fruit-producing industries

— all, all was down the chute. What hurt the crestfallen clergy-man most was that so many of his friends, whom he had made party to his dreams, were stony broke too. After a couple of years of trying (with indifferent success) to pick up some of the pieces and get Eastsound back on its feet, he one day left the island as quietly as possible, determined to give up promoting and stick to preaching.

Gray kept his resolve. He was given a church in the Midwest, in due time was ordained a priest, and lived out the rest of his long life in the humble service of the church.

Most long-time Orcas Islanders had already learned to regard being broke as a normal state of affairs, and the newcomers were quick to adapt to the same notion, so the demise of Elder (now Reverend) Gray's schemes didn't hurt them as much as one might fear. The orchards, of course, didn't know the difference, and kept right on producing fruit, so nobody went hungry. Gradually they produced money again, too, though never in the quantities envisioned by the island's erstwhile promoter.

As late as the first World War, Orcas farms were exporting respectable quantities of apples and prunes and pears, all of which grew easily and sold well for orchardists willing to go to the fuss of spraying their trees, and grading and packaging their product suitably. Until then the Orcas Island style had been simply to pick the fruit when it was ripe, toss it into whatever crates were on hand, and ship them off to market. Insect infestations were at first unknown, so there was no need to spray the trees, or do much of anything else to them between crops but watch them grow.

But it was this very ease with which many islanders had always been able to produce and sell that led to their downfall. For eventually a more aggressive breed of growers in Eastern Washington, by dint of irrigating, spraying, grading and pack-aging better, and just plain working harder, were able to produce fruit that looked better, and sold better, even though many insisted it did not always taste better than the Orcas products. Islanders responded gamely with equal efforts in the attempt to recapture the market, but the Eastern fruit had become the housewife's choice and remained so, bringing an end to the era of commercial fruit-growing on Orcas Island.

Still the trees, hundreds upon hundreds of them, continue to this day to grow, with no care whatsoever, often in defiance of encroaching second-growth forests. These old trees, gnarled, unpruned, topheavy, still yield their fruit in season by the uncounted bushels to feed island families who do not one lick of work on them except at picking time each fall.

13

MAYHEM ON THE SOUTHERN PERIMETER

L̲OPEZ ISLANDERS USED TO SAY their climate was so good, they had to kill a man to start a cemetery.

Perhaps so, but it is more likely the island's colossal ruggedness discouraged all but the hardiest of home-seekers from settling there. As late as 1893 newcomers like Michigander C. E. Cantine found "the forest extending down to the water in a dense labyrinth of trees standing so thick on the ground that it was almost impossible for a person to penetrate it."

Early settlements were invariably at the water's edge, with dark, twisty foot-trails connecting them one to another. It was years before these paths were widened to accommodate wagons though a pioneer recalled that there was one horse on the island as far back as 1878 — "but he was absolutely no good. They kept him there to look at."

Readers of this narrative will recall that Lopez was the scene of the first British-American skirmish over the archipelago's sovereignty — long before the San Juan pig episode. Richard Cussans, the Yankee entrepreneur chased off by Governor Douglas in 1853, was on Lopez to cut spars for San Francisco sailing ships precisely because the timber grew there not only thick, but tall, strong and straight. In future years, once these magnificent forests had at last been cleared away, the good rich soil that produced them would turn Lopez into the Islands' most fertile agricultural center.

Deep in some archival dungeon in Washington, D.C., lies a document purporting to describe the troubles of a Lopez settler named Davis who, in 1865, tangled with Camp Pickett's infamous commander, the martinet Captain Gray, over the alleged theft of one of Davis' goats by a soldier. Davis came off second best in the encounter, of course, and so do we, for there are no further details — not even a first name — of this man who seems to have been Lopez Island's first permanent resident. But he may have been one Benjamin Davis, whose name appears on the Lopez Island census for 1870, with data about his farm that is consistent with the raising of goats.

Adding to this mystery is the fact that an 1859 British Admiralty chart of the region names the most desirable bay on Lopez' southwestern shore "Davis Bay," suggesting that our man — or his namesake — was already esconced there in that year-of-the-pig.

On the other hand a Danish ex-sailor, James Nelson, who is generally credited with being the island's first settler, always insisted there were no other residents on the island when he arrived there in 1862.

A crony of Nelson's was Charles Brown, another Scandinavian seaman who held a contract to haul the mail between the mainland and the San Juan military garrison. His craft was sail-powered, and while snow, rain, nor gloom of night kept him from his appointed rounds, the frequent north-and south-easters were something to reckon with, and Mrs. Brown was kept limp with worry for his safety. So when in 1869 she prevailed on him to leave the sea for something safer, Brown took up land near Nelson's place on the northern coast of Lopez. The same year

208

James Davis (no relation to the mysterious Benjamin) and his wife settled near the bay which bears their name, and by the following summer a half dozen more newcomers were calling the island "home."

This last batch included the genial store-keeper from Vermont, Hiram Hutchinson, who built his trading post at Fisherman's Bay where the village of Lopez now stands. He ran his business largely on the barter system, cash money being in scarce supply thereabouts. Settlers brought in the surplus production of their farms, or the fruits of their hunting prowess, in payment for staple goods they needed. "Hi" would convert this truck to sugar, coffee, beans and nails at Victoria to keep his shelves stocked. One pioneer Lopezian recalled the nearest thing to legal tender on the island in those days was deerskins.

"Addie" Chadwick, who was born, lived 88 years and died all on the same piece of land her father homesteaded at Watmough Head on Lopez, used to tell of her dad's routine on "market day." It was a long hike from the southeasternmost corner of the island to Hutchinson's rustic emporium, and the round trip took a whole day. Chadwick would start out early in the morning, rifle in hand, and in the course of his journey kill the best-looking deer he came across, dress it, and take the meat and hide on to the store. These he would trade for flour, tobacco, and whisky. Then he would pocket the tobacco, drink the whisky, sling the flour over his shoulder and head back down the trail for home.

When San Juan County was organized, after the boundary settlement, one of the first acts of the county commissioners was to tax "Hi" Hutchinson for a liquor license. He paid the price, but the records do not say whether the county got it in dollars or had to take deerskins like everybody else.

The man whose murder enabled Lopez "to start a cemetery" was John Anderson, a sometime shoemaker who came to the island from Port Ludlow in the later 'seventies and took up a farm on the eastern shore, at a peninsular bulge known as Sperry Point. His nearest neighbor was one John Kay, a Norwegian; Anderson was a Swede, and the two never hitched well at all. Both were married to Indian women. Anderson and his wife had two children.

A fence dividing the two farms ran right down to the bay but at very low tides it was possible to get around the end of it. Anderson had a "breachy" cow that learned this trick and all too often, Kay would find it searching for the greener grass on his side of the pale. Finally he shooed the critter into a corral and shut it in.

After a bit Anderson came looking for his cow, discovered it in his neighbor's corral and presented himself at Kay's cabin door with blood in his eye. The two had a heated argument, while Kay's wife looked on apprehensively.

The argument developed into a fist fight and soon Anderson, though he was the smaller man, had Kay down on the floor and was pummeling him without mercy. Kay called to his wife, Eliza Jane, for assistance, whereupon the terror-stricken woman helped him grab a fist-full of Anderson's ample beard, pulling a good share of it out by the roots.

This had the desired effect and in a moment Anderson in his turn was underneath being pummeled by Kay. Eliza Jane turned away and began crying hysterically into a handkerchief as the fight went on.

Abruptly she heard a report and looked up to see Anderson, erect again, reel backwards and fall to the floor. Kay was holding a pistol from which a thin wraith of smoke was wisping upward.

Anderson had been hit in the left breast at such close range the exploding powder set his clothing on fire. Eliza Jane ran for a pan of water and threw it on the victim's chest to extinguish the blaze, but by that time a large area of the helpless Swede's flesh was badly burned. Probably he had already expired from the bullet wound, for the coroner found the slug had passed through or very close to the heart.

All this happened shortly after twelve o'clock noon on Tuesday, May 15, 1882.

At the inquest Eliza Jane told all and Kay was committed to stand trial for murder at the fall term of district court at Port Townsend — the same session at which the Orcas Island blacksmith, Lars Brown, was to be retried for the killing of Yves J'Affret. Kay of course pleaded self-defense but the jury found him guilty of second degree murder and he was sentenced to ten years' hard labor in the Territorial jail at McNeil Island.

Kay was defended at the trial by Charles Bradshaw, "Addie" Chadwick's grandfather, a Port Townsend attorney with political ambitions. Naturally Kay had no money to pay Bradshaw's fee, so the lawyer took title of his former client's property. Adelia's father was given the disagreeable task of seizing Kay's home and possessions, which he did, literally turning Eliza Jane out into the cold of a Christmas day.

John Kay served a small portion of his sentence and was released, after which he returned to the San Juans and squatted at Davis Bay on Decatur Island, not far from his former home. Long years later his old cottage became part of Frank Henderson's summer camp for boys and the tale of the shooting — somewhat embellished, perhaps — has been told around many a beachfire since. Still liveable, the cabin used to house the camp's year-around caretaker.

Kay nearly didn't come to trial at all, for one outraged Lopez Islander was determined to shoot Kay on the spot. He was talked out of it by William Graham, who had the good sense to urge that due process of the law be observed — even on Lopez. Graham also served as foreman of the coroner's jury which indicted Kay.

Violence visited Graham's home some years later, costing the life of his young son and setting in motion a legal hassle that took eighteen years to resolve. William Graham and his family had settled near the village of Richardson, on the southern coast of Lopez Island's fat central trunk, in the 'seventies. William's brother, John, took a home nearby and both families of Grahams — they hailed from Ontario, Canada — were among the Islands' most highly esteemed citizens.

In 1882 (the same year Anderson was killed) a young couple named Martin and Ellen Phillips, relatives of the Grahams, also came to live near Richardson. In due time the pair were blessed with the birth of a beautiful daughter, Edith. Life seemed to hold nothing but the best of good things for Martin Phillips. Then, suddenly, tragedy struck; and Phillips' wife was dead. All of Lopez Island mourned with him.

But with the passing of years Phillips' grief diminished, allowing love to bloom again. And on the day he took a wife for the second time, his Lopez Island neighbors shared in his joy as sincerely as they had grieved with him before.

However, with the wedding festivities over, some of Phillips' young cronies decided to continue their rejoicing in the form of that ancient custom — now happily out of style — known as the charivari. The fact that Phillips himself had been known to participate in the noisy serenading of a number of Lopez Island newlyweds lent to the glee with which eight of the youngsters, armed as usual with cowbells, dishpans and an old service musket, gathered at the Phillips homestead as night-shades fell. A thunderous discharge of the muzzle-loader signaled the start of the clamorous caterwauling, which continued on — and on — and on, below Phillips' matrimonial window.

Now that the shoe was on his own foot, Phillips' enthusiasm for the time-honored practice of the shivaree was abating smartly. Sensing that nothing any less dramatic would break up the party before dawn, he seized a loaded, eight-gauge double-barreled shotgun and burst out of the house with it. Aiming just over

212

the dusk-dimmed figures of his serenaders, he pulled both triggers.

By the time the shotgun's twin reports had finished echoing away, all sounds of hilarity had ceased, and the charivarists were huddled over the prostrate forms of two of their number who were emitting low moaning sounds. Phillips rushed over to them, aghast. "My God, boys! What have I done?" he asked.

Wallace Bolton looked up. "You've just killed two of your best friends," he replied.

Felled by pellets from Phillips' too-closely aimed blast were Johnny Graham, William Graham's son and Phillips' own nephew; and John Hall, nineteen-year-old son of another Lopez family. A third youthful victim, with a flesh wound in one hand, was Dan Barlow.

Phillips flung his weapon out into the brush in anguish and helped carry the two severely wounded boys into the house where their injuries were examined. Johnny Graham seemed the worse off, and was laid tenderly upon the Phillips' nuptial bed. The Hall boy was made as comfortable as possible on the floor beside the stove.

Bolton, Lawrence Gau and the Barlow youngster set off immediately to fetch the doctor over from Friday Harbor, putting out in a 16-foot round-bottomed sailing craft in spite of a stiff northeast gale that was blowing. Barlow, who came from a seafaring family and had been sailing San Juan waters almost from infancy, instinctively took command.

As the boys rounded into San Juan Channel a sudden squall caught their sail, capsized the boat and flung them all into the Sound. The three fought to get hold of the high side of their craft, and then while hanging on with one hand, worked to remove the mast and sail. When they had succeeded, they were able to right the boat — now sail-less and half filled with water. Barlow and Gau pulled with two sets of oars, while Bolton bailed furiously with his hat. Bolton and Gau were imploring their companion to turn back before they all perished in the storm, but Barlow refused.

It was midnight when they reached Friday Harbor, raced up the street and pounded on the door of S. Whittemore, M.D. Whittemore, an ex-Army surgeon no longer in his prime (he himself would be dead in a year) refused to go out in the storm but promised to go in the morning if the wind went down some. The storm did in fact abate and the party arrived at the Phillips home about noon. There the aged doctor examined the youngsters' wounds and declared that he would be unable to treat them without a consultation.

Gau, on the thin edge of collapse, was sent home to bed, but Barlow and Bolton again set out in their 16-footer to get Dr. I. M. Harrison of Eastsound, Orcas Island. They reached the entrance to East Sound all right, but then the wind came up again so they could not make headway against it with their oars. They elected to row along the southern shore to Orcas landing, which they reached toward dark, resigned to trekking overland the rest of the way.

Bolton started out on foot for Eastsound but soon met a man on horseback who, after hearing the boy's story, obligingly lent him his mount.

At Eastsound Bolton learned that Dr. Harrison was at the bedside of a diptheria patient — a daughter of the pioneer hotelman "Judge" Fry — and couldn't leave her, but the crisis was expected that night. The boys caught a bit of sleep on the floor of Walter Sutherland's store at Orcas, and next morning got word from Dr. Harrison that there had been no change in his patient after all, and they had better return without him.

It was five that evening when the two young boatsmen returned, exhausted, to the Phillips home and were put to bed in the barn for the night. The following morning Dr. Whittemore, who was struggling to keep his two patients alive, said he needed more medicine and a reference book from his Friday Harbor office. By now Dan Barlow's own wound was bothering him so much he was no longer able to handle an oar, so another youngster took his place and, with Bolton, set out for "the Harbor" again. On the way the storm, which refused to subside, drove them ashore on Shaw Island where they spent the night. After several more delays caused by the weather, they finally reached Lopez late the next evening, just three days after the tragic shooting took place. There they learned that Hall had already died.

That night twelve of Lopez Island's young men carried Hall's body two miles to the little Center Church, working in relays of fours, reaching the church at midnight where they were met by another party bearing a casket built for them by a neighbor. They remained in the church until morning — as was the custom in those days — to pay final respects to their dead friend. And none mourned more for him than Martin Phillips.

Johnny Graham lingered for something over three years before succumbing to the bullet lodged inextricably in his spine.

Phillips was arrested and charged with murder. He retained to defend him a prominent Pacific Northwest barrister named James Hamilton Lewis who won a not-guilty verdict, arguing that the charivarists were in fact trespassers. The Port Townsend jury was out less than five minutes.

Phillips, unable to pay his lawyer, was forced to give Lewis title to his farm. This led to a lawsuit some fourteen years later, in which Phillips' daughter Edith — now twenty — claimed half of the property was rightfully hers. The farm had been the community property of her father and his first wife, she contended, and as her mother's estate had not been probated, her father could not legally convey Mrs. Phillips' half to the lawyer. As sole heir, Edith claimed that her mother's half interest should now descend to her.

Edith hired a Friday Harbor lawyer and the suit was brought in the superior court there. The sympathies of the local populace were clearly in favor of the "orphaned girl" as the local paper was calling her, the moreso considering Lewis had in the interim become a rather well-known Chicago politician of Democratic persuasion. In Republican San Juan County, this earned him the kind of disesteem reserved for, say, convicted white-slave racketeers.

Lewis sought to have the case moved to more favorable ground by exaggerating the value of the disputed interests, thus securing transfer of the matter to a federal court. However, the ploy failed and the case was remanded to the court at Friday Harbor where Judge George A. Joiner found in favor of the Phillips girl. Lewis appealed the decision in the state supreme court, but lost the case when it was decided in December 1909 — just twenty years after the tragic shivaree.

Just off Flat Point on Lopez' northwest shore lies little Canoe Island, and just beyond that, Shaw — fourth largest of the San Juans. Shaw Island used to be called the "hub" of the islands, for if you use a bit of imagination the archipelago becomes a wheel, with Shaw exactly at the center.

Shaw's settlement was a slow business. As late as 1883 there were only a dozen men living on the island — all but two of them bachelors, and of these most were a pretty rough and shiftless lot. An exception was Hughie Parks, for whom the bay on Shaw's western coast was named. Parks was as hard-working as his neighbors were slothful, and his farm was the island's showplace. Of course his reward was the hatred of his jealous compatriots, who took to pestering him unmercifully. Parks took their molestations with good grace for a while, but after a few years of it, he began to crack under the strain.

The time came when Parks decided to end his life, which he considered intolerable. This was not long after Lars Brown, the Orcas blacksmith, had been acquitted of shooting Yves J'Affret. Parks, apparently feeling he hadn't the courage to take his own life, visited Brown and begged the big Dane to do it for him. But Brown refused.

Parks returned to his Shaw Island farm and when one of his tormenters approached his place, the ordinarily mild-mannered farmer stepped out on his front porch and shot the man dead.

When the deceased failed to return from his presumably nefarious mission, one of his pals came to see what had become of him. Parks shot him down, too, and ultimately a third man as well.

Sheriff John Kelly was summoned from Friday Harbor and, after learning how matters stood, wisely decided not to approach the Parks farm without plenty of assistance. He swore in fifteen or twenty settlers who surrounded the house, and then called to the deranged man to give himself up. His answer was a volley of shots, one of which struck a settler in the leg.

Kelly and the posse kept up their siege for about two days, with Parks shooting at anyone who came within his sight and range. Kelly's men started shooting back, but still Parks refused the sheriff's commands to surrender. At last the sheriff hollered — true to the style of present-day television melodrama — that if Parks didn't come out, they would burn his house. There was no response.

So the men found some bales of hay in the barn, lit them, and rolled them against the walls of the cabin which soon began to blaze brightly. Even then Parks remained inside. It was only after the cabin had burned down completely, and the ruins were cool enough to examine, that Parks' body was found in the cellar with a bullet in it. He had taken his own life, after all.

By the 1890's, many of the chief actors in San Juan Island's Pig War drama had scattered to other parts of the archipelago. It will be remembered that Paul Hubbs, who surely had more to do with that fracas than almost anyone else — including the pig — somehow wangled an exclusive right to occupy Blakely,

Lopez Island's next eastern neighbor. But he apparently did not reside on the island for any length of time. Blakely's first permanent settler seems to have been another prime mover in the boundary dispute (who also, as justice of the peace in 1860, helped Captain Pickett clean up lawlessness; and later pioneered San Juan's lime industry), San Juan's first surveyor, E. C. Gillette. Gillette moved to the island when Hubbs decided to forsake white ways for those of the Indians.

Gillette remained a Blakelyite until about 1889 when he sold out to a tall, red-headed schoolmaster named Richard H. Straub, who was destined to become the central figure in the Islands' most celebrated episode since the Kanaka murders of 1873.

Actually, Straub had preferred a piece of land adjoining Gillette's, and tried to homestead it; but was beat out of it — as he reckoned — by one J. C. Burns, a railroad man who wasn't even home most of the time. Burns' place was run by his wife, Pauline, daughter of the pioneer Lanterman family of Decatur Island.*

There were only a handful of families on Blakely but several of these had children, so Straub — a man of fair education — was hired to teach them in the little log house islanders threw up for the purpose. But bad blood between Straub and the Lanterman clan (though Straub always professed to get along well with the absent Burns) marred the set-up. Gradually sentiment turned against him throughout the island, as a result of various quarrels, until finally Pauline Burns — who was a member of the school board — came out openly against him and tried to get him fired.

A school election was held to decide the issue, at which Mrs. Burns' brother, Leon Lanterman, tried to vote. Straub exploded

---

* The story is told that John B. Lanterman was a stutterer as well as a comedian. Lanterman "ran" sheep on little Frost Island between Lopez and Blakely. Asked how many he had there he replied, "Ei-ei-eighty-four b-b-b-bands." When his questioner doubted so small an island could hold that many he explained "There's o-o-only o--o-one sheep in each b-b-band."

in indignation, pointing out that Lanterman didn't even live on Blakely. But the disputed vote was allowed to stand, and Straub lost his job. After the meeting the deposed schoolkeep traded a few insults with Lanterman and the two were on the point of a fist-fight when they were restrained by the womenfolk present.

About this time Straub's wife died rather suddenly of kidney failure, thus adding to the erstwhile pedagogue's general depression and irascibility. He had no other relatives in the region.

Late in August 1895, Lanterman and a half-brother, Ralph Blythe, came over from Decatur to help their sister harvest the Burns' potato crop. Toward evening, the three were busily hoeing when an ally of Straub's, smooth-cheeked, seventeen-year-old Irving Parberry, appeared in the next field and began making himself obnoxious. In a loud voice punctuated with curses he accused Lanterman of deliberately setting some forest fires which had been raging over the island, and which had caused considerable damage to the Parberry home. Annoyed, Lanterman tossed down his hoe and walked toward the fence to talk to the boy, who was armed with an axe. Nearby Mrs. Burns, who had a presentiment of the tragedy which was about to occur, watched apprehensively. Blythe, who was farther away, began striding toward the fence to see what was up.

He arrived on the scene to see Parberry raise his axe and take a mighty swing at Lanterman. In the next instant, Straub leaped up from behind a nearby log, where he had been hiding, took aim with a rifle and put two bullets through Lanterman's body. Lanterman was able to turn and run a short distance toward a clover field, at the same time calling out in anguish to his sister.

Straub quickly turned his Winchester on Ralph Blythe who dropped to the ground just as the rifle spoke. The shot missed, but Blythe stayed put and played dead.

"Now I'll kill you!" roared Straub to the horror-stricken Pauline Burns, who began running zig-zag across the field to the house as slug after slug whizzed toward her, one of them piercing her shoulder close to the neck. While Straub concentrated on her, he did not notice Ralph Blythe crawl away and then sprint toward the house for a weapon.

Mrs. Burns succeeded in reaching the house first. Believing both her brothers were dead, she collected her small son, Percy, and the two travelled by rowboat to a neighbor's home a mile distant. Meanwhile, Straub again turned his rifle on the body of Leon Lanterman, pumping several more shots into him as he lay prostrate at the edge of the clover field.

With Pauline Burns and Ralph Blythe free to tell their story, Straub knew his life would not be worth much if he remained at large on Blakely. At the trial, Parberry claimed that he, too, was concerned for his own skin, fearing his former mentor might be tempted to do away with a damaging witness. But in fact Straub talked the boy into accompanying him in a bold move. Together they launched a skiff and rowed straight to Friday Harbor, where they surrendered themselves to Sheriff Newton Jones and were lodged by him in the county lock-up.

Lanterman's well-attended funeral took place on Lopez two days later, a Sunday, and was preached by a venerable Methodist missionary, the eloquent Isaac Dillon, whose sermon added still more heat to the flames of passion already burning in the breasts of an enraged citizenry. There was talk of storming the not very substantial jail at Friday Harbor, where Straub and Parberry were imploring Jones to remove them to a safer place. By Monday the streets of the Harbor were filling with purposeful-looking men, many of them newly arrived from Blakely, Lopez and Decatur Islands.

Toward dusk there were disjointed knots of these men gathering ominously a short distance in front of the frail little building next to the courthouse, and their intention was altogether too clear. But Newt Jones had a plan, too. And as the gloom congealed into darkness, covering the approach of the angry assemblage to the jail's front door, Newt was spiriting his prisoners out the back way and into the safety of the forest. There they remained until morning, when they reappeared at the courthouse in time for a preliminary hearing, at which both men were bound over for trial.

Now it was determined to transfer the two prisoners to safer keeping at Whatcom. There was no regular vessel scheduled to call at Friday Harbor that day, and Jones was fearful of keeping his two charges in the local jug for another night. So he contacted the skipper of the U.S. Revenue Launch *Scout* and arranged for the secret embarkation of the prisoners at six that evening. As that hour approached Newt Jones again whisked the two out by the back door and smuggled them down to the waterfront, where a deputy concealed them on a narrow ledge jutting from behind a rough lumber fence.

Somehow word of the plan leaked out, and the two prisoners watched — limp with fear — as an armed and noisy crowd began collecting a mere thirty yards from their hiding place! But they were not discovered, and the sheriff went out bravely to face the mob, to bluff them, keep them busy until the *Scout*'s arrival.

But six o-clock came — and the *Scout* did not. Straub and Parberry, crouching on their little platform, were dissolving into utter panic, expecting each breath to give away their presence and bring the whole lynching party down upon them. They had decided to dive into the bay and swim for it when the revenue boat — twenty minutes behind its time — hauled into view at last. The launch had scarcely berthed when the two prisoners swung on board her with alacrity, and collapsed shivering into the bottom as the *Scout* put out again immediately for Whatcom.

Richard Straub, in those days of speedy justice, was returned to Friday Harbor within the month to face a jury of his peers. At the first moment his attorney moved for a change of venue, claiming Straub could not receive a fair trial in Friday Harbor, and citing among other things the Reverend Isaac Dillon's inflammatory funeral oration. The judge, who was from What-com, denied the motion; but held out the possibility of a reversal of the ruling, if there proved to be any trouble selecting a fair jury.

Friday Harbor citizens were determined to keep the trial at home, and saw to it that the judge found no reason to change his mind. One out-of-town observer commented wryly that for a case which had been the chief conversation topic everywhere in the county for weeks, it was most remarkable how the twenty-four prospective jurors were the very ones who seemed to know nothing whatever about it.

San Juan County's regular courtroom was far too small to accommodate the phalanx of local citizens, reporters, jurists and others who needed or wanted to observe the trial, so court officials agreed to move it across the street to the Odd Fellows Hall. Tickets were printed and handed out to the lucky ones authorized to attend. Some who were not so lucky tried through various devices to get in anyway: one enterprising islander managed to crawl under the stage and stationed himself directly beneath the witness chair. He was discovered by the defense attorney, Charles Repath, however, who raised an even greater ruckus when it was discovered the eavesdropper was one of the prosecutor's witnesses.

The case against Irving Parberry was dropped when he agreed to testify for the prosecution, which he did, stating Straub had forced him at gun-point to take part in the shooting. Other witnesses told of hearing Straub threaten to kill the Lantermans. Pauline Burns and Ralph Blythe gave their account of the incident, which was supported by Parberry's testimony.

Repath put Straub on the stand and drew from him his version of the shooting, which was that Leon Lanterman attacked Parberry, and was shot by Straub, who just happened along at that moment, in the teen-ager's defense. But Parberry had already blunted this claim by testifying Straub had cooked up that very yarn, and coached him in it, while the two were rowing to Friday Harbor.

The jury took seven hours to find Straub guilty of first-degree murder, and the red-headed ex-schoolteacher was handed an appointment with the hangman. After the usual appeals and a plea to the governor for clemency had all failed, the date for the deed was set and Sheriff Newt Jones found himself in the role of executioner.

In contrast with the hanging of Kanaka Joe twenty-three years earlier, Jones determined that Straub should pay for his crime in private. A gallows was erected near the jail in the courthouse yard, and surrounded with a 15-by-25-foot fence of 16-foot-high boards laid closely together. Only persons who had business there were admitted, including officials and a few reporters. Also on hand was Straub's spiritual adviser, Friday Harbor's Methodist minister, T. L. Dyer, whose church and parsonage stood a short distance from the grisly scene.

There is a legend in the San Juans that Straub agreed to advance the time of his execution about an hour, to accommodate reporters who were in a hurry to catch the last steamer for the mainland. In point of fact, Sheriff Jones delayed the hanging long enough to see whether the ship in question might bring a last-minute reprieve. It didn't, and Jones dropped the trap at 11:15 in the morning, April 23, 1897.

Straub was buried in a little plot across the bay at Channel Prairie, on Point Caution, where the University of Washington's Marine Laboratory now stands. It used to be that Friday Harbor children would sometimes row over to visit the grave of Richard Straub and strew wild flowers over it. Now, its location is all but forgotten.

Official records state that twenty persons witnessed the proceedings behind the high board fence. The records are wrong: there were twenty-four. Apparently no one present on that grim occasion chanced to look *above* the fence, up the street toward the roof of Reverend Dyer's house. If they had, they would have spied eight saucer-wide young eyes watching them. They were the eyes of Reverend Dyer's school-age children, viewing in fascinated horror a forbidden scene which none of them would ever forget.

Sidney R. S. Gray, first vicar of Emmanuel Episcopal Church, Eastsound.
Courtesy Emmanuel Church.

Peter Bostian, Orcas Island pioneer, and a covey of nineteenth-century belles.
Bostian was singing teacher to these lovelies.
Courtesy Mr. Ray Kimple, Eastsound.

Henry Thomas Cayou, prominent fisherman, long-time county commissioner,
and one of the Islands' most respected and public-spirited citizens.
He called Orcas Island "home" most of his 89 years.
Orcas Island Historical Society Museum.

He did lot of good deeds for the Island and
was loved by everybody says George L. Keys of East Sound
Grange Master & State Deputy Master of the Grange

East Sound House, Orcas Island, around the turn of the century.
Courtesy Mr. Robert Monroe and the University of Washington.

Harvest time at an Orcas Island orchard.
Orcas Island Historical Society Museum.

The metropolis of East Sound around 1914.
View from water shows, at left, Emmanuel Episcopal Church.
Steeple behind it belongs to Methodist Church up the street.

Opposite view from corner of Methodist Church shows combined telephone "central"
and post office, the Templin's Fair Co. general store, and Orcas Island's
first Model T Ford. *Courtesy Templin's, Eastsound.*

Mr. and Mrs. William Graham and family.
Lopez Island Historical Society.

Hiram Edson Hutchinson, pioneer storekeeper of Lopez Island.
Courtesy Mrs. Eva Rhodes Hall, Lopez.

Mr. and Mrs. Sampson Chadwick, early-day Lopez Island residents.
Courtesy Kenneth and Dan Hume, Lopez.

Early picture of Lopez shows the solitary buildings of "Hi" Hutchinson.
An itinerant water-borne photographer snapped this view, probably in the 1880's.
Courtesy Mrs. Eva Rhodes Hall, Lopez.

Lopez Village at low tide, about 1908.
"Hi" Hutchinson's old home and store are the first two buildings on the left.
Courtesy Mrs. Eva Rhodes Hall, Lopez.

14

THE KING OF SPIEDEN ISLAND

$\mathbb{B}$lowing dust stung at the face of Alfred Chevalier as he stood in the doorway of his simple farm home, its weathered board sides as gray as his spirit, and surveyed the flat Dakota plains. Squinting against the hot prairie sun he tried in vain to find a hint of cloud in the sky. But he watched a distant "willy" lazily scooping up bits of his farm and blowing them away before his eyes. And the parched tops of corn rows waving yonder with the breeze. They were stunted, of course, like everything else that tried to grow in this country, this God-forsaken drought-dry country.

Chevalier turned wearily and entered the house. His wife raised anxious eyes and he slowly shook his head.

"It's no use, Carrie," he said. "We can't stick it here, the place won't support us. Maybe if there were only the two of us; but with nine children.... I think we should move further west. Things are bound to get better for us if we do that."

"Whatever you think best, Al," she answered simply. But she was thinking that he said the same thing when they moved out

225

from Iowa, a few years before. That, and how stooped her once-handsome husband had come to look lately, and how he rarely smiled any more. Just look at the heartaches, Carrie told herself; more than enough to bend any man, even Al. Oh, my Jesus, help my poor Al.

Alfred Chevalier had been born among the snowy hills of Switzerland. There he learned the gentle art of watchmaking, and after emigrating to the New World as a young man he practiced that quiet and dignified profession with a success that encouraged him to ask and win the hand of pretty Caroline Emma, *née* Schüler, whose parents had come years before from Germany. They made their home in Waterloo, Iowa, where they had happy years together, and many children to brighten their hours.

But then misfortune struck, and it would strike again, and again. It began soon after Alfred succumbed to the bright, slick promise of promoters, sold out his business and his home in Waterloo, and joined the stream of "boomers" following the railroad into the Dakotas. It proved a grievous mistake. Somehow speculators had gotten in first and taken the best land. Tools, seed, lumber cost money — which had to be borrowed at usurious rates. One housed one's family in a sod shanty for the first years and spent every daylight hour breaking in the ground. Those years you were lucky just to keep the mortgage man away, and food in your children's mouths.

It was in the midst of these difficult trials that Chevalier's wife fell victim to the hard fate which was dogging them now, ever more relentlessly. The accident took only a moment, but it left Carrie — once so tall, so beautiful — forever hip-lame and twisted. Then their oldest son and pride, George, who had become a strapping teen-ager, went off to work on the railroad which passed at Plankinton, a few miles from their farm. The evil star flashed again: another tragic accident occurred, and young George's legs were crushed, so that neither were any use to him now, nor ever would be again.

Since then George had lain helpless on his couch, one more burden of grief to his father. And now, directly it seemed that the land might begin to pay out just a little, the drought had come to take the crop — and hope, too.

Chevalier called a family circle and told them of his decision. He looked about him. At Albert Florian, whom everyone called Bert, fifteen, from whom so much would now be expected. At Ed, fourteen, who had his dad's thick, wavy black hair and sly smile of an earlier and happier time. At Hypolite, who disliked the name and wanted to be called Paul. (Paul was the religious one, and held a Salvation Army commission.) At their first daughter, on whom they had bestowed a generous supply of middle names, as though to make up for her lack of sisters: Mary Esther Julia May Chevalier, or as she was usually called, May. And at the younger boys, Arthur, Howard, and James. And finally at Carrie, who was holding their youngest, Maude Zelline, barely three months. All nodded solemnly in agreement — even the baby seemed to be cooing approval.

Thus it was that in the winter, when the last of the meager crop had been gathered in, and a few personal affairs set in order, Chevalier packed some clothes in a grip and, accompanied by sons Bert and Ed, set off silently through the snow for the train station at Plankinton. They were headed for a far-off country called Puget Sound where, if the streets were not paved with gold, at least they were lined with trees and grass, for it was said the rain never failed there. Nor jobs. And if all this proved true, Al would soon be sending to Carrie to sell the farm, to bring the rest of the children and join him.

The Chevaliers' destination was Tacoma, the burgeoning Commencement Bay city and western terminus of the Northern Pacific Railroad. Arriving in mid-winter still clad in their Dakota woollens over scratchy long-johns and in winter caps with ear flaps, they felt both conspicuous and overheated as they swung down from the train into mild Puget Sound sunshine. "The City of Destiny" Tacoma was dubbed in the railroad circulars that had brought them to this place; and it was well they did not know how ironic that phrase would sound to them before long.

How the three first fared in Tacoma is somewhat obscure. Years later, Ed recalled working for a time in a brick yard there. But it is clear that when Al Chevalier found permanent work it was at Carbonado, a bustling coal town some miles away in the foothills of the Cascade mountains. It was the biggest mining operation in the state, all owned by the Pacific Coast Coal Company, which employed men by the hundreds to work three shifts a day in galleries extending literally for miles below the earth's surface. Their output kept three steamers busy hauling from Tacoma to the cities of California.

The work was hard, hard, but steady, and the pay reasonable. Moreover the company — which owned the mines, the town, and everything else in sight, including the souls of the men who worked for them — even provided dwellings for miners with families. Row on row these stood, each a carbon copy of its neighbor: squarish, hip-roofed, one door with two windows flanking it on the front, two-by-four yard separated from the wood-slat sidewalk by a single-rail fence. And everything uniformly grimed over in coal-dust gray. Each house measured perhaps twenty-five feet on a side. It was hard to imagine all eleven Chevaliers crowding into one of them. At least, they would be together again. Al was elated. He wrote home to Caroline, told her to sell everything as quickly as possible, and come join him.

But Carbonado proved less and less the paradise Alfred Chevalier tried to tell himself he had found. Mine work was arduous for a man, now fifty, with delicate watchmaker's hands. He found it impossible to keep up with the younger, huskier men, and he smarted under the lashing invective of impersonal foremen always urging him on to work harder and faster. There was little rest: hours were long, and the company seemed not to believe in days off or holidays. And as the weeks wore on, Chevalier grew despondent. Finally, one gray day in February 1891, he placed the barrel of a small pistol in his mouth and pressed the trigger.

Caroline Chevalier knew nothing of this as she, the crippled George, and six small children set out for Tacoma by rail, having sold their belongings for a price that barely covered their debts. Sandwiches and fruit had been frugally packed in baskets against the week-long journey. The family sat on hard, swaying seats and at night leaned against each other to get what rest they could. The baby cried a good deal; but such temporary hardships were nothing, Caroline thought, consoling herself in the belief that Al, with his loving face and strong arms would be meeting them soon.

At Tacoma, of course, Al was not there to meet them. Bert and Ed were, and broke the news as mercifully as they could contrive. And Caroline Emma Chevalier now knew she was left alone with her children, destitute, without money or friends in a strange country that might as well be at the edge of the earth.

Yet from somewhere, far down in an unknown depth of her spirit she found the needed strength — strength to go on, to plan. After another family consultation it was decided to go north, to a place called Roche Harbor, on an island called San Juan somewhere near Canada. Ed and Bert had learned that a Tacoma industrialist, John S. McMillin, had taken over a large lime quarrying operation there and jobs were to be had for the asking. Thus did they come for the first time to the islands they would all grow to know and love so well.

By San Juan standards, things were truly booming at Roche Harbor then. Two lime kilns and four houses had made up the town when McMillin, one-time Indiana lawyer, acquired it in

1886. Now it had grown to a neat cluster of log and lumber-built homes, a church, hotel and store, and enough new, modern kilns to boost the daily output to five times what it was before. McMillin's hard-driving energy and capitalist's wizardry had already turned the place into the largest lime-producing plant in the Pacific Northwest; soon it would be the biggest west of the Mississippi.

But Roche Harbor, like Carbonado, was a "company town." The company owned everything, even the church and the houses; and McMillin owned the company. The work was hard and the hours long. The pay was fair but it had to be spent in the company's store where prices were whatever the company wished to impose. True, you could go to Friday Harbor and buy cheaper, but it was worth a man's job if he got caught at it. It soon became obvious no one could get ahead fast, working for John S. McMillin. So when a lonely bachelor from a neighboring island paid his court to Caroline Emma, she accepted his proposal of marriage, and with her entire brood went off to a new kind of life, as unlike that of the Dakota prairies as one can imagine.

Emma Chevalier's new husband was James Fitch, a large bluff man who raised sheep on the grassy, undulating hillsides of Stuart Island. There were only a handful of settlers on the three-square-mile island just northwest of Roche Harbor, and most of them were unmarried. There was short, spade-bearded Bernhardt Mordhorst and Frederick Hayes, both Germans, who were partners in a fishing enterprise; they shared a rather stylish house at the head of Reid Harbor, a herring-filled finger of salt chuck indenting the eastern end of the island. John Henry Balam, a short Englishman newly arrived a year or two before, also fished some, and ran a farm. Then there were Joe Emanuel and Frank Erdmann (Erdmann would bite Emanuel in the finger one day, and Emanuel would die of it; but that was years in the future).

230

On the north shore were Indians who lived where, talk was, the government planned to build a lighthouse.

The large family from the midwestern plains took to island life as fish to the sea. The Fitch home, filled with noisy and exuberant children, became the island's social center where islanders vied with one another in sharing with the newcomers their own hard-learned treasures of island lore. The Chevaliers were soon taught to row and sail, and how the winds and tides may be judged and used to advantage. They mastered the old-timers' tricks of guessing the weather and learned, Indian-like, to "think like a fish" in order to bring in a good catch every time. Soon, the transplanted flatlanders were holding their own with the long-timers, and loving every moment of their new life.

The good-humored, naturally sociable youngsters made fast friends throughout the archipelago. Ed became a close pal of Bill Rosler, son of a former Pig War soldier who farmed toward the south end of San Juan. One rawly cold day the pair were reconnoitering little John's Island, a slice of forest-covered rock disjoined from Stuart's eastern end by narrow John's Pass. The beach was white with fresh-fallen snow — even the sloping, coursely graveled stretches exposed by a particularly low tide. The boys thought they were alone but discovered they weren't. At the water's edge they came upon a short man with a weather-tanned, cleanly shaven face, wearing old clothes and a broad-brimmed campaign hat. He was barefoot, but seemingly oblivious of the snow which, on being reached by the oozing salt water, was melting at his toes. Working deliberately with a shovel he was digging clams through the slush.

Bill stared open-jawed. "Who in blazes is that?" he demanded.

Ed, who had seen the fellow before, answered: "Why, looka there," he said, as Bill recalled it long decades afterward. "That's Paul K. Hubbs!"

Hubbs, the one-time Indian scout and prime figure in the Pig War drama, was sixtyish now, a bit heavier than of yore. But he was still tough and strong, still leaning more to Indian ways than to white. Up on the shore above the drift-marked high tide line the boys spotted Hubbs' shanty. It was jerry-rigged of various materials so they couldn't say if it was more of a tent or a cabin.

Hubbs was still as likely to turn up in one place as another in the San Juans, but of late years he had come as close to settling down on Johns as he ever would anywhere. He was running a few sheep, had a garden, fished and loafed, and occasionally scribbled a line to a growing manuscript of memoirs. He did not live alone on Johns, but had his current *klootchman* to keep house and provide what companionship he required.

Just how many wives Hubbs had in all his adventuresome lifetime is something no mortal can now say. One or two were white, the rest dusky-eyed maidens of sundry native tribes. In an 1882 letter he kidded about his many "antiquated friends" who formerly had chosen spousal companions at some Indian encampment but "are now surrounded by full-blooded white children with blue eyes." In the same letter he told of once, during an infrequent spell of bachelorhood, visiting a crony whose Indian wife "interested herself in my domestic affairs and enquired why I did not get a kloochman. I replied that I did not want one, which brought from her the retort that I was 'played out' and would soon get a white woman."

Even in advanced age Hubbs was unwilling to let this woman's prophecy come to pass. When he could no longer entice, on his own merits, some dark-skinned charmer to join in a connubial relationship, he resorted to barter. His bride, purchased from an insouciant father at a Canadian reservation, cost him four sacks of flour, some blankets, a gun, powder and shot. The intended didn't think much of the deal, though, and she eloped with a young man of her own race before Hubbs could find an altar to lead her to.

Hubbs followed the pair hotly in pursuit, and on Orcas learned the runaways had just become legally married at the Lummi

Reservation near Bellingham. "I guess there's nothing you can do about it, now," a settler told him.

"The hell there ain't," Hubbs replied. "She's mine. I bought her, and I intend to have her." But whether he succeeded in this purpose is another bit of history lost, it seems, forever. Still, it is a fact that one day about that time Hubbs appeared on Orcas at the home of Oberlin Loos, a justice of the peace. He had a young native girl in tow and had come to get married, he said. Loos sent him off, grumbling, to get a proper license in Friday Harbor before tying the knot.

As year followed on year the Chevalier youngsters grew toward adulthood. Bert became the sailor of the family, fishing from his own trim sailboat, "Dolphin." Ed and Paul went to work at Roche Harbor — Ed in the sawmill, helping to make staves — Paul and his colleagues turning these into barrels in the cooper shop, for shipping the company's lime to far points of the world.

May, on reaching seventeen, met and married quiet, earnest George Washington Smith, son of an Oregon family which had come to Roche Harbor when he was nine. The newlyweds settled down in one of the neat two-room log cabins maintained by the company, for which George was to work faithfully for the next fifty years.

The same year May was married — 1894 — Ed Chevalier, now twenty, went for a row with two pretty young German girls who were daughters of Frank Erdmann's on Stuart. The trio were in high spirits, yarning, laughing and singing in the forepart of the day. But on the return trip Ed had become strangely quiet and thoughtful. The reason was something they had all seen, and the girls guessed it, and teased Ed about it.

Their leisurely row had taken them to a narrow, dagger-shaped island off San Juan's northern coast. Spieden is a curiosity because, while the southern slopes of the east-west oriented island are rocky and almost completely barren, the northern side is covered thick with forest. A central ridge running from end to end divides the island into these two contrasting geographies. But this was not the cause of Ed Chevalier's thoughtful mood. He was thinking of a small Indian encampment they had seen on Spieden's north shore, a camp where just two people lived. One was an Indian woman, stooped with great age. The other was a winsome teen-ager, as pretty and young-looking as her companion was haggard and old. The girl was the most beautiful Ed had ever seen. All the while the camp was in sight, she sat silently working into braids her long black hair which fell clear to her heels.

Before long Ed Chevalier was back on Spieden to get better acquainted. The girl's name, he learned, was Mary Smith. Her father, Robert Smith, had been one of the British soldiers stationed at English Camp during the joint occupation. After his enlistment ended, Smith — rather than return to his home in Wales — had chosen to stay in the Islands. He married a native lass whose people had lived just across Haro Strait on Vancouver Island since before the coming of the White Man.

Smith had moved his few belongings to Spieden. There, choosing a pretty spot amid green trees high on the island's summit, he built a snug log cabin where he, his bride, and his bride's mother lived for some years.

Soon after Mary was born, Smith died. His widow, Lucy, had a hard time of it for a while, caring both for her daughter and her mother. Then as Mary approached womanhood the mother remarried and moved away. The young girl and the grandmother stayed on, and now here was Ed Chevalier visiting them more and more often as he courted the beautiful Mary.

Ed Chevalier was also fascinated with the stories the grandmother could tell, stories of primitive days in the San Juan area with their cruel tribal wars and placid though complicated ways of life before the whites came. And how the coming of the white men meant pain and death for untold thousands of Indians — not because of the whites' belligerence, as in some areas of

234

this continent; but because he brought with him the scourge of smallpox. Epidemics of the dreaded disease, against which the Indians had no immunity whatever, accompanied or even preceded arrival of the first sailors and explorers. Families — even whole villages — were wiped out. Recurring outbreaks of the pestilence in fact is what led to abandonment of the San Juans by most of the natives well before Pig War times.

Ed and Mary Smith were married the same year. The bride waited on little Pearl Island, off the entrance to Roche Harbor, while Ed went to town to see about a minister. The pastor of the Roche Harbor church, T. L. Dyer, lived in Friday Harbor and Ed walked the nine-mile wooded trail to fetch him. The return trip was made in Reverend Dyer's sailboat *Epworth*, an ungainly vessel with the habit of capsizing on the least excuse. Dyer had built the boat himself and nearly lost his life in it several times. But on this occasion it remained upright and brought its passengers safely to Pearl Island, where the happy pair were united in a quiet ceremony. Afterwards they returned directly to Spieden where Ed and his bride set up housekeeping in the same pretty little log cabin, now deep-covered in ivy, that Mary's father had built.

For long years to come Ed and Mary Chevalier truly "ruled" their island kingdom, for they were practically the only inhabitants right from the start. Some years before, Paul Hubbs had induced a nephew to come out from the east, and had set him up sheep-ranching on Spieden; but the man's family lacked enthusiasm for solitary island living and he had already moved off, first to Bellingham and later to more populous Shaw Island. Briefly a retired newspaperman, E. T. Vernon, lived on Spieden, to be succeeded by a Russian of dubious reputation named Anton Cepas.

By this time Ed had children of his own to help run his island fief. He had them keep an eye on Cepas who, like the Chevaliers, ran sheep on the island without benefit of fences. To distinguish their animals Ed branded his by nicking one ear, but the Cepas' mark was removal of the whole ear. As Cepas' flock had a way of increasing unaccountably while the Chevalier herd declined exactly in proportion, the Russian was suspected of some nefarious activities with the cropping shears when the moon was dark, but it was hard to prove anything. Eventually Cepas' poor business tactics and lack of industry led him into debt whereupon Chevalier bought him out and after that he and his family had the island to themselves. That was when Ed's friends began calling him "king" of Spieden, and his sons and daughters princes and princesses.

Toward the end of the century the little chain of islands north of Roche Harbor began attracting more and more settlers. The government built the lighthouse that had been rumored, on Stuart's Turn Point, and as often as not the keeper's family included children. (Ed Durgin, for instance, had eight, one of whom — Helene — would one day write a best-seller about the family's hardships and adventures.*) Then a young couple, Eric and Marie Ericksen — just off the boat from their native Norway — came visiting to Stuart where Marie's brother was an early keeper at the Turn Point light. Delighted with the island they stayed, and both were to live all their long and happy lives there, in the course of which they added eight offspring of their own to the burgeoning population.

By the time Ed Chevalier's oldest "prince," William, was of an age to attend school, one had been started. It was located at the head of Stuart's Reid Harbor, and young Bill daily rowed some two miles over open water to learn his three R's. Often he picked up two or three other youngsters along the way. It was only after two years of overdeveloping his rowing muscles that Bill's dad presented him with one of the small gas boats that were then a novelty in the Islands.

Earlier Uncle Sam had seen fit to establish a post office on

* Helene Glidden, *The Light on the Island.*

Stuart. Bert and Howard Chevalier were given the first contract to haul the mail over from Roche Harbor twice a week, for which they were paid the handsome sum of $2.75 per trip. After the Ericksens came, Marie became postmaster. She held that position for thirty-two years, dispensing the mail without ceremony from the kitchen of her neat home on Prevost Harbor until over-citified postal inspectors insisted the dignity of the United States required a separate mail room. When the new quarters were built, Marie found there was more space there than the mail needed, so she moved the cream separator in, too. Of course the inspectors found out eventually and made her remove the separator.

Meanwhile, Spieden's Ed and Mary Chevalier ("Dad" and "Ma," island people were calling them now) had come to be as widely known and loved as anyone in the San Juans. In the process, they proved how hard a family can work. With their children — they had five — they raised turkeys for market (this was mainly "Ma's" concern); tended a fruit orchard; grew all their own produce; kept sheep and horses, and milked two cows; logged, and cut wood. Winters, when the farm chores were fewer, Ed put his spare moments to use building boats for friends on neighboring islands. While for many years he still held down a full-time job at Roche Harbor, rowing the two miles or so to work and back each day in fair weather or storm.

"Dad" Chevalier also fished commercially. Once he was away from Spieden for three whole months, fishing in Alaska; "Ma" didn't like that very much, and neither did Ed. After that he went in for reef-netting closer to home — around Johns and Stuart, for example — and did so well at developing the technique islanders look on him as the local "father" of reef-net fishing.

When the family had outgrown the little log cabin Mary's father had built, Ed hauled in lumber and built a snug frame house not far away. Through the many years this little blue cottage on top of Spieden's highest hill was to be a never-failing

237

center of hospitality for friends and strangers alike, whether they came purposely to Spieden's shores through sociability or were blown there by storms, as sometimes happened.

One sunshiny, early-fall morning in 1919 a row-boat nosed somewhat awkwardly into Spieden Channel from San Juan's north shore, a stocky, ruddy-faced man at the sweeps opposite his pretty young wife of a few months. All about them were piled their few earthly belongings: clothes, a typewriter, a rented tent that was to serve as home until something more substantial turned up. It was the second time the pair had set out on this trip: the day before a contrary wind had turned them back. They had beached their boat for the night, but — uninitiated newcomers from back East they were — forgot to drag their craft above the reach of a rising tide. Boat and all had gotten a dunking, but now they were on their way again, laughing at their own foolishness. This time they were sailing over a gentler sea on which ducks bobbed lazily.

Their destination was a small dot of an isle the charts call Sentinel. Standing in close to Spieden it does indeed appear to be posted there, guarding one approach to Ed Chevalier's island kingdom. It rises sheer from the bay, timbered on the north and rock-bare to the south, in imitation of its big neighbor.

There is no harbor and the island has no water. It is hard to see how anyone would choose such an island to call home; but Farrar Burn (whose brother Bob was to make the bazooka famous when radio came along) and his wife, June, had sought just such a place. There they could "pull the ladder up after us and live, untroubled by anything." And it was the last island in the San Juans — perhaps in all America — still available for homesteading.

The Burns camped on their gumdrop-shaped island all through the autumn, with eyes only for themselves and the beauty about them. But other eyes were on them. And when chill winter winds

238

began to blow, "Dad" Chevalier looked down from the blue cottage perched on the heights of his domain and ordained that the young couple were to move to Spieden until spring. And they moved. As June would write later in her marvellous "unconventional autobiography," *Living High*, Ed Chevalier's word was a law one did not question.

It was the Chevaliers who saw that the Burns neither starved nor drowned during their cheechako years on Sentinel, who rescued them from the teeth of gales brashly ventured into, who taught them the island lore Ed had learned in his turn thirty years before on Stuart. And when the Burns' first son began to be born, at the height of an historic northeaster, it was Ed Chevalier who chopped ice from the deck of his boat so he could start the engine and go for the doctor. But meanwhile, Mary stayed with June — and delivered the baby herself before the medico arrived.

Perhaps it was the memory of hardships endured in their young years, and the wish to pass on a bit of the happiness and contentment the Islands had brought them. At any rate, taking people like the Burns under their protective wing was a way of life for the Chevaliers. But while those they befriended often appeared briefly on the scene only to fade from it again, it seemed the Chevaliers and their Spieden kingdom would go on forever. Nothing does, of course, and after a near half century on Spieden (more if you figure in some brief stays on neighboring Stuart, Johns, and Pearl) Ed and Mary Chevalier bowed to their years. They retired to a snug home at Friday Harbor, where both lived to a great age, surrounded by their many friends and any number of children, grandchildren and great-grandchildren, and uncountable memories.

15

THE HERMIT OF MATIA

To BE, LIKE EDWARD CHEVALIER, the respected "king" of an island empire; to live cut off from the world's woes by a rolling moat of salt water: that was the dream of yet another man — one who first saw the spring's blue gleam of San Juan inland seas long before the Chevaliers began their trek west from the Dakotas. It was June 4, 1883, when this solid, portly man with the look of the sea about him stood on the deck of the steamer *Evangel* plying between Orcas Island and Roche Harbor. He wore a full, but closely trimmed beard and looked younger than his forty-eight summers.

Upon arriving at Roche Harbor he looked about briefly, took in the rude dock with its clustered barrels ready for shipping, the scattering of outbuildings around one sizeable, solid-looking log structure, the masonry kilns to one side and, backgrounding everything, near high cliffs with their frequent outcropping of white, chalky stone.

He stepped ashore — for he was a passenger now, not a crewman — and strode purposefully up to the log building which proved to be the headquarters, dormitory, and mess-hall of the

Scurr Brothers' lime company. Rather grandly he announced his name: Philip Clayton Van Buskirk, on leave from the United States Navy; and asked to be put up for the night.

Philip Van Buskirk had followed the sea, on and off, since he was twelve. He enlisted in the Marines in 1846, just as the Mexican War was beginning, and served in that fracas as a drummer. Later he touched history when he sailed aboard a ship accompanying Commander Matthew Perry to the far-off and, at that time, still mysterious islands of Japan. (Their mission, which was successful, was to deliver — under arms, if need be — President Pierce's demands to the Emperor for an end to the oriental nation's haughty isolation.)

Van Buskirk left the sea occasionally — once he simply deserted, and again he went off to serve the South in the Civil War: he was captured by the North, exchanged, and discharged. But always he went back to the sea; and now for the past dozen years he had served as a mate in the Navy.

Yet Philip Van Buskirk was scarcely your typical nineteenth century sea dog. Introspective and studious — self-taught in subjects like mathematics, Latin and even Chinese — he considered his less learned shipmates as bores and shunned them. He had little respect for his officers, either, and disliked Navy discipline with a black hatred. He never married. He once carried a torch for the daughter of his commodore's secretary, but was barred from seeing her because of his inferior rank.

At forty-eight, Van Buskirk saw retirement not far over the horizon. He had purchased a farm on the Snohomish River, near present-day Everett, Washington, and there he spent his leaves; but what he really wanted was an island in the San Juans, and after all these years a wife, if possible, to share it with him.

He could do without the wife; the island he must have.

Accordingly Van Buskirk had taken passage to Roche Harbor, which was to be his base for making a systematic reconnoiter of the archipelago's northwest quarter. After some solitary explorations on nearby Pearl Island, he decided to get a guide, and hired Henry Perkins, pioneer settler of Henry Island, for the purpose; and about 2 p.m. of June 7 they set out from Roche Harbor in Perkins' boat.

By 5:30 they were off the north side of Stuart Island, but the current was too strong for them to row against, so they landed in a cove and had lunch until the tide slackened. They were headed for little James Island ("Satellite" on today's charts) at the opening of Prevost Harbor, and finally reached it toward dark. They bedded down beneath a canopy of stars, next a blazing beach fire, with Van Buskirk no doubt dreaming dreams of how sweet his life could be on an island like this one.

Next morning the two men tramped James from end to end but, finding no fresh water on the island, Van Buskirk reluctantly scratched James from his list. He scratched neighboring Johns, too, when he learned the ubiquitous Paul Hubbs and his current klootchman were encamped there in *de facto* possession.

There followed a pleasant little visit with the fisherman partners, Mordhorst and Hayes, on Stuart Island and then Van Buskirk and Perkins set off eastward toward Spieden.

The wind was rising and contrary, but by skillful use of sail and oars alike they made the north coast of the island and were circumnavigating it when squalls forced them to turn back and pass on its southern side, without landing, the island that would someday be Ed Chevalier's. But they learned that Spieden, too, was "spoken for" — by Robert Smith, the ex-British soldier and his wife. And roaming the island just then were Smith's dark-haired children, one of whom would be Ed Chevalier's wife eleven years hence.

Jones Island, lying between San Juan and Orcas and favoring the Orcas side, was the next subject of exploration; but while there were no inhabitants, there was no water either. So a dejected Van Buskirk had Perkins take him back to Roche Harbor, where he put up for another night at Scurrs' bunkhouse.

Early next day the determined sailor hiked across San Juan Island to Friday Harbor where he had breakfast (having found the bread unpalatable at the lime kiln) and arranged for passage on a sailboat to Waldron Island. Waldron was too large for Van Buskirk's purposes, and had eight settlers already esconced — one of whom, a sixty-year-old, deceptively mild-mannered fellow who looked and dressed like Buffalo Bill, was already a full-blown legend of the Pacific Northwest. His name was William "Blanket Bill" Jarman. Years before, as a young British soldier, Jarman had been captured by Indians on Vancouver Island and was ransomed by the Hudson's Bay Co. bigwig, James Douglas, a full decade before the San Juan pig brouhaha. The ransom was a stack of Hudson's Bay Company blankets, allegedly equal to the ransomee's height.

Jarman's fame stemmed primarily from that incident, but he was also noted for a lifetime filled with adventuresome exploits ranging from harmless chicanery and barroom brawling right up to homicide. Van Buskirk, perhaps, was unaware of all this as he sat talking intently with the gathered Waldronites, describing the island of his dreams, asking questions, getting advice. Quite guilelessly he told them where he would be searching next. He scarcely noticed old Blanket Bill, quietly taking in each word.

Van Buskirk's eyes were turned northward and eastward, and his immediate destination now was the reefy Sucia group of islands opposite Orcas' north shore. To reach them he bargained with an Orcas Islander of questionable reputation, "Colonel" Enoch May, who had a government contract to carry the mail between Orcas and Waldron. The "mail boat" turned out to be a smallish, leaking canoe, to which the sea-wise sailor was hesitant about confiding his substantial frame — until he reflected that the cagey Colonel was suspected of making his real living as a smuggler, and the vessel was probably a good deal more seaworthy than it looked. So he took a chance, and arrived safely the next day.

Sucia, too, he found occupied; so he pressed on to the next neighboring island on his circuit, the elongated, 145-acre gem called Matia. And here at last was just the island Van Buskirk had been dreaming of. He felt it in his bones, the moment he landed. There were several good harbors, clean, pebbly beaches, a spring that bubbled a stream of fresh, delicious water. And no settlers! Nobody at all on the island except the surly British Columbia Indian Skookum Tom, who — suspected of murders on both sides of the border — headquartered himself here so he could flee in either direction should the law of one country or the other come after him.

But Tom didn't worry Van Buskirk. What blasted his dreams was a paper, tacked to a stake, with the following

NOTICE

I, William Jarman, have this day taken possession of 160 acres of this island for the purpose of making a home. Dated June first (1) 1883.

Of course Jarman had raced over from Waldron, knowing Van Buskirk was on the way and that Matia was the one island still unoccupied that fit the questing sailor's desires. He posted the notice (the date was an outright fake) not really intending to settle, but hoping to turn a buck or two by convincing Van Buskirk he did, and selling him his "rights." It was a common enough trick; but Van Buskirk thought, naively, that Blanket Bill really wanted to live on Matia. Glumly he returned to Friday Harbor, and caught the first boat to the mainland, consumed in disappointment.

Van Buskirk went back to the sea, with periodic leaves spent at his Snohomish farm, but he couldn't get Matia Island out of his thoughts. So in 1889 he again took passage to the San Juans, this time putting up at the Orcas residence of "Colonel" May near Eastsound. Here he learned William Jarman had abandoned his phony claim as soon as he found out Van Buskirk wasn't taking the bait. After this a fellow named Weir had come along, squatted on Matia briefly and sold out for fifty dollars to a Swede named John Penson. Penson was an ex-sailor, too, who now lived on Matia and made his living fishing. Van Buskirk borrowed a skiff and rowed over to the island to see him, but no one was home.

Van Buskirk estimated Penson's improvements were worth around a hundred dollars, and resolved to make an offer to buy the man out. Unfortunately, though he spent most of a week determinedly chasing Penson all over Orcas Island, he exhausted his leave time without finding the man. Once again he had to turn his back on his island dream, and return brokenhearted to the mainland.

It was not until 1896 that Van Buskirk decided to visit the San Juans again, and this time because of a very odd thing that had happened. His retirement from the Navy had just come through and the ex-sailor, with his thoughts on the future, had become interested in spiritualism. While attending a seance he was confronted with a spectre which brought him a startling message. It claimed to be William Jarman who was urging him, from the world beyond, to revisit Matia where Van Buskirk would find valuable papers in an old cabin. Jarman's "spirit" told how he had been drowned when a boat capsized in 1891; that two white people — a man and his wife — now resided on Matia; and numerous other convincing details. All this sent Van Buskirk excitedly packing for his third trip to the Islands.

He got as far as Victoria when he learned that Blanket Bill, far from having perished in an overturned boat, was still respiring quite normally and living in Ferndale, north of Bellingham.

Van Buskirk's faith in the world of spirits was a bit shaken and he gave up any notion of finding valuable papers on Matia, but curiosity as to what had become of the dream island that might have been his led him to pay it one more visit. He found the island was now the home of a man who truly meant to stay put: Elvin Haworth Smith, a powerful, six-foot-plus Civil War veteran, one-time captain in the Union Army. Like Van Buskirk, Smith adored this little pearl of the San Juans, and he sympathized with the ex-sailor who came so near being its Crusoe. The two men met on Orcas, and Smith invited Van Buskirk to be his guest on the island for a month.

Elvin Smith had risen from a private in the ranks during the Great Rebellion and at war's end was a breveted captain in command of his company. But somehow the commission went unrecorded, an error that no amount of corresponding with all the bureaucrats in Washington City could correct. Smith never got over his bitterness at this turn of events, which sullied not only his reputation but the amount of a potential pension. Along with this disappointment there was an unhappy love affair, and the upshot of it all was that Smith left his Wisconsin home and headed West, to forget.

Smith did his forgetting first in Iowa, where he worked as a newspaperman. Later he became a travelling passenger agent for the Northern Pacific Railroad; and in due time arrived on the shores of Bellingham Bay, where he had a spate of sociability lasting at least long enough to serve as the first secretary of the Fairhaven Masonic Lodge.

At Fairhaven Smith fell in with a lawyer and the two cooked up a scheme to make a few dollars on a land speculation. It was rumored that the U.S. Government, which had reserved Matia Island as a possible lighthouse site, was going to release it for homesteading. The lawyer agreed to put up the money to buy out squatters who had prior rights on the island — a pair by the name of Evans and Lovering, who apparently bought Penson's improvements not long after Van Buskirk had hoped to do the same thing himself. All Smith had to do was move to Matia and live there, pretending to be a *bona fide* settler long enough to secure a homestead, after which the island could be sold at a pretty profit the two men would split. Technically the scheme was illegal, of course, but it was a common enough procedure that flourished wherever cheap government land went on sale. The idea appealed to Smith's recluse-like tendencies, and in April 1892, he transported his worldly goods to "Matty's" — as he pronounced it — sunny shores.

Within two years Smith had so fallen in love with the island no amount of money would have induced him to part with it. So he bought out his partner for $1150 (three times what the improvements were actually worth, Van Buskirk groaned in his diary) and settled down to spend the rest of his days there.

Matia is an island to make any man a poet. Just a mile long and a quarter wide, its shoreline includes quiet coves and sandy beaches on all sides. Inland a spring feeds what was, in Smith's day, a fetching dot of a lake, surrounded by groves of native trees growing in the unspoiled way: straight, high trunks, not cluttered with underbrush, only the clean inviting greensward filling the spaces beneath. Here and there lay a peculiarity of Matia's: large boulders of granite scattered about, as though sewn by a giant's hand to a prehistoric wind. Actually, they were brought down by the glaciers and left behind as a taunt to man's puniness.

Peace lay like a blanket over all of Matia. Any number of beauteous spots could have served as the site for Smith to build his home shelter; he selected one at the east end of a low central ridge, just under a sheer rocky bluff at the head of the island's southeastern harbor. Some earlier squatter had thrown up a rude log shack here, and Smith cunningly built on and around it a snug, neat, permanent dwelling.

From this haven Smith looked out on as precious an expanse of islet-studded sea as can be imagined. Nearest at hand, just to the east of Matia lay, like the tiny period to a fat exclamation

point, diminutive Puffin Island (Smith called it "Little Matia").
Too barren for humans, it was home only for the playful seals
which convened there by thousands, and noisy gulls wheeling
down to lay their great, speckled eggs on any least excuse for a
ledge or crevice. And there were other birds: raucous bitterns
and big-billed sea parrots mingling with the more common shags
and ducks. Sea lettuce grows thick in beds between Matia and
Puffin, and each spring Indians from Canada used to come
sliding down in their long, graceful canoes and collect this,
together with gull eggs and other delicacies.

Nearby the southeast harbor of Matia stretched long and
narrow, and shallow — just a fathom or so at low tide — and
across its entrance Smith could keep a net stretched in order to
capture all the cod and salmon he could use. While a short
distance upland he cleared a plot of five acres or so, fenced and
cultivated it, put in a kitchen garden and orchard. He stocked
the island with sheep, chickens and rabbits (and was sorry for it
later when the island came to be overrun by the latter).

Oddly, Smith was opposed to killing animals and did not keep
them for their meat. His chickens provided him with eggs, and
the sheep presumably yielded their wool; what the rabbits were
for is a bit of a mystery.

Soon after his coming, islanders universally took to calling
Smith "the hermit of Matia Island." Even the county newspaper
put it just that way in type, and Smith himself cheerfully owned
up to the description. Yet he was not all that antisocial. In fact,
he hadn't been on Matia long before feeling some pangs of
lonesomeness. It was then that he invited an old crony of his
from Civil War days and before, John B. Vliet, to come visit
his island paradise. Vliet, who had mustered out of the Rebellion
as a lieutenant colonel, accepted the offer and moved in for an
indefinite stay.

It seems the two men had practically grown up together, and
were virtual foster brothers. That may be so, but after a year or

more of each other's exclusive company the pair found themselves wrangling a good deal over which was the greatest general on the Union side of the War, after which Colonel Vliet and Captain Smith said their strained good-byes. Vliet boarded with an Orcas family for some years and finally went back to Wisconsin.

Now Van Buskirk was guesting on Matia, where the two men found they had much in common, including an interest in matters metaphysical. Smith's notions rarely coincided with those of any established religion, but he did believe in the efficacy of prayer for healing the sick. His hobby, if it may be called that, was putting this belief to work. Each morning about four, the one-time Union Army captain arose and went quietly about his devotions; he believed that was the best time for prayer, as "the earth is quietest then."

The beneficiaries of Smith's lengthy matins were scattered at great distances about the country and all were complete strangers to him. They suffered from sundry ills and through some mysterious grapevine had learned of Smith's reputation as a long-distance faith healer, so wrote him imploring letters asking to be included on his prayer list. Smith made the long trip to Orcas Island regularly every Saturday to collect these missives, and brought them home literally by the water-bucket full. Occasionally he received cash or checks as well, from grateful "patients" who were convinced Smith's intercessions were responsible for their improved health.

Van Buskirk accompanied Smith on these weekly journeys to Eastsound during his month's stay. The two would push off from Matia's southeast harbor in the captain's smallish rowboat and head for Point Thompson, with Smith at the oars and Van Buskirk steering with a paddle at the stern. They made the two-and-a-half mile trip in about an hour and a half when the wind was calm and the tide favorable, tying up on Orcas' North Shore in a small cove near the home of Roger Cockrell. (Cockrell is still remembered on Orcas as the man who tried to shingle his cabin roof starting at the ridgepole.)

From Cockrell's the pair walked a wooded trail two miles to the Eastsound post office. This establishment had just recently moved to its own building next to the Episcopal church, a few rods up the street from Charles Shattuck's store-and-dance-hall which had housed it since pioneer days. Luther Sutherland, whose father, Walter, had succeeded Shattuck as guardian of Uncle Sam's post, was now in command. (Walter Sutherland was an otherwise respectable man whose single vice, a penchant for reading his patrons' postal cards, led one Eastsounder — linguist Richard Geoghegan — to correspond in Volapuk.)

Other than these Saturday journeys to Orcas Island's Buck Bay metropolis for mail and supplies, and evenings spent in the comfort of armchairs before an open fire, or sprawled by a roaring driftwood blaze on the beach, when they would refight the old Civil War battles or trade spine-numbing yarns of the supernatural, Smith and his guest spent most of their time tramping the woods and shores of the captain's island hermitage. Van Buskirk revelled in each detail — perhaps even in the captain's vegetarian menu; but then he was eating his heart out too, in envy and regret that he was the one who would shortly be leaving, and his six-foot host the one who would remain. How he wished it were the other way around! How he cussed old "Blanket Bill" for the mean trick that cost him his island, his very happiness! How he railed at the Fate which kept him from finding that Swede fisherman, Penson, and buying him out when he had the chance. Ruefully the stocky ex-sailor wished for a way to stretch a month into forever.

But inevitably there came a day when Smith's little skiff nosed once more into the quiet cove by George Cockrell's cabin (its shingles relaid now in the more conventional style, one hopes). This time the two shook hands and parted, Smith returning to his "Matty," and Van Buskirk bound for the mainland.

Three years later the portly sailor was back in the San Juans on another visit to Stuart, to the Chevalier home on Spieden, and to Smith on Matia. But these were only social calls, one last bittersweet revel of rubbing shoulders with men living the kind of life he always wanted for himself, but was never to achieve. The fact is that Van Buskirk was a sailor who had missed the boat. Four years later he would be dead, in Bremerton, Washington, at the age of sixty-nine.

Elvin Smith, whose years numbered just about the same as his deceased friend's, continued his hermit-like life on the island of Van Buskirk's dreams for many more summers and winters. Even in his eighties it seemed his strength and energy would never fail him. With a fellow Civil War veteran, George Carrier of Orcas, Smith used to joke half-seriously that he was planning to be the oldest living survivor of that conflict. His habits remained unchanged, except that he finally discarded his oars for one of those new-fangled Evinrudes, and his Saturday visits to Orcas became a bit less regular.

It was because of this fact that, late in 1920, Eastsounders were slow to spread the alarm when Smith failed to put in an appearance for a long time. Finally two of his friends, W. F. Jarman (no relation to Blanket Bill) and George Sutherland, went over to Matia to see what was what.

They found the elderly gentleman in a most dangerous situation. An early-winter storm had torn his one and only boat from its moorings, dashed it against the rocks and smashed it to kindling. For 72 days Smith had been more of a hermit than even he wished for. His groceries had all given out early on. After that he had lived on eggs laid by his chickens; but these were so few, and Smith was growing so hungry, he in desperation discarded his vegetarian scruples and began butchering the hens one by one. (How his source of delicacies from the sea also chanced to fail him at this time is not recorded: perhaps the same storm that destroyed his boat ruined the net.)

After this near-tragic experience Jarman and others tried to persuade Smith to give up his seclusion and stay with them on Orcas — at least for the winter. Smith refused. As a compromise he agreed to have a house-guest again, and his friend from the days of the Great Rebellion, George Carrier, was elected to accompany him home to "Matty."

It was one of those winters when storms trailing one another down the coast from Alaska brought almost continual gales. Smith and Carrier were wind-bound much of the time, and by mid-February the larder was again dangerously low. But it is a meteorological phenomenon in the San Juans that February often sees a long spell of calm, sunny weather. And so when it appeared the series of southeast blows was at last slacking a bit, the two men piled into Smith's new flat-bottomed boat with the two-and-a-half horse outboard and started for Orcas. They were heading for R. H. Anthony's place on North Beach, where Carrier had been a boarder before moving to Matia.

Anthony heard the boat coming and went down to the beach anxiously to see them ashore. The winds were still plenty fresh and the water was corrugated with angry black swells. It seemed there might not be a lull in the gales, after all.

Smith and Carrier landed safely, borrowed a wagon and headed for town with their long, long grocery list. Shortly afterward they came trudging back with as much stuff as they figured the little skiff would hold. Meanwhile the southeaster was kicking up again and the Anthonys urged the pair to stay with them until the weather improved, which they wisely decided to do.

It was many days before the long-awaited calm actually materialized. During the enforced visit, Smith at last rather grudgingly admitted that perhaps he was getting a little too old for Matia, and ought to build himself a little cabin on Orcas to spend his remaining years in — an idea that met with his friends' relieved approval.

On Wednesday, February 23, the winds softened finally to a dead calm which left the water flat and smooth off Orcas' north shore. Anthony helped Smith and Carrier haul their provisions down to the beach and load them into the captain's skiff, jamming canned goods and odds and ends of small items into the spaces around the large boxes, cans and bottles that nearly filled the whole boat. When the two men took their places on the thwarts their heavily-laden craft settled even more deeply into the water. The freeboard looked alarmingly scant. But a glance at the salt chuck's glassy surface seemed reassurance enough that the crossing could be safely made.

Smith observed, however, that the tide was contrary at the moment and proposed to wait for the change. Anthony was dubious. But they said their good-byes and then Smith and Carrier went to a nearby friend's home where they played a few hands of cards to pass the time. The game got hot, the players' whole attention was on their cards, and when several hours had passed they found the tide had changed, but the wind had come up again, too.

The two Matia dwellers returned to the skiff as Anthony, more apprehensive than ever, appeared behind them on the beach. But Smith yanked the outboard into life and waved to him confidently. Then he edged the boat off the shore and set a course east, vectoring the tide he knew would shortly drift him northward to his destination.

Anthony remained at the water's edge watching the heavily loaded skiff bobbing on the swells, listening to the put-put of its receding motor. The late hour had laid a gathering gloom of darkness over the water and after a few minutes the boat was only a dim distant smudge of black against the gray haze. Beyond it the indistinct line of a tide rip was the farthest thing he could see. Approaching that line, the little smudge rose and fell

253

with the chop, disappearing momentarily at the bottom of each descent behind the growing swells. Then the smudge, line, and haze seemed to merge at once into gray nothingness. At the same moment the far sound of the outboard also passed over the threshold separating the heard from the unheard. Anthony pressed his ear to the ground but he still could make out no sounds but those of the sea and the wind.

For a time Anthony's concern that the boat might have swamped in the tide rip alternated with his reluctance to raise an alarm unnecessarily. Finally he went to the telephone and reported what he had seen to the Coast Guard at Friday Harbor.

Unfortunately, their cutter was out of the area for the day.

Next morning Captain William Harnden, of Sucia Island, came to Orcas and hearing of the matter agreed to run over to Matia and see if its two inhabitants were safe. A signal was arranged: three blasts of his boat's whistle would mean the men had not arrived; no signal would mean all was well.

Harnden arrived at Matia and saw no sign of Smith's boat in its usual moorage. He landed, and found nobody at Smith's house. Although it had rained heavily the night before, leaving the shore muddy, no tracks could be seen leading from the water. Fearing the worst, Harnden returned to his vessel and gave three long pulls on the whistle cord.

A Coast Guard search of the whole area revealed not one clue to the fate of the two elderly islanders. Some days later a five-gallon can of kerosene — part of their over-generous cargo — washed ashore on Sucia. And in the spring, at Gray's Point near the Canadian border, some Indians happened upon a piece of a wrecked boat in the sand. Smith's rusty outboard motor, still attached to it, confirmed their tragic fate at last.

There are three graves on Matia's verdant shores. Each holds the mortal clay of a person unknown, a victim of the seas whom the seas also washed ashore, there to await Heaven's last trump. Elvin Smith is not one of these, nor is George Carrier; their bodies were never found. Government gravestones have been placed at Orcas' Mount Baker cemetery in honor of these two gentle men who once bore arms for their country. But the graves beneath them are empty.

The government never did open Matia to homesteaders. In 1936 it was assigned to the Department of Agriculture and designated a bird refuge. Foxes were raised there for a time, and one or two people have lived on the island for brief periods. Currently Matia is a Washington State marine park, by agreement with the federal government. Thus no one before or after him has been so closely identified with the island as "Matty's" pioneer hermit, and probably no one ever will.

16

SMUGGLERS AND OTHER GENTLEMEN

G LEN TULLOCH, ORCAS ISLAND'S
perceptive wit of pioneer days, once observed that the business of
smuggling was "reputable or otherwise in proportion to your
distance from the border." Certainly many of the early islanders
found it not only reputable but plain common sense to sell their
produce wherever they could get the most for it, and buy what
they needed where the costs were lowest, even if it meant hauling
goods back and forth across an invisible international boundary
line. That the practice contravened the customs laws of one or
both of the countries involved (unless, of course, one were foolish
enough to stop at the customs house and shell out most of the
savings in duty) was considered a typical bit of governmental
foolishness scarcely worth noting. Or as another Puget Sounder
of the era put it, "smuggling is a species of law-breaking over
which the Ten Commandments have no jurisdiction."

Of course, there was the sinister aspect. Much of the troubles
of British and American camp commanders alike during the joint
occupation was traceable to the wholesale importation of illicit
liquor — a traffic that would persist in the area, only reaching its

256

peak with the American experiment of Prohibition some seventy years later.

Not only booze but Canadian silks and wool were commodities which commanded better prices in the States than north of the line, and any number of enterprising dwellers of the border area saw fit to turn that fact to their profit from time to time. They did so with only the barest risk of being detected in this form of larceny, the revenue boats being too few and too slow in those days to pose much of a threat. On the other hand, the money to be made was not particularly spectacular, for the difference in price on these items was rather modest.

It was not until the introduction into the Pacific Northwest of large numbers of Chinese laborers that the opportunity for real profits in the smuggling line came along. The first of the Chinese — contemptuously referred to as "Celestials" by those whose ancestors hailed from an opposite direction — entered the country in a straightforward manner and went to work cheaply at unskilled jobs like building railroads or in canneries. Many were opium smokers, thus creating a huge market for that drug, on which the United States placed an import tax of $12 per pound, presumably to discourage use of the stuff. Canada took a different attitude, and not only imposed no duty on opium, but permitted factories in both Victoria and Vancouver to turn out huge quantities of the drug — all perfectly legal north of the border, but contraband the moment it passed to the Yankee side.

In 1882 Congress responded to the anti-Chinese sentiment of its West Coast citizenry — who felt that 300,000 "Celestials" was enough — by promulgating the Chinese Exclusion Act, making the further importation of Oriental laborers illegal, though those already here were allowed to stay. (Except in Tacoma, where lynch mobs summarily loaded the "Chinks" onto a Portland-bound train and then burned the Chinese quarter of town to the ground; similar measures were attempted in Seattle, but were only partially successful; but that is another story.)

257

Nevertheless thousands of Chinese still in the homeland who dreamed of joining their relatives or friends in the American promised land took passage to British Columbia and, once arrived, were perfectly willing to pay from $100 up to anyone who would take them across the border and deposit them safely on U.S. soil.

Thus was the stage set for the golden age of smuggling on Puget Sound, and once again the San Juan Islands — due to their strategic location practically astride the border — found themselves in the center of that stage, playing host to chief actors like Jim "Pig-Iron" Kelly and Larry "Smuggler" Kelly, Bill "Old Man" Jamieson, and Henry Ferguson, better known as "the Flying Dutchman."

The two Kellys were often confused in newspaper stories, and still are in the legends they left behind. They were not related, and differed markedly in the way they plied their craft. Larry was known up and down the Sound as "king" of the smuggling fraternity, apparently because he was heard of the most — the reason being that he got caught so often! Nevertheless, his fame remains such that whenever the roster of Puget Sound *contrabandistas* is called, it is his name which generally heads the list.

Lawrence Kelly was born about 1839, of Irish parents, probably in that country or in England. As a youth he served a hitch in the British army, later became a deep-water sailor. After seeing a good deal of the world he chanced to put in at New Orleans just as the Civil War was erupting. Kelly left his ship and joined a Confederate outfit, the "Louisiana Tigers," with which he fought up to the moment of Lee's surrender on April 9, 1865. He then left the South, reputedly vowing he would "never earn an honest living under the stars and stripes," and returned to the sea.

Later the same year Kelly arrived on the inland waters of the Pacific Northwest aboard the vessel *Young America*. Almost immediately he was attempting his first smuggling caper, sneaking a batch of Canadian silks across to the Washington mainland.

He was promptly caught, and the offense cost him $500 — but without dissuading him from his new-found vocation.

A decade or so later found Kelly living on the southwestern bulge of Guemes Island, across from Anacortes, with his wife, an Indian woman named Lizzie Kotz. There he supported himself and his tawny bride with profits gleaned by hauling a miscellany of contraband items from place to place on the Sound. Those being the days of scant interference from the undermanned revenue service, Kelly used an ordinary fishing sloop in his work, not even bothering to change the bright red paint job which characterized it — and made it quite visible from a great distance away. On those rare occasions when he was spotted by the customs men, he was generally able to outrun his pursuers, or elude them among the Sound's numberless bays and channels, all of which he had come to know like a familiar book. If all else failed, the outlaw goods were dumped overboard at the last moment, for without them, there could be no conviction.

Kelly always stuck to sail in his work and has been called the most skillful small-boat handler on Puget Sound. A crony recalled how the smuggler king would grease his craft with pot black and tallow to cut its resistance in the water.

Those were the days of the revenue cutter *Oliver Wolcott*, a lumbering old tub with a top speed of four knots. Given any wind at all, Kelly's sloop could sail faster than the *Wolcott* could steam, and could navigate in passages too narrow, or water too shallow, for the government vessel to follow.

Eventually, determined revenue officers fitted out one of the *Wolcott*'s small boats with sail, and laid for Kelly. A witness to the encounter which followed left this account of what happened:

"The revenue boat was pretty smart before the wind and there was a smart wind and a freshening sea up in the San Juans. Kelly came bowling down the channel at a great clip. The revenue boat shot out from the little bay where they were watching for [him].

"He was pretty close up on the revenue hiding place when the little boat shot out but it never feased him. He put his helm hard over and swung up into the wind. He just turned tail like a scared jack rabbit and the way that little sloop of his went flying back toward the north was a sight to see.

"Kelly had a boat that would sail into the eye of the wind or just as close to it as anything afloat will sail and he knew how to handle her. She buried her nose in the seas at times till you couldn't see anything but white smother, but she made better weather of it than the revenue boat. Gradually Kelly drew away and the revenue men sailed back into port, sore all over."

Kelly's come-uppance came at last one cold, foggy December night in 1882. Deputy Customs Inspector Thomas Caine learned one of the smuggler-king's tricks was to sneak his boat along the shoals of Swinomish Slough, near LaConner, in the early morning. So Caine staked himself out in the slough and waited quietly. But the wily Irishman must have suspected something, for as he approached the place where Caine was stationed he slipped overboard into shallow water and began pushing the light boat ahead of him, as soundlessly as possible.

Caine heard some faint splashing sounds and suddenly the smuggler's craft loomed out of the fog almost in front of him. The inspector pulled a large service revolver, pointed it and shouted, "I've got you, Kelly!"

"All right," said the king of smugglers. "Put up your iron. I'm your prisoner."

Kelly's cargo this trip was $400 worth of illegal Chinese wine. Worse still, he had a Chinaman aboard, contrary to the months-old Exclusion Act. Fortunately for him, the man was able to convince a judge that he was not a coolie, but a merchant doing business in Portland.* Kelly got off with a $150 fine.

---

* To avoid being classed as laborers, many Chinese attached themselves to small businesses, some of which numbered their owning "partners" in the dozens.

This was a pittance to Kelly, who was doing so well that a few years later he bought up a 320-acre spread on Sinclair Island, also known as Cottonwood, on the eastern edge of the San Juans. The property (prudently placed in wife Lizzie's name) comprised a third of the island, where Kelly — in spite of his profession, if not actually because of it — was considered a citizen of great uprightness and was even elected to the school board.

Kelly's place was on the northwest shore of Cottonwood, where he had a commanding view of the Strait of Georgia, and Canada beyond, which helped him keep tabs on the customs vessels. He was now specializing in the importing of opium, and his usual practice was to haul the drug in relays. After purchasing it at one of fourteen licensed refineries in Victoria, he would head for Cottonwood and bury the stuff somewhere along the beach or on his farm. When the time seemed right he dug up one or more of the caches and headed for Port Townsend, a favorite destination, or Seattle, or elsewhere, and disposed of the drug to an agent for the standard $12-a-pound fee.

Years later, when he had fallen on hard times, residents of Cottonwood used to see him poking about there, hoping to find in some old hiding place a forgotten packet that could be converted into a few needed dollars.

Meanwhile, the customs service was becoming decidedly more aggressive in their war on contrabanders. Gradually, with more manpower and faster boats on the Sound, Kelly and his confreres found themselves being overhauled and searched more and more frequently. Of course, they responded by becoming foxier. Larry Kelly took to tying his opium in a weighted sack and trailing it, submerged, on a line fastened to a ring-bolt under the hull of his boat. Ultimately inspectors caught onto this stunt, and routinely "keel-hauled" suspected smuggling craft. Or, if pursued too closely by the revenue cutter, Kelly would sometimes anchor his cargo to a float and return for it when the coast had cleared.

The cynical mishandling of human contraband became rather

prevalent, with the smuggler-king getting his share of the blame, though there is some doubt whether Larry Kelly went in much for that end of the business. Once a band of Chinese were put off "temporarily" on a lonesome rock in San Juan Channel when the revenue boat was bearing down, but the man who collected their fares never came back for them. They were discovered days later by Reverend T. J. Weekes, emaciated and barely subsiding on clams on a reef which has been called "China Rock" ever since.

Another dodge of those days was to set out from Vancouver Island under cover of fog and, if the revenue boat was known to be in the neighborhood (or even if it wasn't), sail around the Canadian islands a while and land the unsuspecting Chinese passengers — who had, of course, paid in advance — exactly where they started from.

Credit for the increasing competency of the revenue service on Puget Sound goes chiefly to a business-like, clean-shaven son of the famous evangelist, Reverend Henry Ward Beecher. Herbert Foote Beecher began steamboating as a deck-hand on the East Coast, achieving his master's papers in just four years. Ultimately he migrated to Oregon and then to Washington, where in 1883 he purchased the gospel ship *Evangel* (built two years previously as a mission ship) and put her on the mail run between Townsend and the San Juans. In 1885 President Grover Cleveland, in payment of a political debt to Beecher's dad, appointed him Customs Collector of the Puget Sound District.

Beecher brought more to the post than his characteristic energy and a righteous impulse to do his job well. For two years he had been rubbing shoulders and yarning with the Sound's seafaring fraternity, among whom the exploits of men like Kelly were discussed openly and in damning detail, so that he now had a good deal of practical knowledge of their operations. The vigorous efficiency with which he used such information in combatting the smuggling racket led to the seizure, in a little over a year, of more than $150,000 worth of opium alone, whereas the seizures, fines and forfeitures exacted in the District during all the preceding fifteen years only amounted to some $30,000.

Beecher personally seized one opium shipment worth the latter amount in a single operation. For he had determined not only to go after independent operators like Kelly, but to bear down on several large steamship companies that were augmenting their legitimate earnings by importing goods whose description never appeared on a manifest. In this case Beecher raced a suspected freighter in the *Wolcott*, piloting the old tub himself and browbeating the engineer into getting more speed out of her than was ever done before, or since. Beecher won the race and the drug shipment he confiscated was the largest ever seized by the Service to that time.

With this sort of activity threatening their profits, owners of the steamship companies brought political pressure to bear and Beecher's appointment, which was subject to confirmation in the U.S. Senate, failed to be confirmed. An angered President Cleveland promptly reappointed Beecher a special agent of the Treasury Department — a post not requiring senate approval — and charged him with the continued suppression of smuggling on Puget Sound.

A few years later there was a change of administration and Beecher again found himself out of a job. For a time he tried to run a general shipping business at Port Townsend, but a lack of good will from key quarters, plus a habit his ships and wharves developed of catching fire, ended the venture. In one of the area's greatest comedowns, Beecher finally went back on Uncle Sam's payroll — as a pilot on board the *Wolcott*.

It was during the Beecher era that Larry Kelly began to find himself enmeshed with increasing regularity in the law's toils. Every customs man on the Sound had an eye out for him. His over-water movements were closely watched and reported by telegraph. Even Canadian authorities were cooperating in the effort to check-mate his operations. The king of smugglers was making the acquaintance of jails from Victoria to Tacoma, and the increasing fines he paid for his infractions threatened to make him a poor man.

Kelly's frequent tactic in those days was to land up-Sound in an unlikely spot and go on by railroad to his ultimate destination. He usually got away with it, but there was a time early in 1891 when he picked the wrong train. Special Agent Charles Mulkey of Tacoma and an Inspector Fox, of Portland, were passengers on board the Portland-bound rattler when Kelly boarded it at Tenino, carrying a large, brownish, new-looking grip. Mulkey strolled into the smoking car, recognized Kelly and became suspicious of the bag. He opened it and found sixty-five half-pound cans of illegal opium.

Mulkey took the protesting Irishman into custody, along with Kelly's seat-mate, a bewildered gentleman named George Davis, whom Mulkey needed as a witness. Mulkey transferred his prisoners to a north-bound train at Castle Rock and had Kelly before a U.S. Commissioner the same day in Tacoma.

Kelly always maintained Mulkey "jobbed" (framed) him by planting the contraband under his seat when he was in the wash room. The judge wasn't buying any such yarn and handed the smuggler king a ticket good for two years in the institution on McNeil Island, which had now become a U.S. penitentiary.

The Sinclair Island populace, however, who owned Kelly as a smuggler but never knew him to be a liar, believed his story. They got up a petition to have him pardoned, but the effort was unsuccessful.

It was just the beginning of Kelly's hard-luck streak. Two days after his arrest, customs men raided his island home and confiscated his boat. The following year a small son of his drowned tragically in a shallow well on Sinclair. Newspapers took to printing lurid stories about Kelly, naming him "head and front" of a "smuggling ring." Yet money was a serious problem, too: to support his family during his enforced absence, he was obliged to mortgage his island property.

"When I came out the panic was on and I could not raise the money to pay the mortgage, so I lost my home," Kelly stated years later. "Just think of the head and front of a smuggling ring not being able to raise $500."

Actually the Kelly property was sold off in 1896 to the proprietor of a Bellingham newspaper. The family moved to Anacortes where Lizzie took a job in order to support her offspring. Relations between the Kellys grew gradually more strained and finally they all "scattered," as Kelly phrased it.

Still Kelly pursued his chosen occupation with an obstinacy that seems almost admirable. Picked up with $800 worth of opium as he stepped off a steamer in Portland in 1902, he served several months in a county lock-up there. Two years later he was spotted on a train not far from the Canadian border with another satchel-full of the drug on him; that time he leaped from the train, while it was moving at full speed, to escape capture. He was picked up later, still lying unconscious by the trackside, charged, and released on bail.

Kelly jumped the bail as promptly as he had jumped the train and went right back into business.

The following June, Inspectors Fred Dean and Fred King of the revenue service got a tip-off that Kelly had started up-Sound with another load of opium. They took a government gas launch, rigged it to look like a private fishing boat and started patrolling the waters between Seattle and lower Vashon Island. After several days of this they sighted their quarry, running placidly through the Tacoma Narrows, under sail as usual.

Dean and King set a course to intercept him. They did so just as Kelly came abreast of McNeil Island — an omen not unlikely to have escaped any of the actors of this little drama. Kelly grabbed for his oars and tried briefly to elude the inspectors, but the days when he could outrun any customs craft afloat were gone. Glumly he surrendered and remarked to his captors, who were surprised at the small amount of opium on board, that it was all he could afford.

Still it was enough to earn him another stretch at McNeil, the prison doors not reopening for him until March 18, 1907. Even then they didn't stay open long. As Kelly stepped through the gate a waiting U.S. marshal clapped a hand on one shoulder and hauled him straight off to jail in Seattle for an earlier offense — the one he had jumped bail to avoid. The next several years saw his address alternating yo-yo-like between the King County calaboose and the federal one on McNeil Island.

By the time he had his freedom again Kelly was a beaten old man in his seventies who felt it was an auspicious time to retire. It is said he bought a one-way ticket to Louisiana (financed, perhaps, by one last cruise *sub rosa* to Victoria and back, if a 1911 item in the San Juan *Islander* is any clue) and lived out his years quietly in a Confederate soldiers' home.

The legend persists that in his heyday, Larry Kelly once hauled a load of Orientals into the States via the San Juans and, when about to be overtaken by a pursuing revenue boat, dumped his luckless passengers overboard as unconcernedly as he would deep-six any other form of contraband.* Whether the incident occurred at all is problematical; Kelly himself denied that he ever took or endangered life, and his friends held divided opinions about it.

Such an exploit would, however, be in keeping with the career of Larry's namesake, Jim "Pig-Iron" Kelly. "Pig-Iron" (also known as "Red" though his hair and beard suggested that hue only slightly) served his smuggling apprenticeship on the Maine

* The place where the grisly deed was supposedly done is variously claimed to be Peavine Pass, north of Blakely Island; Pole Pass, between Orcas and Crane; or the narrow passage separating Barnes and Clark Islands, between Orcas and Lummi.

266

coast where he dealt mostly in illegal whisky. When things got too warm for him he transmigrated to Alaska for a change of temperature, earning his bread there by the illicit peddling of spirits to the natives.

When "Pig-Iron" arrived on Puget Sound in the late 'eighties he earned his unique nick-name — not by weighting the bodies of Chinese "passengers" on his smuggling forays, as is often supposed, but through the imaginative theft of some ingots from the Irondale smelter, near Port Townsend.

Jim spent the bulk of his time north of the border, where Canadian officials considered him a B.C. resident. But he was a familiar figure on San Juan as well, and had many acquaintances — if not actual confederates — on that island. He catered to his friends by keeping them supplied with Canadian booze and other notions, and they reciprocated by providing meals and beds as the occasion arose.

Kelly spoke frankly of his dealings in contraband, which were no secret to customs officials; but as one of his contemporaries put it, "the trick was to catch him at it." It has been claimed that in twenty years' time every customs man and revenue cutter on the Sound had chased him at least once.

Up to the turn of the century "Pig-Iron" always managed to elude capture or, if boarded, no evidence of wrongdoing was ever apparent beyond an occasional Oriental-style cigarette butt. Once an arrest warrant was issued for him at Port Townsend and an official dispatched to Friday Harbor to look for Kelly — who happened to be on his sloop in that very harbor when the officer arrived. But friends of "Pig-Iron" hustled him inland and secreted him until the officer's departure. Shortly afterward the island's deputy customs collector discovered him asleep on a boat at the north end of Henry Island but, not knowing of the warrant, merely poked around a bit looking for contraband and let him go.

In the early summer of 1902 frustrated customs officials tried a new tack. Suspecting "Pig-Iron" was about due for another trip, they sent a whole covey of inspectors off to Victoria with orders to keep their quarry under observation, follow as he departed with his next load, and apprehend him when inside U.S. waters. But the wily Kelly, who was wise to the shadowing, remained a picture of saintly circumspection. After several weeks the inspectors had exhausted their expense accounts — those being the days of niggardly funding of government agencies — and the operation was called off.

The inspectors had scarcely arrived back in Port Townsend when telegraphic word was received that Kelly was on his way Stateside with a load of Chinese, probably intending to land them at Townsend. The cutter *Grant* and launch *Guard* were promptly ordered out to patrol on a line stretching from Mosquito Pass to Smith Island, in the hope of spotting Kelly's craft.

Meanwhile the deputy collector of customs at Roche Harbor, O. H. Culver (whom we shall meet again in his capacity as editor of the San Juan *Islander*) had reported to the Port Townsend office that Kelly was particularly chummy lately with a certain farmer in the San Juan Valley, and that his boat had more than once been seen moored nearby in Kanaka Bay. Inspectors Thomas Delaney — who had spent his own boyhood on San Juan, his family having arrived there during the joint occupation — and Steve Brinker were dispatched from Seattle. The pair were on the island when word came of Kelly's sortie.

Scouting the Kanaka Bay shoreline Delaney had noticed in a tree overhanging the water an iron staple such as might be used to tie up a small boat. On a hunch, Delaney stationed himself near the tree while Brinker waited at a point farther up the coast.

It was a disagreeable stake-out: the July evening was dark and rainy. But toward eight o'clock Delaney was rewarded by the sight of a long, narrow, black-painted skiff, moving soundlessly through the murk toward the very spot where he stood concealed.

In another minute the boat touched the beach almost at his toes.

"Hello Jim," Delaney said quietly. The two men had met before. "I guess you're up against it this time."

"Hello, is that you, Tom?" replied Kelly. "I guess I am, all right."

"How many have you got?" the customs man queried.

"Six, the sons of bitches. Go down and wake 'em up." For the half-dozen Orientals were in the round bottom of Kelly's canoe-like craft, slumbering peacefully in the sure and certain hope of awakening in the American promised land.

Kelly's passengers were returned to Victoria's Chinatown instead, and "Pig-Iron" was sent to sojourn in the McNeil Island clink for a year.

Some months after his release from that institution Kelly walked into Delaney's office in Seattle, where the former inspector was now Chief of Police. The two chatted a bit and then Kelly asked for a loan of a dollar, promising to pay it back the next day. Delaney laughed. "I've just got a photograph of you, bringing that dollar back, Jim," he said. But he shelled out the cartwheel, just the same.

"Oh, I'll bring it back all right," said Kelly, and sure enough he returned the next day and fished up a dollar from a pocket bulging with gold twenties, leaving Delaney to wonder just what form of larceny had parlayed his buck into so much wealth.

Not that Kelly had forsaken his former occupation, as customs officials had occasion to suspect, and his movements were again placed under stringent scrutiny. Any number of ingenious traps were set to catch him, but none succeeded.

A lack of speedy communications was often a chief factor in these failures, as with other unsuccessful operations of the service. At length the Treasury Department moved to install newfangled Marconi wireless telegraph apparatus at Port Townsend and on the larger revenue vessels. The cutter *Grant* was the first to be so equipped, and in 1904 she made a shake-down cruise around

269

the Sound, with high dignitaries of the government on board sending test messages like:

REVENUE CUTTER GRANT AND OFFICIALS TOUCHED AT BLAINE TODAY. NO NEWS OF ANY IMPORTANCE IN LATEST PAPERS SEEN. ALL WELL, BUT THE COLLECTOR SNORED WORSE THAN USUAL LAST NIGHT.

The radios were a great success, and gave the customs service a decisive advantage over men like Jim Kelly. Indeed it was only a short time before a revenue boat, dispatched to intercept "Pig-Iron" himself, came in sight of Kelly's little craft as it entered Scow Bay, near Seattle, loaded to the gunwales with illegal opium.

Jubilant customs men were almost within boarding distance when Kelly leaped suddenly from his boat, swam furiously for shore and disappeared dripping into the forest.

By the time the inspectors got ashore to search the area Kelly had disappeared utterly. All they could discover, lurking suspiciously nearby, was a mustachioed, barrel-chested individual who spoke like an Englishman and had the manner of a seafaring man. It was pretty obvious the big fellow had spirited their quarry away but there was no way to prove it, and the disgruntled customs men had to content themselves with confiscating Kelly's boat and its illegal cargo.

The broad-shouldered Englishman was actually Jim "Old Man" Jamieson, another adherent of the Sound's close-knit smuggling fraternity. Jamieson had shipped on square-riggers before he joined the club, and rivaled Larry Kelly in his boat-handling ability. But Jamieson was shrewder, and certainly more audacious, reputedly disdaining to land his Chinese passengers at some hidden, exurban rendezvous: it is said he sailed right into Seattle and discharged his human cargo at Schwabacher's dock, like the other freighters.

Jamieson always painted his boat green, to blend with the coastline if seen from a distance. But customs men on the *Grant* spotted it one bright, chilly February day, just as the Englishman set his course from Victoria to San Juan Island. He had crossed the boundary line before he discovered the *Grant* was steaming toward him for all it was worth.

Jamieson had a near-record load of opium on board and didn't care to get caught with it. Swinging about smartly he gave the *Grant* a good race back to Canadian waters, but seeing he wasn't quite going to make it, he began dumping the evidence overboard. It took fifteen minutes of frantic deep-sixing to dispose of the whole shipment, worth something like $20,000.

The *Grant* came alongside almost as the last *tael* of opium hit the drink but the relieved and sweating Jamieson was able to get off one of the few great one-liners in the annals of contrabanding: "It's all right, Cap," he shouted up at the *Grant's* wheelhouse; "I don't need a tow."

Wool was another dutiable commodity often brought into the country without benefit of a customhouse clearance. Dean of this branch of the smuggling biz was a diminutive, gray-bearded Shaw Island man named Alfred Burke. Burke had a long, slender rowboat stained a dull black color; and during each year's shearing season he would quietly ride the changing tide across Haro Strait to the Gulf Islands — appearing, then, at one sheep ranch after another, offering to trade chickens, tobacco or cash for fleeces. In his long black coat and slouch hat he became a familiar figure to Canadian islanders, one of whom recalled that he rowed standing up, without feathering his oars, for fear the sun would reflect from the wet blades.

Burke easily disposed of the wool to San Juan county ranchers who mixed it with their own output, shipping it to mainland markets at a fine profit: wool was selling for some twenty-two cents a pound more in the States than in Canada then. The arrangement was thus lucrative to all concerned, except the U.S. Treasury, whose officials became suspicious when they compared the huge figures for wool output in the San Juans with the modest number of sheep. They knew no flocks in the world could be half so productive!

The government moved in 1905 to break up what they believed to be a full-fledged ring of wool smugglers. On May 13, Inspectors Dean (capturer of Larry Kelly off McNeil Island) and Roy Ballinger left Port Townsend in an open boat, disguised as seal hunters. Their act was convincing. Dean had made his living as a sealer before entering government service. While Ballinger, who had lived in the San Juans (he married a pretty Roche Harbor school-ma'rm) had a ranching background and knew wool.

Under sail and with two pairs of oars, Ballinger and Dean crossed during the darkness to the Canadian islands and began systematic visits to all the sheep ranches they could find.

"We had our pockets full of skewers, wooden pins used in securing meat in form when roasting," Ballinger recalled years later. "And when the ranchers, who were shearing sheep, were not looking, we placed them in the fleece. We would stand around while the men were at work, telling them we were on vacation, seeing the country and doing a little sealing with our boat."

The inspectors spent a couple of weeks at this, traveling back and forth between the Gulf Islands and the San Juans, where they camped Indian-fashion on the beaches. Ultimately their rounds brought them to a South Pender Island ranch where their visit chanced to coincide with that of the short, somber-coated fellow from Shaw Island, Alfred Burke. Ballinger and Dean came upon him as he was loading wool he had bought into his lead-colored dory, struck up a conversation, and had their suspicions aroused.

Toward evening Burke put out into the Strait with his furtive-appearing craft. The two inspectors followed at a discreet distance and as the dory disappeared into the darkness they concluded its destination was Orcas Island. Ballinger and Dean headed for Orcas too, poked around there and at length located half a ton of skewer-marked wool in a warehouse belonging to the storekeeper, W. E. Sutherland.

Burke was arrested at his Blind Bay home, tried for smuggling and acquitted on grounds the inspectors hadn't actually *seen* him cross the border with the contraband. But the government's efforts were not wasted: the wool was confiscated and sold at auction in Port Townsend so that from Uncle Sam's point of view this particular crime paid — and handsomely.

Sutherland was not the only merchant in the Islands to benefit from the enterprise of smugglers. A West Sound pioneer recalled that O. H. Smaby's store in that community never sold sugar except in bulk — because the sacks all had Canadian labels on them. Smaby's source for the sugar, and perhaps other commodities, was probably Victor McConnell, son of a pioneer family. McConnell's dad having died in a shipwreck off Vancouver Island, Victor lived with his blind, respected mother and five brothers and sisters on the island which bears his family's name, until discovery of his extra-mural activities led them to request that he find another domicile.

McConnell is said never to have crossed the border empty: hauled everything from apples to shoes to the Canadian side, in exchange for the sugar and other staples "imported" on the return trip.

Somewhat surprisingly, one of the more popular cargoes when Canada-bound was playing-cards — an item made cheaper by Yankee mass-production methods in the States than in the land of the maple leaf.

The activities of men like Burke and McConnell, and even the two Kellys, were largely looked on with something between tolerance and admiration by San Juan Islands people, who certainly had nothing to fear personally from any of these entrepreneurs. But it was another story with Henry Ferguson, the

273

fast-hitting pirate-smuggler-thief whose wide-ranging exploits earned him the nickname, "The Flying Dutchman."

Ferguson had once been a member of Butch Cassidy's notorious "Hole in the Wall" gang of Wyoming badmen. When vigilantes and the U.S. Cavalry finally made things too hot for them there, Ferguson changed his name to Wagner and lit out for the Pacific Northwest. He arrived in the late 'nineties and promptly embarked on a career of highway and highsea robbery which terrorized island and seacoast dwellers from Vancouver Island to Olympia.

Ferguson's trademark was the stolen boat. He used a succession of them, reworking and repainting each one so speedily it would be unrecognizable overnight. In such craft he sped from place to place on the Sound, smuggling opium and Chinamen, stealing from fish traps and logging booms, looting stores and warehouses, sometimes commandeering whole cargoes from small Sound freighters.

Ferguson's home was in his hat, but he had several hide-outs, including a cabin in the San Juans where he hid his money and received mysterious light signals from the Canadian side. Another retreat was on little Skagit Island, just in the maw of narrow Deception Pass between Fidalgo and Whidbey Islands. It was here that sheriff's officers finally cornered him in October, 1901, and captured him after a prolonged shoot-out. He was prosecuted for a warehouse burglary committed at Stanwood the year before. So for the next several years his hat had stripes on it, and his home was the State penitentiary at Walla Walla.

Skagit Island proved to be the stamping ground of Benjamin Ure, once a wealthy Anacortes landowner whose holdings were lost in a real estate panic. Sheriff Luther Weedin discovered Ure had also been in the customs service at one time, but before that he was a notorious smuggler of fire-water into Camp Pickett during the joint occupation. Now he made a business of sheltering criminals like Ferguson, making his secluded island available as a way-point for stolen and smuggled goods, and a gathering place for the scum of Puget Sound generally.

Weedin put Ure out of business but an indulgent parole board returned Ferguson to society after he served a portion of his fourteen-year sentence, and the "Dutchman" promptly picked up his old career with new vigor.

But Ferguson made the mistake of robbing several post offices, including one at Langley, Washington, for which he was indicted *in absentia* by a Grand Jury. United States Attorney Elmer Todd got a special appropriation to finance a Sound-wide search for Ferguson, but the effort failed. Contemptuously, the "Dutchman" again entered the same Langley post office in 1912 and stole not only the government's cash, but the safe that contained it.

Another costly expedition over Puget Sound waters was authorized but Ferguson remained at large.

Finally in March 1913, Ferguson and an accomplice were surprised by Canadian constables in the act of robbing a store on Vancouver Island. One of the officers was killed in the wild shooting affray which followed, but when the dust settled the "Dutchman" was on the floor with two pairs of manacles about his wrists.

A Canadian court tried Ferguson — alias Wagner — for murder and sentenced him to death.

Ferguson, who had sworn he would never be hanged for his crimes, tried to make good his vow by beating his brains out against the walls of his cell; but alert guards restrained him and on August 28, 1913, after drinking a cup of coffee, he walked unaided to the jail-yard scaffold and paid the penalty for which he had so long been marked.

"Old Man" Jamieson was another who died violently, stopping a slug from a Treasury agent's pistol in a midnight confrontation near Seattle's Alki Point.

Jim Kelly, too, was in action almost to his last breath. In September 1908, Friday Harbor's deputy collector, O. H. Culver, spotted "Pig-Iron" crossing from Victoria in a small boat and alerted customs officials, who again missed catching him with the goods on board. But Kelly's continuing habit of flashing large sums of money about convinced them that the 60-year-old smuggler had not yet retired from his chosen trade and for the next few weeks they kept a particularly close watch on him. Thus a customs man may even have been present at suppertime on the first day of October when Kelly sat down to table on board a pile driver at a fish trap near Seattle. After eating this hearty meal Kelly got up, stretched himself — and fell over dead.

His passing, attributed to heart failure, occasioned a telegram from Puget Sound officials to Washington, in which interlineal sighs of relief, not unmixed with a certain note of admiration and regret, sounded clearly through the jargon of formal text.

Thus ended the prolonged battle between determined government inspectors and the last of the best of the Puget Sound smuggling fraternity. But it was only a battle. The war would flare anew a generation later. For the ill-starred Volstead Act would plunge the nation into an era of speakeasies, bathtub gin, rum-running and hijacking, in which all the exploits of Puget Sound's smugglers would be as nothing compared to the intrepidity of their spiritual successors.

17

JOHN S. MCMILLIN AND THE LIME KILN CLUB

He *was a short, slight man with large, soulful eyes set deeply below shaggy brows and he stepped uncertainly onto the gangplank of the steamer* Evangel *before easing his way down it to the dock at the foot of Friday Harbor's Spring Street. With him was his still-pretty wife of thirteen years, and the pair of them began the steepish climb up from the water along the wagon-rutted main drag. Quiet clucking sounds of disapproval emerged from beneath his generous mustache as they passed the noisy doorways of the little town's false-fronted business establishments, half of which — it seemed to him — were saloons, billiard parlors, and card rooms.*

"Won't do," he muttered, more to himself than to her; "Will-not-do-at-all. What this town needs is the power of the printed word." His life's companion nodded primly in agreement but she was thinking: I hope the power of the printed word will pay the landlord. And the grocer. This time.

This was May of 1890 and the new couple's destination was Will Fowle's candy, bird-seed, and cigar store at the top of

277

the hill. Fowle greeted the two warmly and was soon introducing them around town. The woman, Sarah, was Fowle's sister; her husband was Frank P. Baum, an attorney. The Baums intended making Friday Harbor their new home.

The town was already blessed with two or three resident barristers, and hardly enough legal business to support one; but Baum, in choosing this up-and-coming hamlet, was not expecting to live by solicitor's fees alone. He had scarcely hit town before the whole village was buzzing with an excitement. Friday Harbor was to have its own newspaper.

Baum was a fast worker. He arranged for space in a small structure near the town pump, which edifice he dubbed "the Graphic Building," and installed in it several cases of type and a small hand-operated press capable of printing two 14-by-20-inch pages at once. He set Thursdays as publication day and scheduled the first issue for May fifteenth.

From a Portland firm Baum ordered his "patent inside" — newsprint with national and international news, features and fillers, already printed on one side of each four-page sheet. This was standard procedure for country editors, who set up two pages of local news and printed these on the blank side of the sheet. Baum also ordered page-one preprinted with the name he had selected: The San Juan County *Graphic*.

The paper was late in arriving from Portland and when it did, the word "county" had been omitted from the head. Baum fumed a bit — he had already run off letterheads and envelopes using the full name — but decided to accept the shortened version. When the paper finally went to press, two days late, the Friday Harbor school was let out so all thirty-two of its scholars could visit Baum's "plant" and watch the first issue come off the press. A lot of other people stopped by to see this wonder, including a Lopez man with a boat to catch; Baum gave him some uncorrected proofs to take with him, hoping to get some subscriptions from that island.

For the second issue, Baum had already sold several ads in addition to the big one he ran for his brother-in-law's notions store. But again, the paper failed to arrive on time. On Monday — four days after the *Graphic* should have been "on the street" — Baum turned in desperation to Churchill and Noftsger's general store for a supply of brown wrapping paper on which issue number two was finally printed.

If the *Graphic*'s parlous beginnings were taken as an ill omen, this was the correct reading. Moreover its editor-publisher was a man seemingly marked for repeated disasters. Frank Baum was 38, a Pennsylvania farm boy who had also been a logger, a clerk in a store, and a homesteader on the plains of South Dakota. None of these occupations had brought fame or fortune, so Baum began teaching himself some law during the long, cold Dakota winters and was admitted to practice in 1883. He entered into partnership with a capable barrister in Plankinton, and a natural exuberance together with a fair gift of the gab seemed to be leading him at last to considerable financial success.

But illness struck and Baum decided to leave the Dakotas for a friendlier climate. For the next several years he traveled about in the South, as his funds dribbled inexorably away, finally settling in Thedford, Nebraska. He helped found a newspaper there and served as its first editor; alas, the effort failed dismally. In less than a year Baum, dead broke, caught a train and landed in mid-winter at Newberg, Oregon.

Baum talked himself into the editorship of Newberg's weekly paper and supplemented his income by acting as that town's recorder. In well under a year it appeared that the Newberg *Graphic* was on a collision course with the same kind of rocks on which the Thedford *Tribune* had foundered.* So Baum resigned both positions and here he was, optimistic to the last, trying it again in the little town on Joe Friday's bay.

* But the Newberg *Graphic* survived and is still in existence as these words are written, nearly eighty years later.

The people of the Harbor could live with a weekly that was less than punctual, and sometimes appeared on butcher paper; they could overlook Baum's imaginative misspellings and other scriptorial sins; but there was one peccadillo many of them could never forgive. In a town practically founded on booze, the *Graphic* was a prohibitionist paper!

Baum lined up solidly with the church-going, anti-saloon element (what there was of it) in Friday Harbor, never missing a chance to give in his columns a boost to the spiritual and a knock to the spirituous pursuits of the community and its citizens. Consequently his paper, while perhaps racking up points in Heaven, did poorly in Friday Harbor. That it survived at all was due chiefly to the fact that the *Graphic* was the only paper in the county.

This was a situation destined to change abruptly a few months later with the arrival in town of a high-powered eastern writer named James Cooper Wheeler. Wheeler was a glad-handing pragmatist who would be instantly at home on Madison Avenue today. It was not long before he had induced the anti-Baum crowd to finance a second paper with Wheeler as editor and publisher. The new sheet was to be called The San Juan *Islander* and Wheeler's company shipped in some two tons of equipment for it, installing this in a building a short distance down the street from the *Graphic* shop.

The first *Islander* was pulled from a hand-operated flat-bed Washington press early in March 1891. It was an eight-pager, and left no doubt as to its position on the liquor issue: "This paper will not condemn a merchant or farmer who visits a saloon for relaxation, nor will he set the dogs on a saloon or hotel keeper," wrote Wheeler in his first editorial. "*The Islander* will not extol one merchant who puts ten dollars in the contribution box at church, and cry down another equally good man, who does not happen to belong to his denomination or creed."

In volume one, number one, the *Islander* was already claiming to be "The Leading Paper of San Juan County" and was gibing slyly at the opposition. "The handsome sign that adorns the front of *The Islander* building is attracting general attention," ran a typical item. "It is said to compare very favorably with the circus sign over the office of the little paper up the street." Wheeler also ribbed the *Graphic* for several spelling errors, including a minor transposition of letters in the name of the mail steamer *Evangel*.*

But these were only pot shots. Wheeler's artillery went into action in a piece headed BAUM LIKES ORCAS which took the *Graphic* to task for its preceding week's editorial. In it, Baum had contended new settlers were bypassing San Juan for Orcas Island, to avoid the evil influences "eminating" from San Juan drinkeries.

"If Mr. Baum is so fond of the purity of the moral atmosphere which he says prevails in that 'neck of the woods,' why on earth don't he go over there and start a truly moral newspaper," ran the *Islander*'s rejoinder. "He need not be afraid of offending his friends in Friday Harbor by leaving, either. We could get a band and see him off on the steamer, his departure heralded by the inspiring strains of 'In the sweet by and by,' or something similar."

Baum did leave Friday Harbor shortly afterward, moving his paper not to Orcas, but to Lopez Island. From this somewhat safer distance he continued to declaim against the evils of the saloons at the county seat, even as he began a new phase of his career: that of real estate promoter. Enthused over the idea of building a new town — a moral, non-saloon town, of course — Baum joined with a number of like-minded men and bought up property around a small lagoon on Lopez Island's Swift Bay. William W. Mallory, a Methodist preacher better known in some

---

* The *Islander*'s first issue ran an ad for the *Evangel*, calling it "Regular, Reliable and Safe." A few weeks later that vessel's boiler blew up, killing three men and scalding most of the crew.

quarters as the "Kansas Cyclone," was president of the company; Baum was secretary.

The group called themselves the Port Stanley Townsite Development Company. Baum gave the town its name, after the British explorer Sir Henry Stanley whose book, *In Darkest Africa,* was the current sensation.

Port Stanley came into being in June 1892. Baum got himself appointed postmaster and built a combined post office, store, and residence, which also housed the *Graphic* office. (Country postmasters in those days did not receive a salary, but were paid the amount of their cancellations; hence Baum could begin mailing out the *Graphic* as first-class mail, at no cost to himself.)

The Port Stanley development was barely underway when, in 1893, the same bankers' panic that ended Elder Sidney Gray's dreams of building a picturesque Village de Haro on Orcas, put the Port Stanley company abruptly out of business. Hardly any of the property had actually been built upon. A Lopez tradition says some who had purchased lots sight-unseen finally viewed them — underwater at high tide — and let them go for taxes. Baum's own property was abandoned in 1896.

Meanwhile, the panic had brought about the demise of the San Juan *Graphic* (after another brief interlude of publishing it from a third location) and very nearly did the same for the *Islander.* James Cooper Wheeler departed for more familiar climes in the East, leaving his paper to founder uncertainly for a spell under a succession of local editors. It was a grim time in the San Juans, as elsewhere in the Pacific Northwest.

It is the genius of some men to be able to turn not only good fortune but adversity to their own account. Such an individual was John Stafford McMillin, the big, six-foot-three ex-Indiana lawyer whose name for exactly fifty years was law in the fief of Roche Harbor, San Juan Island. McMillin, upon coming to the Pacific Coast in 1884, had invested in a Puyallup Valley (near

Tacoma) lime concern, was named to its managership, and two years later was sent to scout the Scurr Brothers' San Juan quarries — the ones Israel Katz had for a time been interested in — on behalf of the company. McMillin's encouraging report of well-nigh inexhaustible deposits of the precious rock, coupled with a nearby haven for deep-water ships to haul the finished product, led to acquisition of the Scurrs' operation for $40,000.

The company was reorganized as the "Tacoma and Roche Harbor Lime Company," and McMillin bought into it, subscribing and paying for $1800 worth of its stock. The directors, reposing great faith in the Indianan's manifest business know-how, elected him president of the concern.

Seven years later Roche Harbor was the most valuable lime works in the Pacific Northwest, and far and away the county's largest and most stable payroll. Visitors to the place were startled at the changes those years had brought: in place of a few scruffy shacks to one side of the dock, huge warehouses and neat, business-like structures of varying sizes crowded the whole harbor; the shore-line had been built out some seventy or eighty feet to a sea wall, constructed of huge boulders of non-native sandstone; the two old-fashioned brick kilns the Scurrs had built were dwarfed now by a small army of towering steel giants across the face of the lime-laden eminence behind; while the whole panorama of kilns, shops and wharf was strung together by an impossible filigree of handcar tracks, bridges and trestles.

The centerground was dominated by a massively ornate, white-painted structure bearing the legend: Hotel de Haro. This was the same building that had sheltered the island-seeking sailor, Philip Van Buskirk, some thirteen years previously, in its original role as the Scurr Brothers' bunkhouse. Now that John S. had taken over, the building had been added onto, over and around, and so tastefully furnished and decorated that more luxurious quarters were scarcely to be found north of San Francisco. And far from serving grub so unsavory that Van Buskirk had once skipped his breakfast here, the "De Haro" now sported a Japanese chef who knew all the recipes.

Now in the panic year of 1893 the future of this burgeoning empire looked as bleak as that of countless other enterprises teetering on the rim of bankruptcy. Everywhere, financiers and big-city bankers were responding, characteristically, by hoarding cash and seeking to liquidate their paper holdings of all kinds (never mind that this deepens the spiral of depression where an opposite policy would cure it). So stockholders in the Roche Harbor company were not long in accepting a proposition being put to them by the canny John S.

McMillin's offer was to buy out each of several investors, with the smallest of cash payments and the Indianan's note for the balance. When the transactions had been made, McMillin was found to hold a controlling interest in the company. He then promptly voted himself twice his former salary, and with the increase, began to pay off the notes he had signed. Under McMillin's expert guidance, the company weathered the panic years and emerged stronger than ever — with John S. McMillin himself forever after in firm command.

Another example of McMillin's organizational and financial ingenuity centered about an ancillary company which manufactured barrels for the lime concern. In the midst of the depression John S. learned of a newly invented machine whose revolving knives fashioned barrels from fir or cedar logs. McMillin proposed to directors of his company that the firm buy patent rights to the machine, but the panicked directors declined to do so. John S. and several associates thereupon formed their own corporation, called the Staveless Barrel Company, and issued several thousands of shares of stock, most of which McMillin subscribed for himself, paying into the treasury all of $200 in cash money.

McMillin, acting in his own behalf, negotiated a contract with McMillin, of the Lime Company, to provide the latter concern with hogsheads for its product. Next he sold the contract to McMillin, of the Staveless Barrel Company, for some $200,000 and took that corporation's note in payment. This note he then returned to the company to pay for the stock he had subscribed for.

There remaining in the treasury of the barrel company $200 of actual money, McMillin submitted a bill for that same figure and paid it to himself as a legal fee for organizing the company.

As John S. had foreseen, the Staveless Barrel Company was a money-maker from the first moment and as the proceeds went largely into McMillin's personal coffers year by long year, resentment on the part of minority owners in the Lime Company grew, leading ultimately to one of the Pacific Northwest's more sensational court battles.

McMillin's political acumen was no less evident. A life-long devotee of the party of Lincoln, he was "Mr. Republican" in the San Juans — if not the entire state — for decades. Beginning in 1888, he was a member of every single Washington Territory,* State, and San Juan County convention of the G. O. P.

At election time, Roche Harbor became the focus of such intense campaign hoopla that just about all the votes cast went to Republican candidates. Not that John S. browbeat his populace to vote that way; but under his towering and ever-present influence, it seemed almost un-American to mark one's "X" for any other party. The same kind of frenzy radiated outward so that handsome majorities for the G. O. P. were virtually assured county-wide.

Election days were followed by clangorous band-wagon parades through Friday Harbor to celebrate the victory of Republican candidates. These noisy festivities all but drowned out the occasional disgruntled voice raised to complain of "bossism" in San Juan County where, in those days before direct primary

* Washington became a state in 1889.

285

elections, the successful candidates had regularly been hand-picked by John S. McMillin.

Meanwhile, back at the *Islander* office, a new figure was lately occupying the editorial chair. He was A. J. Paxson, a newcomer from the farmlands of the Midwest, cradle of that third-party protest movement of the 'nineties known as Populism. The Populists espoused a mildly socialistic platform of agrarian reform and the silver standard, issues calculated to bring the corpuscles of conservatives like John S. McMillin to a speedy boil. Paxson went so far as to endorse, in the *Islander*'s columns, Populist candidates for one or two offices in the election of 1894. They lost, of course; and so did Paxson. He was succeeded, within the year, by a trustworthy crony of McMillin's, a Vermonter by the name of Otis "O. H." Culver.*

"O. H." had a solid newspaper background and came to Friday Harbor directly from the managership of a Bellingham sheet. He had also headed the Tacoma bureau of the big Seattle *Post-Intelligencer*. Now he joined with his brother, Fred "F. N." Culver, to purchase the *Islander* plant outright. The first issue after the takeover included a caustic anti-Populist editorial, and copious reportage of the doings of John S. McMillin (which, under Paxson, had been rigorously ignored).

It appears that Culver's income as *Islander* publisher was disappointing to him during the first two years, so it was fortuitous for him to be named, in 1897, Deputy Collector of the U.S. Customs Service, in charge of the Sub-Port of Entry at Roche Harbor. That McMillin pulled strings to get him the post would be difficult to prove; but it is unlikely that John S. *opposed* the appointment.

The fact that the Sub-Port was located at Roche Harbor, rather than at Friday Harbor, which would have been infinitely more convenient for everyone — excepting John S. McMillin —

* Paxson went on to Alaska and ran a roadhouse where the town bearing his name now stands.

was also traceable to the latter's influence. Culver found himself chained to this remote outpost, filling in government forms, while brother "F. N." got out the paper. He was scarcely able to get leave from his station, even to visit his wife when a child was due to be born.

By 1900 "O.H." was fed up with the whole situation, and announced his intention to resign from the Customs Service, sell the *Islander*, and go back to newspapering at Whatcom. Then suddenly, after a decade of stony opposition, the Treasury Department okayed a sub-port for Friday Harbor, and Culver was appointed to run it. He accepted the post, which he established in a corner room of the *Islander* building, bought out his brother's interest in the paper and started in to run it with a vengeance.

The *Islander* even began showing signs of some independent thinking. When in 1902 the county commissioners received imploring petitions from the citizens to do something about the rickety, 1883-built, vault-less courthouse in which the county records were kept, a proposition was placed on the ballot to build a somewhat larger, but wholly modest structure. McMillin cooled the idea, ostensibly favoring a delay until a more expensive brick building could be erected. Cynics suspected John S. was thinking of the $732 in additional taxes his company would be assessed, if the measure succeeded.

Public opinion and the *Islander* favored the proposition, however, which seemed certain to pass — until election day. Voters arriving at their polling places found a letter posted from one of the respected candidates for county commissioner, who had seemed to favor the new courthouse, now denouncing the plan as an unnecessary expense. Confused, they turned thumbs down on the measure, and elected the letter-writer to office.

The *Islander* now lashed out bitterly at the "subservient" candidate, Isaac Sandwith, noting the provocative letter had in fact "issued" from the Lime Company office. Sandwith, snorted the paper, had thus "announced through the medium of the

287

Lime Kiln Club that as commissioner he will take a firm grip on the coat-tails of progress and holler 'whoa!' "

Yet Culver declined to attack John S. personally. "Why indulge in anathemas against Mr. McMillin for exercising his right to fight?" asked the *Islander*. "Like a good mechanic when he has a job to do he simply makes the best use he can of the tools he has at hand."

Direct action was one of the tools McMillin used adeptly. In 1906 a young Irishman named Micky Doyle organized the Roche Harbor workers into a union, and demanded a "readjustment" of wages from $2 to $2.25 a day and a reduction in board and rent charges. A strike was threatened if these demands were not met. While management and labor haggled, McMillin, who had been absent, returned to Roche Harbor and settled the dispute instantly by firing Doyle and everyone else involved on the union side. In all, some fifty men found themselves out of work.

Aside from this minor triumph of antisyndicalism, however, 1906 was a downhill year for John S. Spring found him negotiating with a group of eastern financiers who were interested in buying the Roche Harbor company, with the price tag at something like $800,000. Just as the principals were set to put pen to paper on the deal, McMillin was charged in U.S. District Court at Seattle with fraud!

An injunction, barring the sale pending a hearing of the matter, was based on sensational accusations brought by the Lime Company's minority stockholders.

The charges against McMillin were widely publicized in Puget Sound newspapers — the *Islander* included. It was alleged that he gained control of the company in a fraudulent manner to begin with, and had since been milking it of vast sums which rightfully belonged to stockholders. He was also charged with impropriety in setting up the Staveless Barrel Company as his personal concern, and with operating it "on the profits filched from the lime company."

288

Caroline Schüler Chevalier, age 16 years, mother of Ed Chevalier, the Spieden Island "king." *Courtesy Mrs. Norman Mills, Prevost, Stuart Island.*

E. C. Gillette, surveyor, justice of the peace, and teacher, closely associated with the San Juans' early days. *Courtesy Mrs. Leith Wade, Friday Harbor.*

Ed and Mary Chevalier with their family on Spieden Island.
Courtesy Mrs. Norman Mills, Prevost, Stuart Island.

John S. McMillin, Roche Harbor industrialist
and "Mr. Republican" in San Juan County.
Courtesy Mr. Neil Tarte, Roche Harbor.

Paul K. Hubbs, early San Juan Island settler
and a chief actor in the Pig War drama,
preferred Indian ways to those
of his own race.

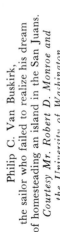

Philip C. Van Buskirk,
the sailor who failed to realize his dream
of homesteading an island in the San Juans.
*Courtesy Mr. Robert D. Monroe and
the University of Washington.*

The family of Reverend T. L. Dyer, Methodist minister at Friday Harbor during the not-so-gay 'nineties. *Courtesy Mr. Earl Dyer, Bremerton, Wash.*

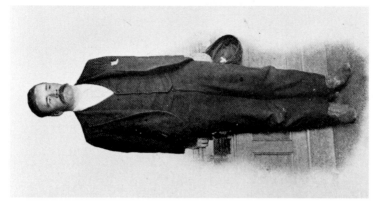

William "Old Man" Jamieson, English-born smuggler of unusual cunning.

Larry Kelly, storied "king" of Puget Sound smugglers.

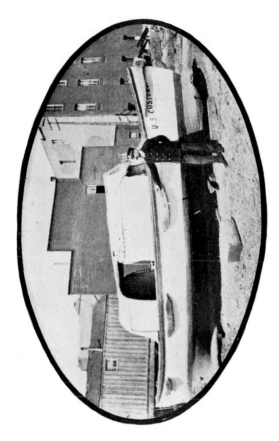

Inspector Fred C. Dean and a U.S. Customs launch — actually the former smuggling craft *Hyack* — following one of Kelly's numerous captures.

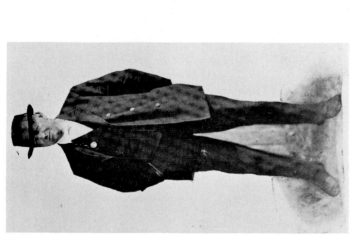

Captain H. F. Beecher led Puget Sound smugglers a merry chase during brief career as Customs Collector.

The busy waterfront at Roche Harbor, San Juan Island, in its heyday as Western America's foremost source of lime. *Courtesy Mr. Neil Tarte, Roche Harbor.*

Another alleged scandal was that McMillin had secretly negotiated preferential rates with steamship and railroad companies while himself serving on the State Railway Commission — a board charged with stamping out precisely this kind of hanky-panky.

The *Islander*'s editorial indignation was aroused all the more when the true value of the Lime Company's Roche Harbor property was revealed to be about eight times what it had been paying taxes on, while the Staveless Barrel Company turned out to be worth fifty times its assessed value.

The *Islander* opined that the revelation "should afford considerable food for reflection to the taxpayers of this county and to those public officials, past and present, who have been wont to fall down and worship the president of the lime kiln club and bask in the sunlight of his gracious presence. Mr. McMillin has for many years exploited the politics of this county for his own personal benefit as systematically and as thoroughly as he has the business of the Tacoma & Roche Harbor Lime Company. For many years seekers for office in the county have made biennial pilgrimages to the throne of the lime king to crave his support and pledge their allegiance as faithfully and as humbly as pious Mohammedans journey once in a life-time across the Arabian desert to worship at the tomb of Mahomet. It may be that this sort of thing will continue indefinitely. If it is what the people want, by all means let them have it."

But the people wanted nothing of the kind. What they wanted — and got — was a tax reassessment of the McMillin empire. They also called a special election and voted ten-to-one to build a new, brick courthouse costing $14,000. Its cornerstone (of Roche Harbor limestone) was laid June 29 by Stephen Boyce, the pioneer sheriff.

Even before the ceremony the *Islander* reported the sale of the old courthouse site to Gene Gould, 25-year-old cashier of the San

Juan County Bank.* A few weeks later Gould announced a piece of the lot had been sold to a newly formed stock company about to start an opposition newspaper in Friday Harbor.

It was common knowledge in town that the new outfit's avowed purpose was to run the *Islander* clean out of business. That periodical's recent switch to an anti-McMillin line notwithstanding, a division was taking place among the G. O. P. faithful of San Juan County, with "O. H." and the *Islander* supporting the regulars, while a growing number of Republicans favored a rump ticket that would expunge "bossism" from the Islands once and for all. Backers of the new paper stood with the rumps.

O. G. Wall and G. A. Ludwig, both of whom learned their newspapering in Minnesota, brought out the first issue of the Friday Harbor *Journal* on September 13, 1906. Wall was editor. "A Square Deal for Everybody" was the masthead motto, and a deceptively low-key editorial promised the *Journal* "would not be blindly partisan, believing that good men are of greater importance than political sentiment."

Culver's editorial reply was bluntly plaintive. "It will [not] be an easy matter to put the *Islander* out of business," he said, adding it was too bad Wall hadn't just offered to buy the paper, since "the publisher of the *Islander* would have been much more pleased to get out of the business than he seems to be to get into it."

Nevertheless the journalistic battle had been engaged and both editors pursued it relentlessly with few holds barred, differing somewhat in tactics but not in determination.

The opposing slates of Republican candidates provided the first battleground. The regulars, in convention assembled, nominated the youthful banker, Gene Gould, for representative in the State Legislature. The rumps opposed him with William Schulze, an

* The bank was established by Gould's father in 1893. When Gould, Jr., was promoted to the post in 1901 he was reputedly the youngest bank cashier in the United States.

erstwhile asssociate of McMillin's whose damning testimony in the fraud case against John S. had made him the hero of the anti-bossism movement. The two factions also were split over most of the other county elective offices.

In November the rumps, who called themselves the "Independent Manhood of San Juan County," won every contest except that for sheriff. Schulze even carried the Roche Harbor precinct — by just three votes.

Schulze's victory occasioned a wild celebration throughout the county. In Friday Harbor, where McMillin's supporters usually staged bandwagon parades after each election success, the Independents saw to it theirs was the biggest and noisiest cavalcade the town had seen. A ship made the rounds of the islands, collecting the jubilant and transporting them to the Harbor for the occasion, which was climaxed by a nighttime torchlight parade and banquet.

Meanwhile the case against John S. continued in Seattle, where the Seattle *Times* bore down hard on his alleged malfeasance as railroad commissioner. Under this fire, McMillin resigned the post and returned the salary he had received from the State.

But on June 19, 1908, Judge C. H. Hanford vindicated McMillin of each of the charges against him. The Lime Company president's stock purchases were legal, the court found, and so were his actions as majority stockholder afterward. As to the staveless barrel affair, the judge found McMillin had urged his Board of Directors to buy the machine, and when they declined, was within his rights in acquiring it for himself. Now that the machine had proved a success, McMillin was entitled to the benefits of his good judgment in making a transaction that was "neither illegal, immoral nor unfair."

Facing about once again the *Islander* filled its columns with praise and congratulations for the Roche Harbor magnate's victory; the *Journal* was even more friendly, and made a point of referring to the *Islander*'s "vicious and sensational attack" on McMillin earlier.

But by now the *Journal* had found an even more damaging issue on which to attack its opponent, stemming from the fact that O. H. Culver, while holding a nonpartisan government post as deputy customs collector, was engaging in politics by publishing a partisan newspaper, in contravention of the civil service rules. The hue and cry raised by the *Journal* and its backers led to an official reprimand for Culver and a reported warning that further political activity would cost him his job. Consequently, "O. H." dropped his name from the *Islander*'s masthead and announced his brother "F. N." was taking over as manager.

But the *Journal* was not satisfied. What with the customs office and the *Islander* occupying the same quarters, it looked suspiciously as though Culver's disassociation with the paper was largely a nominal one. Further complaints were made and in March 1909, customs inspector Roy Ballinger arrived in town to relieve "O. H." for a few weeks.

Culver was "interviewed" in the *Islander* and let it be known that he was off on a two-month vacation.

Bosh, quoth the *Journal*, and trotted out its biggest and blackest type to headline confirmation that the Civil Service Commission had in fact suspended Culver from duty and pay for sixty days.

Amid rumors (which finally saw print in both sheets) that John S. McMillin was "after the scalp of Mr. Culver" the next blows fell in relentless succession. The *Islander*, which had for years been the official paper of San Juan County, found itself replaced by the *Journal* in that function. Culver took the matter to court, contending his rates were lower than the *Journal*'s, but the case was thrown out. The *Journal* responded with the charge that the reason the *Islander* could undercut its printing rates was because of the "shameful rental" of $25 a month Culver was collecting from the government for use of the "little 10 x 12 corner in his print shop" as a customs house.

When the *Journal* dug up figures showing that receipts to the government from customs transactions at Friday Harbor were less than Culver's salary as deputy collector, it appeared for a time that the post might be abolished. The *Islander*, pointing out the prestige that would be lost to Friday Harbor if this happened, likened the *Journal* to a "dirty bird [befouling] its own nest." This ploy of the *Journal's* was quickly blocked by the Treasury Department, however, which ruled the Friday Harbor sub-post essential in view of the "facility with which smuggling" was carried on in the area.

With the untimely death at 44 of F. N. Culver, the mantle of nominal managership was passed to the brothers' aged father, G. N. Culver. However, the *Islander's* wounds were mortal, and everyone knew it. The paper was sold in 1913 to a Seattle man, John Dickie, who tinkered with it for about a year before allowing it to pass mercifully into newspaper limbo.

There, perhaps, it communes yet with the bones of that great host of fallen frontier newssheets, including its own victim of an earlier decade, Frank Baum's San Juan *Graphic*.

18

THE LIFE OF FRONTIER PREACHERS was notoriously hard. Depending on the denomination, financial support from the home church organization varied between insufficient and none at all. Ministers depended mainly on the collection plate for basic living expenses, and when times were bad — which is to say practically always — the wolf was never far from the parsonage door.

It was worst with the Methodists. When the Reverend John Tennant and his Indian wife finished their first year of service on Orcas and Lopez Islands, this devoted man of the cloth advised his Presiding Elder to reappoint him, for the Tennants had learned to survive on clams, and "any other man with a family would starve to death on that field."

Tennant concentrated on Orcas, launching the county's first church of his persuasion into a precarious career at East Sound in 1887. John S. McMillin, a life-long Methodist, saw to it a quaint little chapel of bird-house architecture was built at Roche Harbor about the same time, and invited Tennant's successors to preach there on a circuit-riding basis. A newly-built Presbyterian church centrally located on Lopez Island likewise made its

294

pulpit available to the itinerant proclaimers of Methodism from time to time. Conspicuously absent from the list of places where the prohibitionist-minded Methodists were preaching was the little saloon town at Joe Friday's harbor.

The tough-minded man of God who determined to do something about the latter circumstance was a snaggle-toothed son of a Willamette Valley pioneer, whose father in turn had been a hunting partner of Daniel Boone. Reverend Andrew J. McNemee is said to have been no great shakes as an orator, but "Brother Mack" was a fighter.

Mack had decided early to become a preacher after visits to the home of an Oregon minister. But it was not the parson himself who influenced the thirteen-year-old most. "When I went to the front door the old gentleman would meet me and often give me some tracts and along with them some good advice," he recalled long years afterward; but "when I went to the back door Grandma Royal would give me an apple, or some cookies, and I always liked her kind of religion."

It became Mack's kind of religion, too. So much more adept was he at giving than at receiving, he probably came as close to starving to death as any circuit-rider since the Apostle Paul. Mack hated to take up a collection, and was known to hand money back when the giver looked poorer than he.

Mack rode circuit in the wild country around Whatcom for a few years before tackling Port Townsend and his first church-building job. He spent every cent he owned on the building and did most of the work on it, and when it was nearly finished the good people of the church turned him out. They wanted a married man, whose wife could play the organ and teach Sunday School. McNemee was a bachelor.

Broke and with only one suit of second-hand clothes to his name, Brother Mack was staked to train fare to Portland by the International Order of Good Templars, the temperance lodge. In Portland his brother wrote off the hundred dollars Mack already owed him and loaned enough more for a new suit and transportation to his next assignment.

McNemee's new circuit was to be Lopez and San Juan Islands, and his arrival there was scarcely auspicious. Mack landed at Lopez on a Saturday in the early autumn of 1889. His predecessor, the Reverend Eugene Stockwell, seemed in a hurry to leave and caught a boat for the mainland the same day.

Mack preached his first sermon at the Center Church the next day. Afterward he visited a man Stockwell had pointed out as a prominent member of the Lopez flock.

"I had no more than got seated when he commenced telling me about the poor sermon I had preached," McNemee wrote in his memoirs, "and said, if I could not preach better than that, the sooner I left the Island the better."

Mack had hoped to get supper and a bed for the night at the home of this pillar of the Lopez congregation, but after a bit more conversation with the cantankerous islander the parson was obliged to leave and search for hospitality elsewhere.

It was nearly dark as McNemee started down the unfamiliar island trail toward the home of the next neighbor, a mile and a half through the woods. He got lost on the way but finally stumbled into the cabin of James Blake at nine o'clock, nearly exhausted, and having gone most of the day without a meal.

Blake fed him and put him up for the night, but McNemee didn't do much sleeping. His Presiding Elder had warned him that "they were a rough class on the San Juan Islands" and Mack was learning his superior was right.

"I made up my mind that I would go to San Juan," McNemee recounted, "and if I met another such reception from the people there, I would leave for British Columbia and go off into the woods and never tell anyone that I was a preacher."

McNemee took passage to San Juan the following day landing, fortunately, at Argyle, where he was so cordially received by the

Tucker brothers, Clarence and William, that Mack determined to make his home there.

Reverend Stockwell had secured some partially cleared property at Lopez on which to build a Methodist church but there were two catches. Of course one was money, or the lack of it; the other was that the property's donor insisted on the building's containing a schoolhouse as well.

"I did not see how I could build a church that would cost at least $1,800 or $2,000 with only $365 subscribed and besides I did not want to combine a church and school house in one building," wrote McNemee, and he decided to concentrate on getting a church built at Friday Harbor instead.

One of Methodism's stalwarts had obtained property in Friday Harbor two or three years earlier. Covered with second growth fir and brush it was perched on a hilltop overlooking both the village and the bay. McNemee set out singlehanded to clear two acres of this and then put in four months of hard labor on the church building, besides meeting his preaching engagements on both islands, and helping in a volunteer project to build a wagon-road from Friday Harbor to Argyle.

Apparently Mack had scant assistance from the faithful around Friday Harbor. Those of a spiritual bent were already attending the little Presbyterian church in the valley; while the unspiritual were taking umbrage at McNemee's penchant for anti-saloon temperance sermons. When the structure was finished, the plucky preacher found himself personally answerable for $360 still owed for materials.

It was the usual practice to invite one of the luminaries of Methodism on Puget Sound to conduct the ceremonies dedicating a new building, but Friday Harbor seemed so far away and the lack of enthusiasm was so apparent that McNemee was hard-pressed to get anyone to attend. Finally Reverend W. H. Johnstone agreed to come all the way from Eastsound.

Only a scattering of people were on hand for the dedication, which McNemee celebrated by contributing $175 of his own money toward retiring the church debt. The sum was more than three times the amount he had received in "salary" via the collection plate during his year in the San Juans.

McNemee had borrowed the $175 and it was many years afterward before he was able to pay it all back.

Three months later Mack was reassigned to the Islands for a second year and instructed to go over to Lopez and build a church there. McNemee responded that he was already hundreds of dollars in debt and couldn't afford to build another church right away, so he was relieved and transferred to the town of Edison, in Skagit County.

Once again Brother Mack was forced to borrow funds to get to his new post, and the day he left Friday Harbor he called on a few of the people who were actually sorry to see him go. One was the storekeeper, N. E. Churchill, who told him: "Now Mack, I am no church member but I am a friend to you and I want to give you some advice as I used to live in Edison and know the people there. If you will attend to your preaching, the people will treat you well, but as certain as you go to railing against the saloons like you have done here in Friday Harbor, they will put you under the ground before you have been in Edison three weeks."

McNemee's trials and ultimate successes in Edison are beyond the scope of this book, but it can be said that he did not give up railing against the saloons and the people of Edison did not put him under the ground in three weeks. It seems that after the San Juans, Mack was equal to most anything.

Reverend McNemee's successors pursued, with varying degrees of nonsuccess, the ecclesiastic battle against the sins of the saloons and their habitués, which Brother Mack had inaugurated. Most of the parsons that followed stayed their single year and moved on to less obdurate corners of the Lord's vineyard. An exception was the Reverend Thomas L. Dyer, whom — together

298

with his temperamental sailboat *Epworth* — we have met in an earlier chapter. Dyer stayed four years in Friday Harbor, embracing exactly the period of financial panic which began in 1893 and ended with the arrival on Puget Sound of the famed "ton of gold" steamer *Portland* heralding the Alaska stampede.

Dyer's collections in those depressed days never amounted to much and with ten offsprings in the family, a good deal of secular moonlighting was imperatively called for. The Dyers kept a garden, a cow and some chickens, of course; and on top of that he taught at one of the little schools out in the country; and then on Saturdays he would take the *Epworth* for a day's fishing and clamming, often hooking onto a drift log to tow in to the mill. You got a dollar apiece for logs, delivered that way.

The sawmill was between the Dyers' church and manse and the bay, and was run by their nearest neighbors, a Seventh-Day Adventist family. The Browns had four children who were the Dyer youngsters' constant playmates — except on Saturdays and Sundays. It was a lark for the Dyer progeny to try to tease the Brown moppits into violating their Saturday Sabbath by a game of ball or jacks, while the Adventist youngsters just as gleefully returned the compliment each Sunday.

A trace of the same impishness crept into the grownups' relations as well, though the two families were the best of friends. The sawmill's noisy machinery was clearly heard in Dyer's church each Sunday morning, so that the reverend used to grumble privately to his family that Brown "would run his sawmill on Sunday if he never run it any other day of the week." Brown also had a habit of blowing the mill's whistle especially lustily at the dot of noon on Sunday, and this became the compelling signal at which Dyer was obliged to cut short his sermon and dismiss the service.

It was a time, in America, of great religious revivals — a concomitant, perhaps, of the painful translation of a countrified

299

society and its obsolescent values into the new age of the Machine and the City. In such an era of drift man reaches instinctually for an anchor and so heeds the call of the evangelist more than in the fat times. In the 'nineties they thronged to hear the high, hoarse voices of men like Moody, Torrey, and Chapman, and the latter's protegé, a flamboyant newcomer, the ex-baseball player William A. Sunday.

They preached in the great cities of the nation, those giants. But backwater communities like the San Juans sometimes had their own, home-grown kind. On Lopez the Methodists and the Presbyterians once joined to sponsor open-air revival meetings at a clearing on Fisherman's Bay, known as "Red Charlie's" Grove. Islanders spruced up the grounds in preparation and met to begin the affair.

But organizational trifles introduced and insisted on by parliamentary-minded Presbyterians held up the commencement of preaching, and the crowd grew restive. Until, it is said, a young islander leaped impatiently to his feet.

"Damn the Presbyterians!" he shouted. "Let's start the meeting."

A universal target of all revivalists' oratory being the saloon and its evils, the movement found scant support in Friday Harbor. But there were some converts. Charles McKay, the massive, lusty ex-miner who helped twist the British lion's tail back in '59, in his maturity espoused Christian Science and took to publishing long temperance essays in the San Juan *Islander*. McKay ticked off the results of liquor, as he had observed them, during his decades on San Juan: three saloon-keepers dead, one of them a nephew of his; nine good men drowned while under the influence; and a long list of decent, hard-working youngsters turned into drunken bums, one of them McKay's own son. The aging pioneer — a noted Ned-raiser himself in the old days — figured drink had cost him personally "over three thousand dollars to help those whose families were in distress caused by liquor selling."

But hardly anyone was listening.

Friday Harbor at the turn of the century was perhaps ahead of its times in one regard only: it had that newest marvel of the mechanical age, the automatic vending machine. The product it dispensed was, predictably, alcoholic. You thrust in your nickel, the gears whirred, and out came your mug of foaming suds. The "booze machine" was considered a boon by those too impatient to stand in line at a bar, while also decreasing the time required to transform a thirsty working man into a participant in the general atmosphere of noise and mayhem that kept the county's seat lively.

The constant revelry with its harvest of broken homes and heads finally wrung a wry editorial comment from the *Islander*'s proprietors in 1907: "A considerable sensation was aroused in religious, irreligious and literary circles some years ago by the publication of a book entitled 'When Christ came to Chicago.' Some newspapermen and others were skeptical enough to doubt that he was ever there. If the brilliant author were to come here and write on the subject 'When the Devil Came to Friday Harbor' no such doubt would be expressed."

Spearheaded by organizations such as the W. C. T. U. and the Anti-Saloon League, a nation-wide movement toward legalized temperance was underway. In 1910, Washington joined the list of states which passed local option laws entitling counties and incorporated towns to decide, by direct vote of the people, whether to deny licenses to sellers of alcoholic beverages. As Friday Harbor had incorporated itself the preceding year (with Gene Gould, the youthful banker, as its first mayor) the stage was thus set for a local-option battle.

The likelihood of a dry victory looked dicey at best, but the temperance element was determined to make the best possible fight. They could derive some cheer when the Culvers, reversing a policy which had virtually birthed their paper to begin with, aligned the San Juan *Islander* cautiously with the dries. The *Journal* remained circumspect.

The Town Council set Tuesday, May 10, for the special election. As the date approached, the *Islander* made a sensational announcement: the then most famous evangelist in the United States, none other than the colorful Billy Sunday, had been engaged to speak at Friday Harbor — on the day before the election!

No one doubted that the Reverend Mr. Sunday's address would be his famous anti-saloon "booze sermon" which had stunned audiences from coast to coast, turned lifetime tipplers into pledge-signers and left in its wake a yard-long list of hard-drinking towns that had voted dry in elections just like the one about to take place at Friday Harbor.

Sunday was then preaching daily at mass revival meetings at Bellingham, where his energetic oratory drew hundreds to "hit the sawdust trail" to evangelical Christianity. (In fact the term "sawdust trail" originated in Bellingham, where Sunday drew a parallel between the newly-saved, walking down sawdust-strewn aisles to shake the evangelist's hand, and the habit of certain Puget Sound loggers who were said to leave a trail of the stuff when entering an unknown woods, in order to find their way home again.)

Theoretically, the colorful revivalist conducted his strenuous preaching campaigns six days of the week, resting on Monday. Yet his long-established habit was to use this "day off" in the interest of combatting his perpetual foe, the booze business.

"I have sworn eternal and everlasting enmity to the liquor traffic," Sunday was fond of declaiming. "As long as I have a foot, I'll kick it; as long as I have a fist, I'll hit it; as long as I have a tooth, I'll bite it; as long as I have a head, I'll butt it;

and when I'm old, and gray, and bootless, and toothless, I'll gum it till I go to Heaven and it goes to hell."

Apparently no village was too small to merit Sunday's coming there to aim an ecclesiastical boot at its hooch trade; or perhaps Friday Harbor presented an extraordinary challenge. Bellingham dignitaries having planned to bring Billy and his party over to Orcas anyway, to enjoy a day on the water and scale the heights of Constitution for the view, it was only a further step to prevail on the famous preacher for an address on a favored topic.

Andrew Newhall, a San Juan Island ship-owner and determined dry, made the steamer *Islander* available to Sunday and a party of forty-five for the day, hiring on a special crew for the occasion and paying all the expenses of the trip himself. "What it cost him he alone knows, and he won't tell," the Bellingham *Reveille* reported.

Sunday and his entourage were received and fed on their arrival by the Ladies Aid of the Methodist Church and the Ladies Guild of the Presbyterian Church, and then were escorted to the jam-packed Odd Fellows hall where every seat had been filled long before. Sponsors of the affair had seen to it that registered voters (and their wives, whose influence was acknowledged even in those days before universal suffrage) were given first crack at the available space. It was a warm day. All the standing room was taken, and in the open windows latecomers sat straddling the sills, while outside the disappointed stood in little clusters about the doors and windows.

The meeting opened with the singing of several patriotic and gospel songs, an invocation, and the introduction of Sunday by the Reverend S. G. Jones, current pastor of the Friday Harbor Methodist Church.

The town's saloon keepers, a bit awed by the attention that was falling to them, had elected to close up shop for the day of the great evangelist's visit. "Saloon Men at Friday Harbor Take to the Woods," headlined the Bellingham *Reveille*, and

303

Sunday began his talk with the remark that he was "glad that if by coming here I drove that gang out of town, if even for a day."

Sunday's "booze speech" was a set talk that normally took better than an hour to deliver. He had given it dozens of times with scarcely a variation, either in the text or in the gymnastic whirlings and gesturings that accompanied it. But Billy had allowed fifty minutes for the Friday Harbor address, and he set about to get the whole speech in, resorting to a machine-gun delivery that left his hearers as breathless as himself.

Billy fired barrages of figures to prove the hooch trade "the most damnable, corrupt institution that ever wriggled out of hell and fastened itself on the public." Seventy-five percent of all idiots came from intemperate parents, he assured the spell-bound audience, the legislature of his home state — Illinois — having appropriated six million dollars in 1908 alone just to care for them.

"One hundred and ten thousand in the United States die drunkards' deaths each year. That means a funeral procession 3,000 miles long."

He quoted a Roman Catholic archbishop as stating that seventy-five percent of all social crimes and eighty percent of the poverty in America "is caused by drink."

In Iowa, he reported, the whisky business increased taxes by one billion dollars. While in neighboring Kansas City, after a year of prohibition, bank deposits increased nearly two million dollars, "and seventy-two percent of the deposits were from men who had never saved a cent before, and forty-two percent came from men who never had a dollar in the bank." Business increased 209% and court expenses declined by $25,000, he said.

Now Billy was removing his coat and flinging it from him, perspiration beads whipping off his face as he whirled into a series of ghastly pictures to show the results of intemperance,

304

pictures of drink-crazed men committing murders and repenting — too late — at the threshold of the gallows; of drunks axing their aged mothers and gunning down innocent babies; of good men enticed into drink and ultimately gaining "a free pass to hell" and potters field graves for their suffering widows; of hungry, ragged "whisky orphans" shrieking over their father's coffin; of bodies of "the drunken dead" crawling away "into the jaws of death, into the mouth of hell."

Billy had them now. He had them all. Every move as he raced about the platform, every syllable hurled from clenched teeth and snarling lips found their target in the conscience of each hearer. Eyes blazing, he turned to the near seats — the ones reserved for voters — and thundered: "Say, if the man that drinks the whisky goes to hell, the man that votes for the saloon that sold the whisky to him will go to hell." The man that votes for that dirty business *ought* to go to hell, he said, "and I would like to fire the furnace while you are there!"

Sunday's finale was a comparison of the "Gin Mill" and its consequences with the production of legitimate industries. Every other plant on earth, he said, turned out a product worth more than its raw material. While the raw material of the saloon — the boy — was made into "bleary-eyed, low-down, staggering men and the scum of God's dirt." Calling five rather frightened youngsters up to the platform he pointed to their scrubbed faces. "Say," he said, lowering his voice to the merest whisper, "I would not give these five boys — and I don't know any of them — for all the saloons and distilleries this side of hell."

When Billy finished there was scarcely a dry eye or a wet vote in the house. Many came forward to sign pledges. As Sunday and his party left the hall to reboard the *Islander*, virtually the whole audience followed them to the dock and there burst spontaneously into "God Be With You Till We Meet Again." There were "three cheers for Billy Sunday" as the *Islander* pulled away, and scores of handkerchiefs waved a farewell until the steamer was out of sight.

The next day Friday Harbor's manhood went to the polls and voted almost three-to-one to outlaw "the whisky gang" and their "rotten business."

The weather went dry that spring too — no rain for several weeks and gardens were in bad shape, with the almost-unheard-of threat of a crop failure due to drought facing island farmers. But rain began to fall again the last week in May, and the other dry spell lasted just about as long. Friday Harbor's whisky-sellers, having taken to the woods, there began engaging in that enterprise known as the "blind pig" — rustic forerunner of the speakeasy. Yet the streets of Friday Harbor were quiet at night, with many of the womenfolk maintaining it was the first time in years they could go abroad without fear of insult. Charles McKay said he had been on the island for half a century and had never known Friday Harbor to be as decent a place as it was now.

Prohibition fever was spreading to the rest of the San Juans,* and in November a local-option issue went on the ballot county-wide. By then the spell of Billy Sunday's oratory had waned somewhat, along with the resolve of some of Friday Harbor's erstwhile tipplers. The prohibition issue passed, but this time the margin was a bare eighteen votes in the township. Throughout the Islands the vote was less close, as the archipelago went legally dry from Point Lawrence on the east to Roche Harbor on the west. (Not that the latter place was affected in the least: John S. McMillin hadn't allowed booze in that town from the moment he took it over in 1886.)

Not one to let grass grow under his feet, Sheriff Ed Delaney

---

* On Orcas, Robert Moran, the retired Seattle industrialist and ex-mayor, went strolling with a house guest who remarked that he was drinking a bit of sea water as part of "the cure." "I've been taking two glasses every morning," he confided. "Would you advise me to take a third?" Moran cast his eye over the waters of East Sound and replied thoughtfully, "I really don't think one more would be missed."

began raiding the blind pigs even before the election was held. One of the largest of these spirituous retreats was discovered in a shack on little Brown's Island* just at the entrance to Friday's Bay. Several wagon loads of illegal hooch were seized, boated back to the Harbor and placed for safe-keeping in the county jail.

On the night of the election, the guardians of law and order being perhaps preoccupied with vote-counting and seeing whether their jobs were safe or lost, enterprising (and thirsty) thieves filed through two sets of locks and made off with six cases of the confiscated firewater — surely one of the few recorded instances of anyone breaking *into* a jail.

Next day Delaney's suspicions were aroused when the young son of a prominent townsman was reported grievously ill with symptoms strongly suggesting acute overindulgence. A quiet inquiry disclosed two of the sufferer's close friends were prostrate with the same malady. Delaney had an off-the-cuff chat with the youngsters and the next night five of the missing cases reappeared quietly on the courthouse steps. The now-vanished contents of the sixth having already inflicted a punishment well suited to the crime, the three sheepish islanders were let off with fines and another lecture.

Such near-comic episodes provided the populace with a merest glimpse into the kinds of troubles that awaited them during the nineteen-year headache of state and national prohibition. By initiative measure, all of Washington was to go dry in 1914, while the eighteenth amendment to the U.S. constitution would make teetotalism the law of the land in 1920. In microcosm the San Juans were discovering what the nation would learn in pain and anguish: one does not get rid of an entrenched social evil merely by passing a law against it.

* Since renamed Friday Island by real estate promoters.

19

THE NOBLE DISASTER

No ONE CAN SAY PROHIBITION was rammed down the throats of the American public. Landslide local-option votes had spread a patchwork of legal sobriety across the land long before Mr. Volstead put pen to paper on the subject. The Eighteenth Amendment was ratified in all states but two, many of the legislatures — Washington's included — voting unanimously in favor. Such was the overwhelming popular support for what Herbert Clark Hoover called in his enthusiasm "a great social and economic experiment, noble in motive and far-reaching in purpose."

But local option was one thing; border-to-border abstinence was another. Many a man who once voted to drive the saloon out of his home bailiwick, secure in the secret knowledge that he himself could slip away and bend his elbow in the other fellow's town when the spell was on him, found the universality of the new statute intolerable. In such a circumstance he indulged himself to bend the law, ever so slightly, thereby giving secure employment to those who could cheerfully shatter it to bits.

A goodly share of the shattering took place in the waters of western Washington and British Columbia where the San Juans, as in the bad old days of Chinese and opium smuggling, found themselves center-stage again. In the Pacific Northwest, "just off the boat" generally meant one's booze had been newly spirited across the salt chuck border in a fast night-time dash through the archipelago's twisty channels.

Rum-running into Washington State was big business even before national prohibition. It was relatively safe, then, for the Coast Guard was still trying to patrol Puget Sound and the Straits with the same old, tired boats in which the revenue service had chased the likes of "Pig-Iron" Kelly and Henry Wagner.

Still there were occasional captures. The *Journal* ran a local-boy-makes-good item once in 1917 when the *Scout*, whose commander then was the son of a prominent Lopez farmer, overhauled a launch in which 750 bottles of choice liquors were found concealed. A year later the tables were turned as the *Arcata* seized $6000 worth of Scotch and Canadian whiskies from a boat whose master turned out to be a Friday Harbor merchant, Sam Bugge. Bugge had represented San Juan County in the State Legislature in an earlier decade, which indicates the stature of some of the men being lured by the profits offered in this fast-burgeoning industry.

Passage of the Eighteenth Amendment created a vastly-increased market, ensuring even greater profits for everyone in the business. A bottle of the "real thing," costing a mere fifty cents or so in hundred-case lots in Victoria, fetched perhaps $2.25 on delivery to an intrepid American smuggler, the loading taking place at night in some lonesome, prearranged rendezvous. The "rummy" paid in cash, of course, then made his bee-line — without benefit of running lights — for the U.S. side. There he might dispose of his liquid cargo to a shifty-looking gentleman driving a fast late-model car, and collect maybe $7 the copy. Ultimately this same four-bit booze would be dispensed by your friendly neighborhood bootlegger or hotel "bottle man" for something closer to twelve bucks.

Apparently no one in government foresaw the enormous enforcement job national prohibition would entail in the Pacific Northwest, which is remarkable considering the vastness of the bootlegging industry engendered by Washington State dehydration alone. But those early lessons went unlearned in high places, and it was several years before the pleas of the enforcers for more muscle could be responded to. Meanwhile, seizures by the thinly-spread Coast Guard, for example, occurred largely through accident. Once the venerable tugboat-like cutter *Arcata*, having anchored off Marrowstone Point in a fog, discovered herself lying a few yards away from a rummy which had heaved to for the same reason. *Arcata*'s skipper made that seizure (twenty-four cases and the rum vessel itself) with the cutter's longboat.

On another occasion the harbor cutter *Guard* confiscated $6,000 worth of liquor from a speedboat at Minor Ledge, the deserted shoal east of Smith Island. The Coast Guard version of the capture has the rummies "stealthily" carrying their contraband across the beach at the time, but the Friday Harbor *Journal*'s contemporary report says the rum-runners had been shipwrecked for two days and were so glad to be rescued they couldn't have cared less about losing their booze. The *Journal* also pointed out it was the Coast Guard's first capture in nine months.

Eventually, of course, Coast Guard forces were beefed up — not only by new 75-foot "six-bitters" but through conversion of some of the confiscated ex-rummy vessels into government patrol boats. These craft were speedy and carried business-like armaments, thus driving some of the smaller fry from the game; while the big fellows responded with greater speed and cunning, some going so far as to equip their low-lying craft with armor plate. One of the major operators, a Tacoma brewer whose manufacture of legal .4% "near beer" constituted an ironically appropriate front, invested in a fleet of twin-engined craft that could make nearly forty knots, outrunning just about anything afloat.

But the rummies depended on stealth as well as speed. Oftentimes this meant a cautious exchange of recognition signals before the midnight rendezvous with the Canadian supply boat, at some secluded cove in the Gulf Islands, where a hundred or more "cases" of hard liquor were loaded aboard. (Actually the almost universal container was the homely gunny-sack, either the standard-size bag holding an even dozen bottles or a smaller version in which six were sewn end-to-end, sausage-like, the original six-pack. The gunny-sacks were easier to handle and in case the evidence needed to be ditched hurriedly the sacking would not disintegrate in water.*)

Across the way, a confederate on the north shore of one of the San Juans would be scanning the murk for Coast Guard vessels. Seeing none, he would flash the "all clear" upon which the rummy poured the coal to twin Van Blerck or Liberty engines and in a matter of minutes the illegal merchandise would be beached near the look-out's feet.

The empty rum boat would be on its way again in a moment while the partner loaded the contraband into a waiting automobile and departed at top speed for the southern shore, where another fast boat waited to relay it to the mainland. Islanders learned to ignore those noctural autos speeding hell-bent through the gloom, and warned their children to keep away from the windows if they awoke to hear them roaring by in the night.

Most of the operators maintained hiding places where their goods could be quickly cached in case of pursuit, and a good deal of ingenuity was displayed in selecting them. One of the more successful caches was on D'Arcy Island on the Canadian side;

* To give some idea of the magnitude of the trade, one Victoria dealer in burlap claimed to have sold 3,000 bags a week to just one of his customers.

D'Arcy being a leper colony site in those days, no one risked coming around to investigate!

Another imaginative cache was at Obstruction Pass on Orcas Island where an enterprising fellow constructed a very special kind of outhouse. Half of the two-holer was conventional, but the other half concealed the entrance to a short tunnel where the "merchandise" was hidden. Very effective, providing one didn't forget which half was which.

When pursued too hotly, it was sometimes necessary to deep-six the evidence and take one's chances of recovering it later. Such was the case one dark night off the southwestern Orcas shore when a party of rummies hastily tossed their burlap-wrapped cargo into shallow water, moments before being over-hauled by the persistent guarders of the coast. The pursuers did not observe the dumping operation; but a watchful Orcas Islander did, and when the boatmen returned to retrieve their bottled goods, every bag of it had disappeared. The rum-runners hunted for days, to no avail; but they were looking in the wrong place. They should have been searching the local Deer Harbor speakeasy, where quarts of the finest were on sale with new labels warning customers to destroy the bottles after use, so the rummies couldn't trace them.

In the Islands, the local speakeasy was usually to be found in the nearest village store. For reasons that are apparent, hard liquor was easy enough to come by. But there was little trafficking in imported beer, the profits being so much greater with spirits,* so most of what was sold was of local manufacture. But there were also stills all over the place, and one of them was immortalized in a song parody known to islanders throughout the county:

> "We'll build a sweet little still
> In old Argyle mill
> And let the rest of the world come buy."

* Those few who ran "beer boats" were held in contempt by just about everybody.

The Argyle mill had no still, the miller having abandoned his obsolescent profession to become a highly-respected officer of the local bank, but the rhyme was too fetching to spoil over such a trifling detail.

It is of course no secret that some of the very authorities charged with detecting Volstead Act violations were themselves among the violators. Others, though not actively engaged in the booze traffic, were sometimes willing to look the other way for a consideration. One Orcas man used to tell of bringing his small fishing boat alongside an apparently disabled craft he thought needed help. The islander was wearing an old Navy jacket and was mistaken by the skipper — who proved to be a rummy — for a Coast Guardsman.

"Well, help yourself and let me go," said the rum-runner matter-of-factly, whereupon the Orcas man assumed what he hoped was an official look, threw a gunny-sack full of Canada's best over his shoulder and departed with all the haste he could manage.

Figuring ways to con a few free sacks of hooch from the rummies — who were in no condition to complain to the law over their losses — was one of the sports that made the 'twenties roar. Loyal Larson, who spent the bulk of his four score and four years carrying the mail in the San Juans, used to tell of one such episode. The plotters learned that a certain liquor carrier was using a deserted stretch of beach on San Juan Island for his "drop" and did not bother actually caching the bottles unless a warning shot, fired by a sentinel on a distant vantage point, warned of approaching danger.

Posing as customers, the hooch-thieves were able to overpower the sentinel. They themselves fired the alarm signal and watched patiently as the rum-runner crew scurried to convey the goods into the cache. Then the rummies hurriedly abandoned the

313

scene, leaving the enterprising thieves to collect a considerable haul of free booze.

The polite term for such activities is hijacking, and anyone who was on the inside of the business in those halcyon days will assure you that the hijacker presented a far greater danger to the rum-trade practitioners than all the law enforcement agencies put together. It was as much on account of the liquor pirates, if not moreso, that the rum crews resorted to ever faster boats, thicker armor plate, and more potent weapons for themselves as the prohibition years advanced.

A typical hijack operation occurred one blustery Wednesday in November 1922. A rum-runner calling himself Harry Talbot, from Los Angeles, cleared Vancouver in the Schooner *Daisy* with $50,000 worth of liquor supposedly bound for Estenada, Mexico.* Talbot's true destination was some quiet island meeting with an American boat — a rendezvous he did not keep, for while negotiating narrow Active Pass between Mayne and Galiano Islands, he was suddenly overhauled by a faster craft, the crew of which relieved him at gunpoint of his entire cargo.

Talbot was forced roughly from the *Daisy* into the hijack boat, which turned and headed for American waters at high speed. After a good deal of brutal treatment Talbot was given his choice of being thrown overboard, or put ashore on one of the U.S. islands. It was not a difficult choice to make, and before long he was found scrambling up the rocks to the Turn Point light station on Stuart Island. Islanders conveyed him to San Juan, whence he made his way back to Vancouver, battered, boatless, and bereft of his booze, but glad to be wearing most of his original skin.

Turn Point, being the nearest spot in the San Juans to

* Canadian supply boats generally operated legally as "coastal traders" with their liquid cargoes fully detailed on manifests giving some such destination as "Panama" or "Mexico." No one seemed to raise an eyebrow over 40-foot gas-engined craft, capable of only 20 knots or so, making three or four round trips a week between B.C. and Latin America.

Canadian waters, was witness to more than one drama of the sort. It was on September 17, 1924, that Chris Waters, keeper of the Turn Point light, noticed a small craft drifting northward up Haro Strait on the morning tide. Waters figured the boat's engine had broken down and kept an eye on it. Several hours later the vessel was within a quarter of a mile of Stuart, and still drifting. Waters decided to row over and lend a hand.

No one answered the lightkeeper's hail as he came alongside. Clambering over the rail he made a quick search of the craft and found it deserted. The anchor chain was down, but the anchor seemingly not grounded.

Waters returned to Stuart, left the lighthouse in charge of an assistant and went off to get Eric Erickson at Prevost. Erickson had a gas boat, in which the pair overtook the derelict and towed her in. On closer inspection they found the anchor was not dragging, but gone, the chain having been severed.

That's not all they found. Brownish stains on the deck and hatch cover looked suspiciously like blood, while a pencil-size hole in the foc's'le door could only have been made by a bullet. Going below they found more stains — bunks and bulkheads were splashed with them — and on an opened Adventure Magazine lay a man's cap half filled with the still sticky, reddish-brown goo. It was enough to make the islanders' own blood drop a degree or two in temperature.

Papers and furniture scattered over the deck added to the evidence a mortal fight had taken place, no doubt between hijackers and their rum-boat victims.

Waters notified the Coast Guard, which sent a cutter to take charge of the vessel, the fish-packer *Beryl-G*, owned by William Gillis of Vancouver. Gillis and his son, William Jr., were supposedly using the craft to haul cannery supplies. Both men were missing — nor was either to be seen ever again.

Because of the Canadian registry, provincial police were invited into the case along with U.S. authorities. The ill-starred craft ultimately was towed by the *Arcata* to Friday Harbor where it remained tied up at the customs dock below Spring Street for several weeks. As the county fair was in progress, the much-publicized vessel became the grisly object of considerable interest, vying with the pickled pears and out-sized cabbages for fair-goers' attention.

First, of course, the boat had been combed for clues. The most promising item found was a camera containing a partially-exposed roll of film. Police had the pictures developed and one of them showed in close-up detail a low, squarish boat, its boiling wake curving away from the photographer. A bit of the Gillis boat's rigging showed too, proving that the pictured vessel had just left the *Beryl-G*'s side.

B. C. sleuths identified the pictured vessel as one of the 40-knot speedsters of the Tacoma "near beer" man, Pete Marinoff. An inspector contacted Marinoff and found him cooperative: he was as anxious as they to see the hijackers put permanently out of business.

The Tacoman disclosed that Gillis' job was to ferry liquor from the supply ship *Comet*, standing off Vancouver Island in international waters, to various Gulf Islands rendezvous points where Marinoff's crews took over. The last pickup from Gillis had been made on the 15th, two days before the blood-stained *Beryl-G* was found adrift.

Marinoff also ticked off the names of underworld figures he judged capable of hijacking and murder. Among them was tall 39-year-old Owen B. "Cannonball" Baker, an ex-McNeil Island inmate. Baker and an unknown companion had relieved Marinoff before of booze as well as cash money in a Seattle holdup.

From a Canadian-born laundry worker and sometime rummy, the provincial detective wrung the names of several disreputables who had been pirating liquor in the Gulf Islands area. One of them was "Cannonball" Baker. Another was Baker's sidekick, also a McNeil Island alumnus, named Harry Sowash.

316

Meanwhile, in Victoria, police were questioning an immigrant fisherman who had commissioned an Oak Bay boatworks to alter the appearance of his fishing boat — just two days after the Gillis hijacking. The man also had been heard to mutter that he "needed a good lawyer." And a Victoria customs official recalled that a few days before the Gillises had disappeared, he had run into the fisherman — whom he knew personally — in the company of an American introduced to him as Owen Baker.

Other evidence was amassed implicating the fisherman, who soon chose to unburden himself of a bizarre and complicated tale of deceit, piracy, and murder.

Baker's rather clean-cut appearance inclined him toward the impersonation of law enforcement officers — a technique he had used more than once to pry free booze from hard-working rummies. But most of his jobs had been small ones, netting mere peanuts. Finally he had hit on a scheme to make some real money.

Assuming the identity of a U.S. official, Baker arranged to meet a visiting B.C. police officer in a Seattle apartment. Claiming he wanted the information in connection with Volstead Act enforcement, Baker asked the Canadian to supply him with whatever data the Provincial Police had regarding the location of liquor caches on the B.C. side of the border. Poker-faced, the officer obliged with a list of probable locations.

Baker then gathered some rum-row associates together, chartered a gas boat called the *Dolphin*, and headed for Vancouver Island.

At Victoria they contacted the immigrant fisherman, whom they hired to accompany them in his vessel, the *Denman-II*. They told him their mission was to get actual motion picture film footage of American rum boats in action, at the behest of a Hollywood company which was paying handsomely to use it in a movie. Intimating the operation had the blessing of the provincial police, Baker let the *Denman*'s owner observe him enter the

Victoria police station and emerge again clutching a list of places to be investigated.

The two vessels began visiting these locations, the *Dolphin*'s crew searching each one for hidden booze, but coming up empty-handed every time: the savvy Canadian official had fed Baker nothing but misinformation.

Sowash and Baker, frustrated by the turn of events, now abandoned subtleties for direct action. In the course of their peregrinations they had several times observed the *Beryl-G* at anchor. They decided to knock over the Gillis boat.

The *Denman* was chosen for the job. About 10 p.m. on September 15th Baker, Sowash, and a companion named Charlie Morris instructed their fisherman dupe to take them to the east side of Sidney Island, opposite Stuart. Arriving about midnight they moored near the place where Gillis had been seen earlier, working over his engine.

Baker and Morris had blue suits on and Morris was wearing a gold-trimmed, official-looking cap. Baker pulled guns and a pair of handcuffs from a satchel and the two, together with Sowash, got into a skiff and rowed quietly into the night. The perplexed fisherman was ordered to bring up the *Denman* on a flashlight signal.

A quarter hour passed when sounds of shooting reached the *Denman*, and moments later a light flashed. Before the *Denman*'s agitated skipper could decide what to do next, the skiff — with Baker in it — came alongside. Baker leveled a pistol and ordered the fisherman to "Go ahead!"

As the fishboat approached the *Beryl-G* Morris could be seen walking young Gillis at gunpoint across the deck and into the forward cabin. "We had to shoot the old man a little in the arm," Morris called across to the *Denman*. Actually, William Gillis was below, his lifeless body oozing blood into his cap and overflowing onto the magazine he had been reading.

Baker and Morris transferred the *Beryl-G*'s liquor to the other

318

vessel while the two craft, lashed side-by-side, headed east toward little Halibut Island. There the Gillis boat was anchored and Sowash ordered the younger victim topside. As he stepped out on deck Sowash struck him a savage blow over the head from behind. "The cold-blooded murderers!" exclaimed Morris, aloud, as young Gillis crumpled.

Baker and Sowash shook hands over the boy's silent form and went below to get the older man's body. The two victims were then handcuffed together and — as a precaution against their bodies floating to the surface — both were ripped open with a butcher knife. The two killers attached the *Beryl-G*'s anchor to them and dumped father and son overside.

Brandishing the dripping butcher knife before the eyes of the terrified fisherman, Baker ordered him to take the *Denman* to nearby islands where the liquor was cached, then on to Anacortes. There the hijackers debarked — after a final threat to "plug" the panic-white fisherman if he ever talked.

The *Denman*'s skipper headed for the San Juans where he spent a day thinking things over and trying to get a grip on himself. Opting to keep quiet about the whole affair, he returned to Victoria and saw about getting his boat's appearance altered.

When the fisherman's tale was told, police rounded up Charlie Morris easily enough, but Sowash and Baker had vanished. Rewards were offered and a gigantic man-hunt spread across North America. Locally, authorities spent a month and a day fruitlessly dragging the salt chuck for the Gillis bodies, but swift tides and voracious sea creatures had removed every trace.

Baker was tracked to the New York waterfront by Seattle detectives who captured him on December 27, 1924. A month later New Orleans police recognized Sowash, who was netted by chance during a routine roundup of transients.

Sowash, Baker and Morris were tried in Canada and convicted of capital murder. Morris appealed and got his sentence commuted to life imprisonment, but the others paid society with

319

their lives. It is said that Baker's last words, directed to the hangman, were "Step on it, Buddy. Let's get on with it."

While police on both sides of the border were relentless in their persecution of outlaws like Sowash and Baker, attitudes toward "legitimate" liquor runners ranged downward from reluctant enforcement through tolerance to actual participation. For years, the undisputed king of Puget Sound bootleggers was baby-faced Captain Roy Olmstead, boy wonder of the Seattle Police Department, whose far-flung operation rivaled — in size and organization — that of any Capone or Dutch Schultz. But unlike those gangsters, whose hallmarks were the murdered mobster and blinded customer, Olmstead ran an honest shop. You could always buy a bottle from an Olmstead man and be sure the contents were neither watered, nor would they dissolve the enamel from your teeth.

Nor would Roy Olmstead permit his associates to resort to gunplay — even to "pack a rod." His success at eluding both hijackers and the law depended on careful planning, secrecy, and top-notch operators.

One of Olmstead's lieutenants, reputedly the most successful rum-runner on Puget Sound, was a short, heavy-set San Juan County man named Prosper Graignic. Graignic's dad was a French sailor who jumped ship at Victoria in the 1870's, married a native girl and settled down on Waldron Island's North Bay. The large family they reared there grew up, it would seem, with sea water instead of blood in their veins. One of Prosper's brothers is said to have sailed the family sloop to Victoria and back at the age of seven. Another, though deaf, earned his way as a fisherman; his knowledge of local tides and currents is described by island people as "uncanny." Even the girls in the family learned, early on, to be as much at home afloat as on dry land.

Prosper's entry into the rum trade was not auspicious. Acquiring a 45-foot gas "yacht," the *M-846*, he had her cabin enlarged and installed twin 300-horse Sterling marine engines. Leaving Seattle's Lake Union about noon of a June day he headed north for Discovery Island, near Victoria; four or five truckloads of hooch were to be boated there from Vancouver and divvied up between Graignic and several other operators.

Arriving at that destination during the night, Graignic and his crewman-companion retired to their bunks for some shut-eye. But early the next morning Chief Constable John James Otway Wilkie of the Provincial Police discovered the *M-846* illegally moored in Canadian waters, arrested the pair, and turned them over to immigration authorities. Graignic was obliged to pay a $400 fine for entering Canada at other than a designated port.

Upon paying the fine, Graignic's B.C. lawyer approached immigration officers and openly asked them how a U.S. vessel could visit Canada and secure a load of liquor "without getting into trouble." He had thus already violated rule number one, for the Canadians promptly reported the conversation to American authorities.

Returning to Discovery Island, Graignic found his boat adrift and had to hire a launch to chase it. When the *M-846* was recovered, eight miles away near Hein Bank light, the Waldron Islander headed home empty and entered the United States — legally, according to the book — at Port Townsend. But officials at that port, who knew exactly what he had been up to, seized the vessel on grounds it was "being used in foreign trade." Graignic paid another $500 fine to get his boat out of hock.

But Prosper Graignic survived the novice stage of his career and in the long run his knowledge of local waters and unerring skill at boat-handling enabled him to land load after load of burlap-wrapped Canadian spirits on the American side, virtually at will, thus contributing heavily to the estimated two hundred cases a day being delivered to Olmstead in Seattle.

Graignic's forte was the ability to navigate in weather neither the Coast Guard nor Sound pirates would dare face. Time after time when vicious southeasters turned the Straits to boiling foam and monster waves drove every other skipper on the Sound to anchor in the lee of the nearest island, Prosper would pile sack on sack of booze into the *Baby Bottleman*, the *Elsie* — named by Olmstead for his wife — or some other craft and head unchallenged for the U.S. side. And he always got there. (Except for the day in 1924 when the high-performance engines of the *Elsie* caught fire, burning the boat to the water, and Graignic barely escaped with his life.)

For the rare occasion when Graignic was about to be overhauled he had a slick device for getting rid of the evidence in a hurry. Sacks were tied together at intervals on a line passing over rollers to the stern of the boat. Cutting one line would cause the rope to pay out and the whole load to be dumped. If his pursuers didn't look sharp, they would never see it happen. And by picking shallow water to dump in, Graignic could always come back later and retrieve every sack.

Of course the truth about Captain Olmstead's extracurricular activities was bound to come out — it was Seattle's worst-kept secret anyhow — but even his dismissal from the force simply enabled the pleasant-mannered ex-cop to devote himself more fully to his private endeavors. And his vast connections within all levels of officialdom weren't hurting him, either. The stacks of money just grew and grew in the old clothes hamper he carelessly called "the bank."

Some of this money he invested in Seattle's pioneer radio broadcasting station, KTCL, partly for fun and partly as a hedge against the future. There is an undying legend in the Puget Sound country that Olmstead used the station to transmit, in the guise of bedtime stories for children, intelligence information about the movements of Coast Guard vessels; but there is no proof that this was ever done. Actually, there was no need to, for Olmstead conversed quite openly with his employes by telephone, safe in the knowledge that wire-tap evidence had been outlawed in Washington State.

Federal authorities tapped his phone anyway, but even this was used to Olmstead's advantage. Calling an employe from home he would give detailed instructions for a booze pickup. "I got you the first time, Roy," the fellow would say breezily. Then Olmstead could go to a pay phone, call back and give a different set of instructions. Prohibition agents spent many a wet night at some phony rendezvous, while the actual hand-over of liquor took place far, far away.

Desperate for a conviction, prohibition agencies built a case on conspiracy to violate the National Prohibition Act, rather than actual violation of it, and got Olmstead and ninety members of his organization indicted in November 1924. Graignic was to be among the defendants at what the Seattle papers were calling the biggest liquor trial in U.S. history. "Whispering wires" evidence, though technically illegal, was by various devices introduced at the classic trial, which drew as observers awed law professors from the nearby University of Washington. Olmstead was convicted, sold his radio station to pay the lawyers, and did time on McNeil Island before receiving a pardon from President Franklin Roosevelt. The wiretap aspects of the case led to its review by the U.S. Supreme Court, and to a landmark decision holding such evidence is not barred by the Constitution's fourth amendment.

Prosper Graignic, like many another of those indicted with Olmstead, jumped bail and fled to Canada, where Graignic had a brother working in a Sooke, B.C. cannery. A few weeks after the historic trial Olmstead, who had put up the collateral for Graignic's forfeited bail bond, himself participated in a two-nation scheme to net his former associate. Driving to Vancouver, B.C., Olmstead and Deputy U.S. Marshal A. B. McDonald boarded the steamer *Princess Victoria*, Seattle-bound via the British Columbia capital. Meanwhile Canadian immigration officers obligingly arrested Graignic for improper entry, ordered him deported, and placed him on board the *Princess* boat when it arrived in Victoria.

Deputy Marshal McDonald remained in seclusion while Olmstead hunted up his ex-associate and the pair occupied a stateroom together until 6 o'clock the next morning, when the steamer was in American waters off Port Townsend. At this point McDonald burst into the cabin, placed Graignic under arrest, and had him up before a Seattle judge later the same day.

Graignic promoted $7,500 for bail and went to plying his accustomed trade until the last weeks of 1927, when the law's arm finally got him into a courtroom to face a file of damning evidence. The Waldron Islander drew three years and a day on that grim little island south of Tacoma. He served half of the sentence, was paroled, and lived a thoroughly circumspect existence thereafter.

Between the determined prosecution by Prohibition forces of organizations like Olmstead's, and vastly multiplied patrol activities by the Coast Guard, the torrent of booze flowing through Washington's inland sea had by the close of 1924 slowed to a persistent but puny trickle. "Puget Sound is drying up" reported the Friday Harbor *Journal*, quoting "the booze men themselves." While according to the Bellingham *American*, as many as twenty-six relentless Coast Guard crews now guarded Puget Sound waters against the transcursions of foreign spirits.

Those rummies who persisted in the game were obliged to resort to elaborate new tactics, such as the false-compartmented boat. But even so, sharp-eyed Coast Guard crews often found them out. One such vessel, the *Alice*, was spotted off Upright Head, Lopez Island, in 1926. J. L. Gunderson, in command of the CG picket boat 2354, thought it odd that the 50-foot *Alice* was riding so low in the water, with no cargo apparent on her deck. He whistled her down for an inspection, which turned up no evidence of liquor — or any other explanation for the sparsity of freeboard.

Smug faces on *Alice*'s crew turned to dismay when the determined Coast Guard officer drove the suspect vessel up on the beach for a thorough look-see. At length the hiding place was discovered: 22-foot-long, narrow compartments had been built into each side of the hull below the waterline, just wide enough to receive the liquid cargos one sack at a time. The sacks were attached by ropes to an iron ring at the opening, to facilitate their removal at journey's end, the whole apparatus being concealed during the trip by a board nailed over the opening.

Gunderson's men seized 115 cases of illicit potables and *Alice* herself, an ex-Navy motor-sailer, was confiscated and pressed into the anti-booze service.

Such were the dying gasps of the rum trade through San Juan waters, as elsewhere. But the prohibition experiment too was terminal: mounting public revulsion over the mood of gangsterism, official corruption and grass-roots scofflawry rampant in a turbulent and agonized society spoke death to the Great Test, the efficacy — if not the nobility — of which was by then almost universally in question. Then the Wall Street humpty-dumpty toppled and as the minions of financial empire scrambled vainly to reassemble the debris, the bread-line crowd howled for the right, at least, to its liquid solace. In 1932 Franklin Roosevelt, besides declaiming against the fear of fear, pledged an axe to the Act of Mr. Volstead; but Congress beat him to it by pulling the budgetary teeth of the Coast Guard and other enforcement agencies. Prohibition was dead, the cadaver to be buried the following year upon ratification of the Constitution's twenty-first amending. In the San Juans as across the nation, the demise of the Noble Experiment was feted with many a high-held toast, and usually to the self-delusory tune of Tin Pan Alley's latest: "Happy Days Are Here Again!"

20

THROUGHOUT THE SIXTY-ODD years of its existence the Friday Harbor *Journal* has, in its editorializing, specialized in concise observations of the puckish and pithy, if not always prescient, variety. There was the day a *Journal* editor, his crystal ball obviously tuned to some wavelength other than that of the coming 1940's, penned this gem:

What would we do with the Philippines? Why, bless you: . . . we would give them to Japan; and if Japan refused, we would lick her and make her take them.

The writer of these immortal words was probably not Virgil Frits, the island boy who joined the paper in 1907 and for most of the following half-century *was* the Friday Harbor *Journal*. Frits went in more for the homely but perceptive one-liner, such as:

The abolition of the woodshed, as heating plants come into general use, in our opinion may have serious effects upon the education of children.

Frits provided his own topper in one inspired editorial comment, one day when a column lacked half-an-inch of being filled:

If you agree with everything the editor writes, you have no more sense than the editor.

The *Journal's* stock-in-trade has always been the social note of the "Mrs. Thomas Jones spent Monday of last week on the mainland shopping," and "Horace Woonspeth reports that the spring rains have slowed rutabaga growth on the southern end of the island" type. But having participated in the bloodier stages of the *Journal's* mortal combat with the San Juan *Islander*, Frits was able to call up hidden fires of editorial belligerence when the occasion arose.

Virgil Frits' entrance into the newspaper game coincided more or less with the emergence on the Northwest scene of the big International Workers of the World union — a socialistic, anti-employer movement embracing such revolutionary demands as the eight-hour day and sanitary standards for lumber camps. Generally speaking, the "wobblies" achieved little for their efforts except cracked skulls and bloodied noses; certainly they earned scant support, if any at all, among conservatively-minded San Juan Islanders, and positively none in the editorial sanctum of the Friday Harbor *Journal*.

I. W. W.* agitation mounted during the First World War and reached a climax in Centralia, Washington, on Armistice Day of 1919. A confrontation between some wobblies and a group of parading American Legionnaires resulted in several shooting deaths, one emasculation and a lynching. Although the unionists were the attackees, not the attackers, the altercation resulted in the arrest of hundreds of I. W. W. people as well as a few non-members who were merely suspected of harboring radical notions of one kind or another.

Though it does not seem that the union had any members in the San Juans, the *Journal's* indignation toward wobblies in general exploded at white heat.

It seems deplorable to advocate mob violence [ran the paper's comment] but when such outrages as the recent trouble at Centralia occur, it seems this is the only course to take. The time is coming

* Critics insisted the initials stood for "I Won't Work."

when every man caught with an I. W. W. card in his possession will be given an application of tar and feathers. There is no room among decent people for such trouble makers and the quicker a community makes it so hot for them that hell will not be a comparison, the quicker much of our industrial unrest will cease.

Ordinarily such a comment (with which perhaps 90% of the county's population were in agreement) might have passed without critical notice. But by an improbable coincidence the *Journal* was just then an object of disaffection on the part of the county's prosecuting attorney, having published in its columns the text of a recall petition being circulated against the prosecutor. The hapless attorney had found himself in the middle of one of those periodic school controversies which seem to be a staple of life on Orcas Island, where two teachers had been fired as radicals. (Their crime: requiring students to read a book written by Woodrow Wilson.)

The teachers appealed to county school authorities, who reinstated them, and Orcas Island patriots, somehow blaming the prosecutor for this outcome, determined to oust him from office.

The attorney replied by filing charges against the *Journal* for inciting a breach of the peace, in publishing the I. W. W. outburst.

The prosecutor next found *himself* charged in court with "misfeasance, malfeasance and corruption" in the performance of his duties, in that he "used the power and functions of his office as a means to vent his spite and ill will against those toward whom he held grievance."

The *Journal* publishers, Frits and G. A. Ludwig, pleaded innocent. Their trial took place within the month and a jury of twelve local people decided, after twenty minutes' deliberation, that the words "...mob violence...is the only course to take...." did not constitute the advocacy of mob violence.

The charges and recall movement against the prosecutor were dropped, since an election was about due anyway, with the chances of his re-election roughly equal to the possibility that Puget Sound salt water would suddenly transform itself into bonded Scotch whisky.

The prosecutor was not re-elected, and Puget Sound did not lose its unalcoholic salinity. But changes of another sort *were* in the making on the Sound — changes which portended fundamental alterations in the Islands' way of life.

For long years the economy of the San Juans had been built almost wholly around the freight-and-passenger boats running out of Seattle and Bellingham. Sometimes several boats a day plied the lower Sound waters, with landings at every little dock from Olga, on Orcas Island, to Argyle, Roche and Friday Harbor on San Juan. They were steamers, those vessels now scarcely remembered, and voracious: each wharf or crib dock was piled high with precisely stacked lengths of island fir to fire their gluttonous boilers.

Schedules were a sometime thing in those packet boat days with Seattle-bound passengers obliged to budget hours of waiting time for the old *Evangel*, or the *Islander*, or the *Mohawk*, the *Lydia Thompson* or the *Rosalie* to make an appearance. Occasionally a boat wouldn't come in at all, if the skipper — for steamboat captains were an independent lot — took a notion to skip one port in favor of a longer call at another.

Each vessel, like the temperamental skippers, had its own personality. The *Rosalie*, a veteran of the Seattle-to-Skagway run in Alaska gold rush days, was the best loved; while island people reserved their greatest scorn for the antiquated "Lydia Pinkham" whose cranky ways were a perennial source of aggravation.

Both the *Islander* and the *Mohawk** were built at San Juan

* The *Mohawk*, built at the Albert Jensen shipyard on San Juan, was originally named *Islander* after the earlier Orcas-built vessel. When the diesel engines with which she was first equipped proved unsatisfactory, she was converted to steam and renamed.

County shipyards, and many of the best of the Puget Sound boatmen were island products as well. Of these, the most famous was "Captain Sam" Barlow.

Sam Barlow was one of seven sons of a pioneer Lopez family. All seven of the boys took naturally to seafaring careers, brother Dan having appeared in our narrative already as the boatman hero of the Lopez "chivaree" shooting tragedy. Sam's sea-going initiation took place at age three when he set out with a brother on a world cruise. Their equipment was a canoe with one paddle, and soon they had lost the paddle. The watchfulness of an older sister saved them from disaster that time, but it was Barlow's own island-learned skill that enabled him later to put in 47 years and 20,000 voyages through Puget Sound's island-studded waters with nary a mishap of consequence.

Old-time Puget Sound steamboaters — as many as are left — can yarn by the hour about Captain Sam's exploits. It is said he once performed a marriage aboard the *Lydia Thompson*, taking literally the law permitting the master of a vessel on the high seas to tie such a knot. Puget Sound is scarcely the high seas, but Sam steered the *Thompson* for a wide place in the Strait of Juan de Fuca and spliced the happy couple as effectively as any Cunard Line four-striper.

Around the turn of the century gasoline-engine craft were beginning to appear on Washington's inland sea. Captain Bill Kasch of Anacortes placed a petrol-powered boat on the San Juan run for the first time, the diminutive *Anglo-Saxon*, earning his family's bread with this boat and its successor, the *Yankee Doodle*, for many years.

But it was not the advent of gasoline vessels that doomed the steam-powered boats. It was the booming popularity of the family automobile. By the early 1920's the products of Henry Ford *et al* had revolutionized land transportation; now the proliferating horseless carriage was demanding a new kind of

330

service, linking the Puget Sound country's separated land masses with water-borne, auto-carrying sea "bridges."

The era of the ferry-boat was at hand.

It was Captain Harry W. Crosby, a relative of Bing's (and an owner of the unpopular *Lydia Thompson*) who organized the first ferry run through the Islands as an experiment. Its terminals were Anacortes and Sidney, B.C., exactly as is the case now, more than four decades later. Crosby began the service with a 97-foot converted kelp harvester, the *Harvester King*, powered by a single diesel engine that turned up fewer horses than does the power plant of a modern family car. She carried some dozen vintage automobiles on her decks and required five hours to make the crossing.

Opposite the *Harvester King* Crosby placed the chartered stern-wheeler *Gleaner*, which carried twenty-five cars. Each vessel made one crossing a day.

Crosby's ferry service was a summer-time operation only, and as such it was a fine success. Thus encouraged he sold the *Harvester King* and replaced it with a 36-car auto ferry, *City of Angeles*, newly converted from a freight-and-passenger steamer the Puget Sound Navigation Company had just retired from the San Juan service. As her running mate Crosby acquired the ancient passenger boat *Robert Bridges*, renamed her the *Mount Vernon* and had her converted to a 26-car single-ender. Meanwhile both Orcas and Roche Harbor built ferry slips to accommodate these vessels.*

Crosby's highly successful operation was sold during the subsequent winter hiatus to the big Puget Sound Navigation Company, lineal descendant of the famous Black Ball Line of clipper ships and a first cousin to the prosperous, Seattle-based Alaska Steamship Company. A succession of ever-larger and

* Conflicting evidence holds that Friday Harbor either resisted an opportunity to have the San Juan landing, or — as is most likely — was outmaneuvered for it by John S. McMillin.

faster vessels, all flying the Black Ball flag, continued the run for the next thirty years, during which time the old freight-and-passenger steamboats gradually went the way of the dodo bird and the mustache cup.

Other ferry routes have been tried from time to time, notably involving a Bellingham terminus and a landing at North Beach on Orcas Island, but none of these short-lived experiments has had the success of the tried-and-true run from Anacortes to Sidney via the San Juans. Since 1926 the ferries have stopped at Upright Head, on Lopez; Friday Harbor replaced Roche Harbor as the San Juan landing point around 1930; and Shaw Island was added that year. Otherwise, except for two changes in the dock location at Anacortes, the route has remained precisely the same until the present time.

But not the ownership. In the late 'forties a difference of opinion arose between the Puget Sound Navigation Company and Washington State transportation authorities over proposed rate increases, which the company insisted were needed to stay in business. Denied the fare boost, company president Alex Peabody threatened to cease operating the San Juan and other ferry routes and sent dismissal notices to seven hundred employes.

The Department of Transportation relented, permitting a provisional rate hike on condition patrons were given chits with their ticket purchases, redeemable for any difference in fares when and if the company could be persuaded to see things the State's way. The company could not. Finally, on June 1, 1951, the State of Washington bought out the entire ferry system, repainted the boats with Washington's colors, green and white — and promptly raised the rates again.

Meanwhile, coincident with Captain Harry Crosby's primitive venture, another new island industry had been a-borning. Its unlikely birthplace: around a bridge table in Spokane, Washington. The four players included one who rarely lost a hand, and three who rarely won one except as the fortunate fellow's partner. The flow of money at the conclusion of this foursome's periodic card meets was decidedly unidirectional.

Consequently, when this bridge adept remarked one day that he would like to start up a business in the distant San Juan Islands, his partners jumped at the chance to fund the venture for him, thereby saving themselves further losses. Or so his story goes.

The bridge expert's name was John M. Henry and his plan was simply to buy up as much land as possible in the central San Juan Valley and plant it all to peas. "Pea" Henry, as he was universally known in the Islands, had not picked the location by whim. Considerable experimentation and soil study had led him to the conclusion that no superior spot for the raising of peas could be found on the Pacific Coast. "Pea" Henry's ultimate plan was to add his own cannery to the set-up, which was viewed with tremendous enthusiasm in the county.

And with good reason. Within three years around 1,200 acres were under cultivation and the San Juan Islands Canning Company plant, employing some 150 people, had boosted its annual pack to about 50,000 cases. The firm called their brand of peas "Saltair" and, as "Pea" Henry had foreseen, the product won nation-wide notice as just about the finest canned peas obtainable.

"Pea" Henry's elaborate empire grew steadily through the 'twenties and when the Great Depression struck the San Juans, his was one of the few bright spots in the local business picture.

But not for long. As the rest of the nation contended over the N. R. A., the C. C. C. and the W. P. A.,* San Juan farmers found themselves locked in combat with a nonalphabetic adversary, the pea weevil. It seems the same ideal conditions which made the peas grow large and sweet encouraged a super-migration

* For the benefit of younger readers: National Recovery Act, Civilian Conservation Corps, and Works Progress Administration, controversial anti-Depression programs of President Franklin Roosevelt.

of the big-snouted, beetle-like bugs. And in those pre-insecticide days there was no getting rid of them. Reluctantly, "Pea" Henry moved his plant to a mainland location where the peas thrived less well, but the weevils proved more controllable.

The demise of the San Juan Islands Canning Company was a near-catastrophic blow to that island's economy, leaving the Roche Harbor Lime and Cement Company's as virtually the only sizeable payroll left. It must be said, to the everlasting credit of John S. McMillin, that the lime baron went far out of his way during the Depression to create as many jobs for island people as he could. Many projects of questionable utility were undertaken by him largely for make-work purposes — though at the same time allowing him to carry out a reputed vow to avoid paying dividends to minority stock-holders.

One of McMillin's projects in the hungry 'thirties was construction of a family mausoleum on a height above Roche Harbor, near the family home he called Afterglow Manor. This columbarium, replete with Masonic symbolism, and constructed of Roche Harbor cement products, was completed early in 1936. McMillin presumably had no inkling that his own death was imminent, but by the same year's end his life reached its conclusion and his own ashes were first to occupy a niche in the resting place he designed.

The McMillin empire thus passed to a son, Paul, who presided over it no less forcefully than his father, if a 1938 Associated Press news story is to be believed. On checking into a Kansas City hotel, it seems, Paul gave his residence as "Roche Harbor, Washington," but the clerk asked for a street address.

"Just plain Roche Harbor will get it," replied McMillin. "I own the whole town."

Islanders who did *not* own a town — or much of anything else — found the Depression years slightly more endurable than did their city cousins. It was the 1890's all over again, and the old maxim about nobody starving if he could wait 'til the tide went out, still held true. A house or cabin roof for shelter, a bit of ground for a garden and access to a beach where meaty bivalves spouted their invitation to dig, and a man could survive. So could his immediate relatives, and also his not-so-immediate ones if he acceded to their pleas, penned from the hungry cities. If one tired of clams (one always did) a juicy venison steak was a welcome variation on the menu. Of course this usually entailed a rupture of the game laws, for the deer season was a brief and annual affair.

But an unwritten island law stated that killing an out-of-season deer to feed one's hungry family was no offense. On Orcas Island, at least, and it was probably true elsewhere, the game warden used to shoot a few himself and pack them around to families who were having an especially rough time of it, usually explaining the gift with some cock-and-bull story that fooled nobody.

On Orcas, the nearest thing to a John S. McMillin was Robert Moran. Third of ten children born to an immigrant family, his rags-to-riches career began on the Seattle waterfront at six o'clock on a rainy-cold, dreary November morning in 1875. That was the time of Moran's arrival by steerage from New York, via Panama and San Francisco. In Moran's pocket was a single dime, and the seventeen-year-old lad had not had his breakfast. Nor had he any prospects whatever for a job, or a place to lay his head.

Moran's hunger-sharpened olfactory apparatus picked up the scent of pork sausage, flapjacks and coffee, and he followed his nose to the establishment of the huge and jolly Bill Grose, colored proprietor of the pioneer hotel-and-eatery known as "Our House." Moran negotiated a credit arrangement with the genial innkeeper, ate heartily of the grub Bill shoved at him through the half-moon kitchen window, and set out to find employment.

335

It was a humble and short-lived job, and so was the next, and the next. But Moran had the kind of drive you spell with S's and C's, and it led him as inexorably to success in business as his tantalized proboscis had steered him to Grose's Front Street chophouse. By 1882 Moran had his own marine repair shop at Yesler's Wharf, and in 1889 he was elected mayor of the burgeoning metropolis. That was the year of Seattle's disastrous fire, and it was Moran who gave the heart-rending order to dynamite several downtown blocks to contain the blaze.

By 1904 Moran was a wealthy and powerful man — and a sick one. Doctors diagnosed the problem as heart disease and gave him a short time to live. So Moran disposed of his shipbuilding empire and retired to the property he purchased from the Orcas Island lumber manufacturer, shipper, and prohibitionist, Andrew Newhall.* The huge estate, located on Orcas Island's Cascade Bay, he renamed "Rosario" after the Strait which bounds the Islands on the east.

But like Paul Hubbs of an earlier time, Moran confounded the medicos and regained his complete health, once he had traded the grinding pressures of business for the calming atmosphere of island life. During the nearly forty years he lived on Orcas he was regarded by many (not all) of its people as the island's greatest benefactor. He spent a reputed million dollars, if not more, on Orcas: by building roads and then giving them to the county — along with the equipment that built them; by sharing his water rights with the neighboring village of Olga and helping build that community's public water system, the first such on the island; by providing jobs during the hungry Depression years.

Moran's outstanding act of philanthropy has to be his gift to the State of Washington of 2600-acre Moran State Park, comprising virtually all of scenic Mount Constitution. Ironically,

* Newhall retired to the "Idlewild" property of the recently deceased Edward Warbass near Friday Harbor.

O. H. Culver in the *San Juan Islander* office, about 1906.
Courtesy Mrs. George Hipkoe, Bellingham.

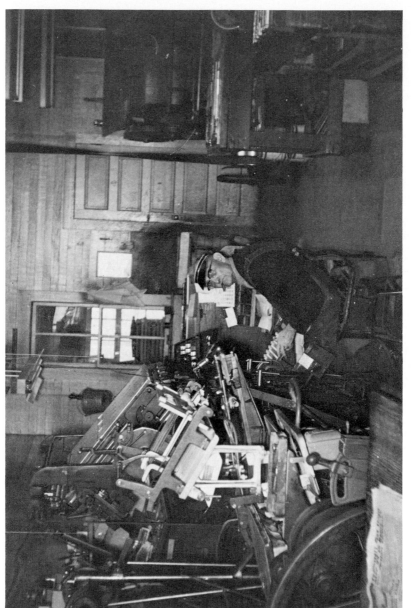

Virgil Frits, editor-publisher of the *Friday Harbor Journal*, shortly before his retirement in 1958. *Photo by author.*

Above: photo of fast boat leaving the side of the *Beryl-G* helped identify hijack-murderers of rum-running days. *Courtesy Mr. Cecil Clark, Victoria.*

Right: Prosper Graignic, of Waldron Island, "ace" of Puget Sound rum-runners. *Courtesy Mr. William Chevalier, Sr., Friday Harbor.*

The *Lydia Thompson* ran — sometimes — between Seattle and Whatcom (Bellingham) via the San Juans in the 'nineties. Fares were considered needlessly high and she was not exactly the most popular boat around. *Courtesy Joe D. Williamson's Marine Photo Shop.*

Andrew Newhall of Orcas bought the 87-ton *Buckeye* and placed it on the San Juan-Whatcom route in competition with the *Thompson*, forcing freight and passenger rates down. The somewhat ungainly vessel foundered in Bellingham Bay in April 1895, with the loss of one life, but she was favored by island people anyway. *Courtesy Joe D. Williamson's Marine Photo Shop.*

Newhall ultimately replaced the *Buckeye* with the 163-ton *Islander*, built for him at Newhall (now Rosario), Orcas Island, by J. A. Scribner. After Newhall's retirement the vessel was sold, leaving islanders again at the mercy of mainland transportation companies. *Courtesy Joe D. Williamson's Marine Photo Shop.*

In 1921 the Jensen shipyard at Friday Harbor launched a second *Islander*, largest vessel ever built in the San Juans. Pure spring water was used for the gala christening, at which attorney Ivan L. Blair spoke glowingly of the prosperity the home-owned vessel was sure to bring island businesses. But this was not to be: sound enough of hull, the new *Islander*'s diesel engines caused such continued trouble she was finally sold. Converted to steam and renamed *Mohawk*, she ended her career as an ocean-going tug. *Courtesy Joe D. Williamson's Marine Photo Shop.*

Robert Moran, and friends, at his Orcas Island estate.
The figurehead was salvaged from a sunken sailing ship, the *America*.
Courtesy Mr. Reeves Moran, Orcas.

Robert Moran's residence at Rosario, Orcas Island.
It has since been converted to a resort-hotel.
Courtesy Mr. Reeves Moran, Orcas.

Boaters enjoying a picnic ashore on Matia Island, now a marine park.
Washington State Parks and Recreation Commission.

Valley Church, San Juan Island.

Moran had some trouble convincing State authorities to accept the gift; yet in recent years the park has become one of Washington's most-visited recreational areas, with tents, trailers, camper trucks and even buses thronging its campsites from spring to fall.

In fact, "recreational" has become the keyword in the development of the San Juan Islands throughout the present century. With the blight of spreading urbanization always at their heels, denizens of Puget Sound cities have been forced to scramble farther and ever farther afield to find the expanses of quiet green and blue that once marked every inch of the region. Spared — thus far — from the blight because it was a backwash (read: because the barons of industry had not yet found a way to make much money from it) the San Juan archipelago finds itself in the final third of this hundredyear a chief target of the harried, serenity-seeking retiree or vacationing megalopolite. Every ferry trip brings him by the hundreds in the season, and the wintertime decrescendo becomes less marked year by year.

He also comes by private boat — from small, underpowered outboard craft to palatial steam yachts, swarming through the waters of every bay, channel and strait on fine days. Even sailboats (which have the right-of-way) are sometimes so thick the State ferries have to twist, zig-zag and backwater to avoid them.

To accommodate these water-borne pleasure-seekers, the State has established a long list of Marine Parks, many of them equipped with moorage floats or buoys, pit toilets, camp stoves and picnic tables and even running water. The roster of San Juan island-parks sounds almost like one of Philip Van Buskirk's home-seeking itineraries: Matia, the apple of that sailor's wistful eye, is now one of the most popular of the saltwater parks. So are the 520 acres of the Sucia group,* and the 179-acre Jones

* Yacht clubs and boating enthusiasts throughout the Puget Sound region combined to buy Sucia and presented it to the State for use as a marine park.

Island. The long, narrow strip of land separating Reid Harbor and Prevost Harbor on Stuart comprises another 78-acre park for amateur mariners. While other whole-island parks include Clark, James, Posey, and Turn Island, as well as many smaller and facility-less islets which are part of the San Juan Marine District.

For land-lubbers, the most significant new retreat in the area is the San Juan Historical Park on the sites of the old English and American Camps. Authorized by Congress, to commemorate the Pig War events of 1859-1872, the Park comprises some 1200 acres on the southern end of the island, including the old Hudson's Bay Company's Bellevue Farm, San Juan Town, Pickett's brave redoubt overlooking Griffin Bay, and Lyman Cutler's farm-site, where the pig-shooting episode brought the affair to its head.

Another five hundred acres to the north contain the British campsite and cemetery. The waterfront blockhouse and other buildings on this property are being restored, along with some trails and garden-sites, and visitors' facilities are yet in the planning stage.

Reactions of local residents to creating a "Pig War national park" in their midst are varied. There is an element of pride in having the area's colorful past thus commemorated, but the pride is mitigated somewhat by still-unresolved problems. Dependent on property taxes to pay for governmental services, San Juan County sees the 1700-acre Park as a sizeable deduction from its tax base — thus causing another rise in already-skyrocketing taxes on island homes. Cars used by increasing numbers of sightseers hasten the deterioration of county roads — which must be kept in repair at a further cost to local taxpayers. Avalanching visitor populations also mean rising law-enforcing problems and costs, and a diminution of the uncrowded condition which brought most of the residents here in the first place.

Not that off-island visitors are unwelcomed in the San Juans:

indeed, next to real estate sales and development, tourism and tourist-dependent businesses have become the county's economic mainstay. Even Roche Harbor — whose lime deposits, once thought to be "inexhaustible," have long since passed the point where they can be worked with economy — has evolved instead into a mecca for yachtsmen, fliers, and retirees. The Hotel de Haro, refurbished, retains its quaintly plush turn-of-the-century atmosphere and, nearby, the former McMillin family home has been transformed into an elegant waterfront eatery. Similarly on Orcas, the Moran estate at Rosario serves now as one of the Pacific Northwest's favorite family resorts.

(Casual visitors are less welcome on privately-owned Blakely, now a "fliers' island" where the imaginatively-architectured summer homes of Puget Sound aviators line both sides of an island-bisecting airstrip.)

As the nineteen-seventies get underway, Industry has not yet intruded its smokestacks, noise and water pollution into the San Juan Islands area (though with the breeze in the southeast the gas refineries at Anacortes are already much in evidence). Yet even this unthinkable prospect nearly became reality with the announcement of plans to construct a large aluminum processing plant on bucolic Guemes, a Skagit County island at the San Juans' immediate doorstep. Shocked, disbelieving Northwest residents from Vancouver, Wash. to Vancouver, B. C. emitted such prolonged and heartfelt howls of protesting anguish that company moguls gave up the idea — but only *after* Skagit County officials accorded the project their unqualified blessing. Out of the matter grew an almost hysterical movement to "Save the San Juans" while Seattle newspapers churned out thousands of words urging enforced comprehensive planning as a means to ensure the Islands against industrial encroachment.

Few hue-and-criers stopped to consider what are perhaps the two main lessons to be learned from the Guemes episode. First, that island *already had* a comprehensive plan supposedly protecting it from heavy industry, but when the opportunity presented itself, county officials — understandably allured by the jobs and dollars the venture would generate locally — proved only too willing to scrap the plan out of hand. Second, and more surprising, was the fact that island and mainland people alike turned out to be less than agreed on just what it is the San Juans should be saved *from*.

Island-dwellers want to save their right to go on island-dwelling, without being forced to sell due to astronomical property taxes, resulting from inflated land values brought about by increasing population and industrial pressures. But they also need to save the means to earn their livelihood, which means looking to these same pressures to generate jobs.

Mainland people want to save the unspoiled character of the Islands for boating, camping and hunting trips; while island people want their own enjoyment of their homes and surroundings saved from the growing inundation by outsiders, whose fun they resent having to help support with their taxes.

Both islanders and islanders-to-be are hoping to save the cherished right to build their own house and live in it, to dig their own well and dispose of their sewage as they see fit, as has always been the way in the Islands; while at the same time clamoring to be saved from the pollution that results from too many people already doing these same things in too small a space.

On such a tenuous basis of pluralmindedness, but prodded by dark warnings that if local officials didn't draw up a plan for the "orderly development" of the San Juans someone in Olympia, or in Washington, D.C., would do it for them, well-intentioned county leaders hired a consulting firm to devise such a plan. Grass-roots support for this move was widespread — until residents got a peek at the resulting document.

Replete with zoning restrictions, building codes and all the other bureaucratic impositions which are the mark of big-city regimentation of life's small details, the comprehensive plan was — islanders decided — one of the things they most wanted to be saved from.

Declining to be told how many dogs or cats or horses they could possess, or how close together two-by-fours must be in a woodshed, they joined almost to a man in demanding that the plan be scrapped.

It was.

Meanwhile, runaway development of the area continues at an accelerating pace. Everywhere in our island Eden, ribbon-flagged surveyors' stakes popping up like fall mushrooms proclaim more and yet more subdivisions in the making. It is indeed the time of the singing of chain saws, and the voice of the bulldozer is heard without cease in our dying land.

County officials at Friday Harbor struggle to keep up with the deluge of new development plat filings. They, newspapers and citizens groups join to wring hands in alarm and talk of stemming the tide — with about as much chance of success as old King Canute, standing toe-to-toe with the North Sea.

To the northwest, Canada's Gulf Islands are undergoing precisely the same ordeal, the population sprawl having proven immune to political frontiers and now extending from Seattle-Tacoma all the way north to Vancouver and oozing ever closer to Victoria. While the spectre of full-scale industrial encroachment looms more and more ominously, through growing pressures to provide sites for processing and moving newly-discovered Arctic oil; by development of British Columbia's gigantic port facility at nearby Roberts Bank; and by Canadian agreements to allow off-shore oil explorations on its side of the border. With the same pressures being felt on the U.S. side, one wonders wryly whether "Judge" Warbass' prediction of ships rounding the bend every five minutes at Friday Harbor may come true after all.

As the 'sixties drew to their uncertain close, professors at the University of Victoria asked a computer to project the Gulf

Islands' future. The machine pictures those Islands by 1980 as just another overpopulated, overpaved, near-treeless bedroom community adjunct of British Columbia's urban nightmare — a latter-day Coney Island. Appalled, B.C. officials slapped a freeze on further subdivisions in the area pending the development of a government plan to control the islands' growth.

They also joined with concerned government and university experts on both sides of the border to urge an international conference leading to *joint* planning for the entire area — embracing the San Juan and Gulf Islands and even part of Vancouver Island. Such a plan could be expected to preserve adequate public recreational areas, limit subdivisions and control lot sizes, rule out heavy industry within the entire area, provide for policing and road maintenance, and deal with problems of sewage, water supplies and the like. U.S. and Canadian government participation at the federal level would be the key aspect of the plan.

More than a century ago, two great nations contended over this cluster of quiet islands, set gem-like in their sun-dazzled seas. Today, two nations' shared concern for the future of this island paradise may be its last best hope to survive.

SOURCES AND ACKNOWLEDGMENTS

A book like this one is not so much written as it is compiled. Without the tireless assistance of scores of librarians, archivists, and other keepers of historical records, there would be no book. While it is impossible to mention everyone who has helped in this project, I do wish to express my special gratitude to Mrs. Hazel Mills and her associates of the Washington State Library in Olympia; to Mr. Willard Ireland and his staff at the Provincial Archives, Victoria; and to Bob Monroe and others of the University of Washington Library, Seattle.

Special thanks are also due to Mr. Cecil Clark of Victoria, a former deputy commissioner of British Columbia's police force, who provided many details for the chapters on smuggling and rum-running.

Material on the "Pig War" and its aftermath is published *en masse* in printed volumes of U.S. Senate and House documents, identifiable by serial numbers, and available in many large libraries. Those most useful are Serials 1024, 1056, 1097, 1316, 1341, and 1350. Others containing information relative to affairs described in this book, but with much duplication of the above volumes, include Serials 752, 837, 984, 1014, 1027, 1031, 1051, 1057, 1349, 1361, 1393, and 1399. There is also relevant material in the Official Records of the War of the Rebellion, Series I, Vol. Fifty, Parts I and II; and in unpublished correspondence preserved by the National Archives and Records Service: Records of the War Department, Post Letters of San Juan Island.

The above sources present the matter largely from the American point of view. Many of the same items, along with much additional material presenting the British view of the case, are found in the San Juan files of the Provincial Archives of British Columbia, Victoria, B.C.

I have also made liberal use of newspaper files, particularly those published in Washington Territory from about 1858, and the Victoria papers of the same period, principally the Victoria *Colonist*. Much information was gleaned as well from surviving issues of the San Juan *Graphic*, the San Juan *Islander*, the Orcas *Islander*, and, above all, the Friday Harbor *Journal*. As to the latter, it was through the kindness of the then publisher, the late Robert Hartzog, and Mrs. Hartzog, that I was able to retrieve over fifty years' back issues of the *Journal* from their various cobwebby hiding places. Collating, binding, then reading and indexing them all cost me a winter's work, but was well worth it.

In addition to the above, the following sources were consulted:

BAGLEY, CLARENCE B. *Indian Myths of the Northwest*. Seattle, 1930.

BRIER, HOWARD M. *Sawdust Empire*. New York, Alfred A. Knopf, 1958.

BROUGHTON, WILLIAM R. "Broughton's Log of a Reconnaissance of the San Juan Islands in 1792," edited by J. Neilson Barry, Washington Historical Quarterly, XXI (January, 1930).

CALKINS, R. H. *High Tide*. Seattle, Marine Digest Publishing Co., Inc., 1952.

CATTON, BRUCE. *The Coming Fury*; *Terrible Swift Sword*; *Never Call Retreat*. Garden City, N. Y., Doubleday & Co., Inc., 1961, 1963, 1965.

CLARK, NORMAN H. "Roy Olmstead, a Rumrunning King on Puget Sound," Pacific Northwest Quarterly, LIV (July, 1963).

CROSBY, H. R. "The San Juan Difficulty." Overland Monthly Magazine, March, 1869.

344

DANNER, WILBERT R. *Limestone Resources of Western Washington*. Olympia, Washington State Department of Conservation, 1966.

DAVIDSON, GEORGE. *Coast Pilot of California, Oregon, and Washington Territory*, United States Coast Survey, Washington, 1869.

EDSON, LELAH JACKSON. *The Fourth Corner*. Bellingham, Wash., Cox Brothers, Inc., 1951.

EGERTON, MRS. FRED. *Admiral of the Fleet Sir Geoffrey Phipps Hornby, G. C. B. A Biography*. Edinburgh and London, Blackwood & Sons, 1896.

FIRTH, LILA HANNAH. "Early Life on San Juan Island." Seattle, The University of Washington Library. (1943?).

FLUCKE, A. F. "Early Days on Saltspring Island." British Columbia Historical Quarterly, XV, Nos. 3 and 4 (July-October, 1951).

GIBBS, JAMES A. JR. *Sentinels of the North Pacific*. Portland, Oregon, Binfords & Mort, 1955.

GIBBS, JAMES A. JR. *Shipwrecks of the Pacific Coast*. Portland, Oregon, Binfords & Mort, 1957.

GULF ISLANDS BRANCH, B.C. HISTORICAL ASSOCIATION. *A Gulf Islands Patchwork*. Sidney, B.C., Peninsula Printing Co., Ltd., 1961.

HALLER, GRANVILLE O. "San Juan and Secession." The Tacoma Sunday Ledger, January 19, 1896.

HAYNOR, NORMAN S. *Ecological Succession in the San Juan Islands*. Publications of the American Sociological Society, XXIII, 1929.

HINES, H. K. *Illustrated History of the State of Washington*. Chicago, Lewis Publishing Co., 1894.

HOWAY, F. W. "The Negro Immigration into Vancouver Island in 1858." British Columbia Historical Quarterly, III No. 2 (April, 1939).

Illustrated Supplement to the San Juan *Islander*, Friday Harbor, Washington, 1901.

JEFFCOTT, PERCIVAL R. *Blanket Bill Jarman, northwest washington mystery man.* Ferndale, Washington, Cox & Ebright, Inc., 1958.

JEFFCOTT, PERCIVAL R. *Nooksack Tales and Trails.* Ferndale, Washington, Sedro-Woolley Courier-Times, 1949.

JONES, H. K. *Illustrated History of the State of Washington.* Chicago, Lewis Publishing Co., 1894.

KINGSTON, C. S. "Juan de Fuca Strait: Origin of the Name." Pacific Northwest Quarterly, XXXVI (April 1945).

LUDWIG, CHARLES H. *A Brief History of Waldron Island.* Seattle, 1959.

McCABE, JAMES O. *The San Juan Water Boundary Question.* University of Toronto Press, 1964.

McDONALD, ANGUS. "A Few Items of the West," ed. by F. W. Howay, William S. Lewis and Jacob A. Meyers. Washington Historical Quarterly, VIII (July, 1917).

McKAY, CHARLES. "History of San Juan Island." Washington Historical Quarterly, II (July, 1908).

McNEMEE, A. J. *Brother Mack, the Frontier Preacher.* Portland, Oregon, T. G. Robison, 1924.

MEANY, EDMOND S. *Vancouver's Discovery of Puget Sound.* Portland, Oregon, Binfords & Mort, 1957.

MILLER, HUNTER. *Northwest Water Boundary.* Seattle, University of Washington, 1942.

MILLER, HUNTER. *San Juan Archipelago*. Bellows Falls, Virginia, Wyndham Press, 1943.

MONROE, ROBERT D. *Sailor on the Snohomish. Extracts from the Washington Diaries of Philip C. van Buskirk*. Seattle, University of Washington Library, 1957.

MORAN, ROBERT. "An Address at the Fiftieth Jubilee Meeting of The Pioneers Association of the State of Washington, June 6th, 1939, in Seattle."

MORGAN, MURRAY. *Skid Road*. New York, The Viking Press, Inc., 1960.

MURRAY, KEITH A. *The Pig War*. Tacoma, Washington, Washington State Historical Society, 1968.

NEWELL, GORDON, editor. *The H. W. McCurdy Marine History of the Pacific Northwest*. Seattle, Superior Publishing Company, 1966.

ORMSBY, MARGARET A. *British Columbia: a History*. Vancouver, The Macmillan Company of Canada Ltd., 1958.

PETHICK, DEREK. *James Douglas, Servant of Two Empires*. Vancouver, Mitchell Press Ltd., 1969.

SNOWDEN, C. A. *History of Washington*, 4 vols. New York, The Century History Co., 1909.

SPLITSTONE, FRED JOHN. *Orcas, Gem of the San Juans*. East Sound, Washington, Fred T. Darvill, 1954.

Told by the Pioneers, 3 vols. Olympia, Washington Pioneer Project, 1937-1938.

TUNEM, ALFRED. "The Dispute over the San Juan Island Water Boundary." Washington Historical Quarterly, XXIII (January-October, 1932).

VAN BUSKIRK, PHILIP C., the diaries of. Seattle, University of Washington Library.

VANCOUVER, GEORGE. *A Voyage of Discovery to the North Pacific Ocean and Round the World . . . in the years 1790 . . . 1795 in the Discovery Sloop of War and Armed Tender Chatham.* London, 1798.

VOSPER, LLOYD. *Cruising Puget Sound and Adjacent Waters.* Seattle, Westward Press, 1947.

WAGNER, HENRY R. *Spanish Explorations in the Strait of Juan de Fuca.* Santa Ana, California, Fine Arts Press, 1933.

WALKINSHAW, ROBERT. *On Puget Sound.* New York, G. P. Putnam's Sons, 1929.

WALSH, SOPHIE. *History and Romance of the San Juan Islands.* Anacortes American Press, 1932.

WASHINGTON STATE ASSOCIATIONS OF COUNTY COMMISSIONERS AND COUNTY ENGINEERS. *The Book of the Counties, 1953.* Olympia, 1953.

WHITEBROOK, ROBERT BALLARD. *Coastal Exploration of Washington.* Palo Alto, California, Pacific Books, 1959.

WILKES, CHARLES. *Narrative of the United States Exploring Expedition,* Philadelphia, 1850.

WILLOUGHBY, MALCOLM F. *Rum War at Sea.* U.S. Government Printing Office, 1964.

WRIGHT, E. W., editor. *Lewis & Dryden's Marine History of the Pacific Northwest.* Portland, Oregon, The Lewis & Dryden Printing Company, 1895.

OTHER BOOKS

Burn, June. *Living High.*

Cook, Beatrice. *Till Fish Us Do Part; More Fish to Fry.*

Finney, Gertrude. *Stormy Winter.*

Gilbert, Kenneth. *Triple-Threat Patrol.*

Glidden, Helene. *The Light on the Island.*

Holland, Melvin Ned. *The Haunted Island.*

Lockett, Sharon. *The Strong-Box Mystery.*

Mayse, Arthur. *Perilous Passage.*

McDonald, Norman C. *Song of the Axe.*

Montgomery, Elizabeth. *The Mystery of Edison Brown.*

Richardson, David. *Magic Islands.*

Wetherell, June. *The Glorious Three.*

Wheeler, James Cooper. *Captain Pete of Puget Sound.*

INDEX

Pictures and their captions are referred to by the nearest preceding page of text. Thus *288+4* means the fourth page of pictures following page 288, etc.

352

357

359